NetWare Workstation Troubleshooting & Maintenance Handbook

The Communications Book Series

The Computing That Works Book Series

For more information about other McGraw-Hill materials, call 1-800-2-MCGRAW in the United States. In other countries, call your McGraw-Hill office.

NetWare Workstation Troubleshooting & Maintenance Handbook

Edward Liebing
Charles D. Knutson
Michael Day

McGraw-Hill, Inc.
1221 Avenue of the Americas
New York, NY 10020

1234567890

Cover design by Kate Hennessy Johnson. The editor for this book was Vince Sondej and the production supervisor was David B. Doering. It was composed in PageMaker 3.01 by Doering & Associates.

Library of Congress Cataloging-in-Publication Data

Liebing, Edward.
    NetWare workstation troubleshooting and maintenance handbook/
Edward A. Liebing, Michael Day, and Charles D. Knutson.
        p.   cm.
    Includes index.
    ISBN 0-07-607027-1   :
    1. Microcomputer workstations.   2. NetWare (Computer operating
system)   I. Day, Michael, 1961-   . II. Knutson, Charles D.
III. Title
QA76.5.L5135   1990
005.7' 1369--dc20   90-6617
                                                     CIP

For information about our audio products, write us at:
Newbridge Book Clubs, 3000 Cindel Drive, Delran, NJ   08370

ACKNOWLEDGEMENTS

The authors wish to acknowledge the efforts of many friends and associates who have contributed to the creation of this book. Their contributions have had a tremendous positive impact on what you now see before you. Some have provided technical expertise, while others have read and re-read the manuscript at various stages of the project. Vince Sondej and Barbara Hume have served tirelessly as our editors. Dave Doering performed the layout and design work. Most of all we wish to thank our wives—Maddy Liebing, Alana Knutson, and Melinda Day—who generously supported our writing habit from beginning to end.

The following people, many of whom work for Novell, have directly contributed to this book.

DOS and NetWare section
James Brown, Grant Echols, Howard Johnson, Tony Lindsey, and the LANswer people for their technical reads.

OS/2 and NetWare section
Larry Angus, Danny Brand, Matt Brooks, Lee Cormier, Andy Lawrence, Russ Marsh, Ken Nielson, Blain Ogden, Bevan Rowley, and Earle Wells for technical and conceptual reviews as well as moral support. The OS/2 Requester development team for building a product worth writing about.

Macintosh and NetWare section
Scott Ivie, Tim Barnard, and Milt Anderson. All engineers who have worked on Macintosh development, inside and outside of Apple, from 1984 to today.

Table of Contents

Section 2 - OS/2 and NetWare

FOREWORD

As a system supervisor, you are responsible for maintaining and troubleshooting the workstations on your network. If you know DOS fairly well, and if you enjoy solving hardware and software problems, you can most likely keep up with the growing technology known as local area networks.

While NetWare v2.0x allows only DOS workstations on the LAN, NetWare v2.1x also allows for OS/2 workstations and, with NetWare v2.15, Macintosh workstations as well. NetWare 386 v3.0 allows DOS and OS/2 workstations, with a future interest in incorporating Macintosh and UNIX workstations.

You may know quite a bit about setting up and maintaining DOS workstations, but you may not know how to set up and maintain OS/2 or Macintosh workstations. The *NetWare Workstation Troubleshooting and Maintenance Handbook* is to help you understand the basics of the three workstation environments that NetWare supports. A clear understanding of these basics will leave you better prepared to set up and maintain the workstations on your NetWare network.

The handbook is divided into three sections; each section addresses a different workstation operating system. The first section of the book is designed to help you better understand how DOS and NetWare environments can work together, as well as how to diagnose and troubleshoot any workstation problems you may encounter on the network. The handbook also covers NetWare error messages for workstations.

The second section of this book describes the OS/2 platform, the software and hardware differences between DOS and OS/2, and the process of setting up and maintaining an OS/2 workstation environment. The third section tells you how to set up, maintain, and troubleshoot Macintosh workstations on NetWare.

This book deals only with workstation diagnostics and troubleshooting. The *NetWare Server Troubleshooting and Maintenance Handbook* describes the intricacies of the NetWare operating system for NetWare versions 2.1x, including information on diagnosing and troubleshooting problems that occur at the server.

Edward A. Liebing
Charles D. Knutson
Michael Day

June 1990

Section 1

DOS
and
NetWare

1 Disk Operating System

DOS (Disk Operating System) is the basic software that operates most IBM and IBM-compatible workstations. DOS creates an environment for other programs to run in.

As an analogy to an operating system, imagine a room full of tables. On each table is a number of working tools; one table contains scissors, paste, tape, rulers, and like utensils, and another table contains a hammer, chisel, hand saw, screw drivers, and similar tools. Depending on what you want to accomplish, you choose a table and do the work necessary to complete your determined task. In many respects, DOS is the room and the tools within the room, and each program or utility is like a person using those available tools to complete a specific task.

In this example, you are limited by the constraints of the room and the available tools. You certainly couldn't build a full-scale airplane or a sloop if the room were too small, or if the tools didn't suit the task at hand. So it is with DOS and its available applications. DOS was written to take advantage of the 8088 coprocessor chip, which is limited to an eight-bit internal instruction set. This means that the DOS environment is limited to 1MB (1024KB) of memory: 640KB of addressable main memory for applications and utilities, and 384KB of system or reserved memory. (There is also 64K of memory beginning directly at 1024KB that is known as High memory and is addressable from real mode as well.)

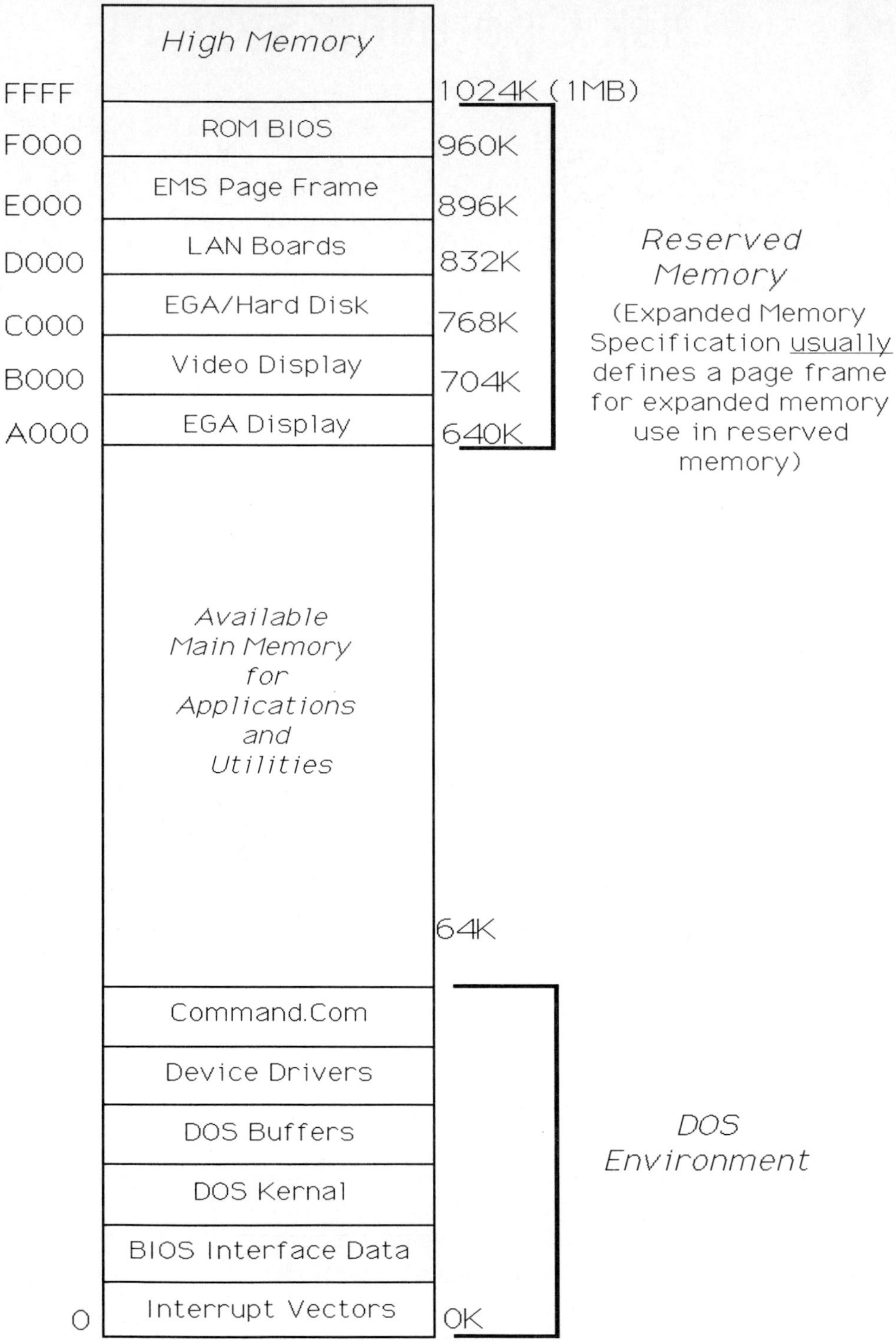

High Memory		
FFFF		1024K (1MB)
ROM BIOS	F000	960K
EMS Page Frame	E000	896K
LAN Boards	D000	832K
EGA/Hard Disk	C000	768K
Video Display	B000	704K
EGA Display	A000	640K

Reserved Memory

(Expanded Memory Specification <u>usually</u> defines a page frame for expanded memory use in reserved memory)

Available Main Memory for Applications and Utilities

64K

Command.Com

Device Drivers

DOS Buffers

DOS Kernal

BIOS Interface Data

Interrupt Vectors

0   0K

DOS Environment

Figure 1: Memory allocation in a workstation.

The 640KB limit has become a problem only in the last few years, as applications have begun to expand their capabilities and their memory requirements. Once programs have used up the available 640KB of space, your workstation may not be able to do everything you want it to do.

DOS Versions and Their Utilities: A Quick List

DOS includes an extensive list of utilities to help you maneuver around in its environment and perform certain functions, such as listing files in a directory, printing files, copying files, and so forth. For those of you already familiar with DOS, here is a quick list showing which DOS utilities are featured in the many versions of DOS. Below is a list of DOS commands for MS-DOS and PC-DOS versions 2.0 to 4.0x. (While some of the commands appeared in versions of DOS before v2.0, they are documented here as part of v2.0.)

This list does not include the minor utility enhancements throughout the different DOS versions; it only indicates when the utility became part of the DOS repertoire.

This handbook also divides the list of DOS commands into two logical parts: internal to COMMAND.COM and external to COMMAND.COM. Internal DOS commands are part of the COMMAND.COM file and are always immediately available; external commands, found on the DOS diskettes, are the DOS utilities with .COM and .EXE extensions. To run these utilities, you must use the DOS diskettes or have access to a directory containing those files.

Internal DOS Commands

Command	Function	DOS Version
BREAK	allows for a controlled break function within a program	2.0 and above
CHCP	a system command that selects a code page for devices	3.3 and above
CHDIR	displays full directory path	2.0 and above
CD	changes directory within a given directory path	2.0 and above
CLS	clears screen and brings DOS prompt to upper left corner	2.0 and above
COPY	copies the file(s) from one place to another	2.0 and above
CTTY	changes keyboard and screen control to an auxiliary console	2.0 and above
DATE	displays date and lets you change date	2.0 and above
DEL	deletes a file or files in a specified directory	2.0 and above
DIR	lists directory of files, or only specific files in a specified directories	2.0 and above
ERASE	erases a file or files in a specified directory	2.0 and above
EXIT	terminates the current copy of COMMAND.COM if it was involved as a child process	2.0 and above

MKDIR	makes a directory (can also be MD)	2.0 and above
PATH	searches through designated directories for *.COM, *.EXE, and .BAT files	2.0 and above
PROMPT	changes the DOS prompt line	2.0 and above
REMARK	places remarks (can also be REM)	2.0 and above
RENAME	renames files (can also be REN)	2.0 and above
RMDIR	removes a directory (can also be RD)	2.0 and above
SET	sets "environment" variables used by some programs; also displays current values of set variables	2.0 and above
TIME	displays the system's time or changes time	2.0 and above
TYPE	lets you see what's in a file	2.0 and above
VER	shows the operating system's version	2.0 and above
VERIFY	ensures that the data you are copying is correctly copied	2.0 and above
VOL	displays the name you called your volume	2.0 and above

Other internal DOS commands that are used mainly in programming batch files include CALL, ECHO, FOR, GOTO, IF, PAUSE, and SHIFT.

External DOS Commands

Command	*Function*	*DOS Version*
APPEND	locates files not in your current directory that do not have a .COM, .EXE, or .BAT extension	3.3 and above
ASSIGN	routes disk I/O requests to another drive/directory	2.0 and above
ATTRIB	marks file attributes on a single file or on all files in a directory	3.0 and above
BACKUP	backs up files on a disk drive to another drive	2.0 and above
*.BAT	creates a series of DOS commands that can be executed together	2.0 and above
CHKDSK	displays disk space and bytes available on local disk (if using NetWare); also displays total memory and available memory	2.0 and above
COMMAND	initiates another command processor	3.1 and above
COMP	compares information in two sets of files (PC-DOS only)	2.0 and above
DISKCOMP	compares disk content to another diskette	2.0 and above
DISKCOPY	copies entire diskette to another disk	2.0 and above
DOSSHELL	returns you to the DOS shell after executing commands at the DOS prompt	4.0 and above
EXE2BIN	converts .EXE files to .COM files (MS-DOS only)	2.0 and above

FC	compares information in two sets of files (MS-DOS only)	2.0 and above
FDISK	sets up DOS partitions on hard disk drives	2.0 and above
FASTOPEN	stores in memory where directories and last-opened files are	3.3 and above
FIND	looks for a "string" of characters in files and saves to another file	2.0 and above
FORMAT	initializes a disk acceptable to DOS	2.0 and above
GRAFTABL	loads language characters for graphics	3.1 and above
GRAPHICS	prints graphics to a printer	2.0 and above
INSTALL	loads TSR command normally used in AUTOEXEC.BAT, including FASTOPEN. EXE,KEYB.COM, SHARE.EXE, NLFUNC. EXE	4.0 and above
JOIN	allows two directories to be viewed as one	3.1 and above
KEYB	used to load non-U.S. English keyboards (PC-DOS only)	3.0 and above
KEYBFR	used to load MS-DOS keyboard layout for France	3.0 and above
KEYBGR	used to load MS-DOS keyboard layout for Germany	3.0 and above
KEYBIT	used to load MS-DOS keyboard layout for Italy	3.0 and above
KEYBSP	used to load MS-DOS keyboard layout for Spain	3.0 and above
KEYBUK	used to load MS-DOS keyboard layout for U.K.	3.0 and above
LABEL	lets you label diskettes and hard drive volumes	3.0 and above
MEM	displays used and unused memory	4.0 and above
MODE	used to set up printers, monitors, and asynchronous communication devices	2.0 and above
MORE	sends data to the screen and pauses after each screen load	2.0 and above
NLSFUNC	supports extended country information	3.3 and above
PRINT	sends files to printer for printing	2.0 and above
RECOVER	recovers data from a file that has a bad sector	2.0 and above
REPLACE	allows you to selectively copy files to a target drive or diskette	3.2 and above
RESTORE	used with BACKUP: restores backup files to a directory	2.0 and above
SELECT	formats and copies one diskette to another; also creates AUTOEXEC.BAT and CONFIG. SYS files	4.0 and above
SHARE	supports file sharing	3.0 and above
SORT	sorts data from an input device to an output device	2.0 and above

SUBST	substitutes a directory path for a drive letter	3.1 and above
SWITCHES	sets up conventional keyboard functions when you install an enhanced keyboard	4.0 and above
SYS	transfers OS files (IBMBIO.COM and IBMDOS.COM)	2.0 and above
TREE	shows directory and subdirectory structure	2.0 and above
XCOPY	copies file(s) in a directory as well as subdirectories	3.2 and above
XMAZEMS.SYS		
	supports Lotus, Intel, Microsoft (LIM) board for Expanded Memory Specification (EMS)	4.0 and above
XMAEM.SYS	emulates IBM PS/2 80286 Expanded Memory Adapter /A (only used in 386 systems)	4.0 and above

Many good books can tell you how to use the DOS utilities and how to set up DOS on standalone computers. This book, however, focuses on setting up, maintaining, and troubleshooting supported workstation operating systems on a NetWare environment. The rest of the text will deal with that subject.

2 The DOS Workstation

Personal computers have been around in one form or another since 1977. But in 1981, IBM introduced its version of the personal computer: the IBM Personal Computer, or IBM PC. IBM chose DOS as its computer operating system and licensed DOS from Microsoft. When you buy PC-DOS, you are buying IBM's version; when you buy MS-DOS, you are buying Microsoft's version. But they offer essentially the same functionality.

Microsoft was quick to publish DOS's application programming interface (API), which made it possible for programmers and developers to write applications for the DOS platform. Literally thousands of applications and utilities have been written to take advantage of the DOS environment. These applications and utilities offer a wide selection, from games to spreadsheets to word processors to databases. Many applications and utilities come with graphics and special mouse features. All work within DOS's constraints, and for the most part, applications written to DOS v2.x also run under DOS v3.x; however, the networking capacities of DOS v3.x caused most DOS v2.x applications to be rewritten. (Application and DOS incompatibilities also made their appearance with DOS v4.0x.)

With the PC inception, IBM took an approach unique at the time: the IBM PC was an "open architecture" system, which meant that anyone could make hardware for it or even copy its design (copies are known as PC compatibles). This approach led to strong hardware support for the PC line; now you can buy monitors, keyboards, memory, disk drives, and other peripherals from a long list of manufacturers.

The IBM PC quickly evolved into the IBM PC XT (eXtended Technology), a machine which supported hard disk drives. In 1984, the XT gave way to the IBM PC AT (Advanced Technology), a machine which contained Intel's 80286 microprocessor. In 1986, Compaq introduced the DeskPro 386, a personal computer based on the 80386 microprocessor. In 1989, Intel's 80486 microprocessor made its debut in a number of personal computer lines.

It wasn't until IBM began losing market share that IBM management changed their minds about open architecture, dropped the IBM PC line, and introduced the IBM Personal System /2 (PS/2) line. PS/2s are a complete line of personal computers containing 8086, 80286, 80386, or 80486 microprocessors. PS/2s differ in architecture from the PC line, and IBM licenses the architectural specifications to those vendors wishing to make hardware products for the PS/2 line.

But the PS/2 line also runs DOS, which means that all applications written for DOS run on the PS/2 line. Along with the PS/2s, IBM announced OS/2, an operating system designed to take full advantage of the processing power and functionality of the 80286 microprocessor. (IBM says that OS/2 v2.0 will, in the same way, take full advantage of the 80386 and 80486 microprocessors.)

See page 133 for OS/2 workstation requirements.

The Workstation's Operations Manual

Most personal computers come with some form of hardware quick reference or operations guide. These manuals (which sometimes come with diskettes) tell you how to assemble your computer and how to install hardware components such as memory boards, floppy disk drives, and network interface boards. The manuals also show you how to troubleshoot hardware failures. Browse through at least one of these manuals to become familiar with the type of information they contain.

While most computers are similar in appearance, each computer carries its own peculiarities and therefore requires its own information on installation procedures. For example, a Compaq computer's Operations Guide includes an introduction, Compaq's program files, Compaq's utilities, and the appendixes. The appendixes include a "Getting Started" manual, a "Memory Expansion Installation Guide," a "Fixed Disk Drive Installation Guide," and a "Technical Overview," along with three diskettes containing diagnostics and user programs.

The IBM Guide to Operations for the IBM PC XT contains chapters on basic computer use, setup, operations, troubleshooting (along with a diagnostics diskette), and options—for example, switch settings, computer relocation, and keyboard templates.

With the IBM PS/2 line, you get a Quick Reference and a Reference Diskette. The Quick Reference manual covers getting started, installation procedures, troubleshooting, and additional material about cover-lock keys, diskettes, moving the computer, and other information. There is also a technical reference manual specific to each PS/2 machine, covering the technical aspects of programming on that machine. While this manual is overkill for most supervisors, it does include some useful charts dealing with low-level memory mappings.

But for the most part, the Technical Reference is for programmers. As a systems manager, when you purchase manuals you need to keep in mind the way you troubleshoot your workstations. If you must find out which component failed in a malfunctioning computer, it will help you to run the diagnostics diskettes that comes with many types of PCs. These diskettes can be helpful in pinpointing the failed component. But if you only need to find and replace the failed computer, the diskettes and manuals may be unnecessary.

Here's a list of manuals that will assist you in maintaining and troubleshooting a DOS workstation:

1. The hardware quick reference or operations guide for the workstation;
2. A current DOS manual;
3. The network interface board supplement either from Novell or from the board vendor;
4. The DOS Technical Reference manual (optional but useful);
5. A hardware technical reference manual (optional).

Hardware for the Workstation

DOS runs on the IBM Personal Computer (PC), PC XT, PC AT, and compatibles. DOS also runs on the IBM PS/2 line of computers and compatibles. The basic hardware differences between the PC and the XT involve hard disk drive capabilities. Both computers use the 8088 processor, which addresses 1MB of physical memory. (DOS reserves 640KB for applications and 384KB for reserved memory, which is addressed by LAN boards, monitor boards, and other devices.) The 8088 processor is also capable of different internal speeds (for example, internal application instructions in turbo XTs can run at 10MHz); however, for both the PC and the XT, all bus I/O for installed boards (such as a network interface board or a memory board) is limited to 8-bit transfer at 6MHz or 8MHz.

The IBM PC AT computer offered two advances over the PC. The 80286 microprocessor has 24 address lines, making it capable of 16MB of physical memory addressing, and the microprocessor is capable of moving data 16 bits at a time, both internally and externally. These capabilities make it possible for the AT to address up to 16MB of memory. The AT also runs in two modes of operation: real mode, which works within the 1MB confines of DOS (leaving 640KB reserved for applications), and protected mode, which allows the 80286 microprocessor to access the 16MB of extended memory in the same way it accesses real mode memory. (For more information on operating systems using protected mode capability, turn to the OS/2 section of this book.)

Internally, the AT was much faster than the PC or XT, principally because of the faster internal clock speeds the AT could achieve. When the AT first appeared it ran at 6MHz, which seemed significant compared to the PC's 4.77MHz speed. Then came 8MHz ATs without "wait states" (pauses between memory references), allowing programs to run discernably faster. Now, 25MHz ATs run DOS applications and utilities at speeds much greater than most people can fully utilize.

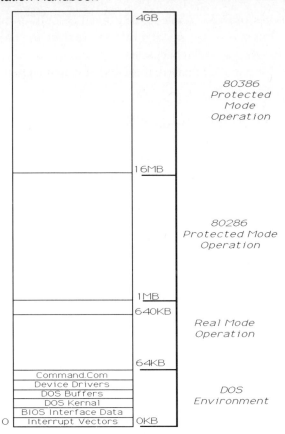

Figure 2: The 80286 microprocessor is capable of 16-bit instructions and of accessing 16MB of extended memory in protected mode. The 80386 and 80486 microprocessors are capable of 32-bit instructions and of accessing 4 gigabytes of extended physical memory and 64 terabytes of virtual memory.

Here's a list of workstation components and some common errors you may experience in working with each component. Because of the diverse nature of personal computers, these pages can offer only guidelines to better general workstation maintenance. Whenever economically practical, try to keep on hand a few extra components for each of your computer types.

Floppy Disk Drives

IBM PC and compatible workstations and IBM PS/2 and compatible workstations have two types of floppy disk drives—5.25 inch and 3.5 inch. Each disk drive type can come in either a low-density or a high-density capacity. The term "density" refers to the amount of information a floppy disk is capable of storing: 5.25-inch diskettes can hold 360KB of information when formatted on a low-density disk drive and 1.2MB when formatted on a high-density disk drive; 3.5-inch diskettes can hold 720KB of information when formatted on a low-density disk drive and 1.4MB when formatted on a high-density disk drive. (The term "double-sided" simply means that the drive reads both sides of the disks.)

The chief cause of drive read and write errors is dirty drive heads. Every 100 hours of computer run time, you should clean the floppy disk heads with a cleaning diskette and rubbing alcohol or the equivalent. (Follow the instructions on the cleaning diskette.) For a machine that boots from a hard disk drive, you won't need to clean the floppy drive heads as often; even so, keep them on a regular cleaning cycle.

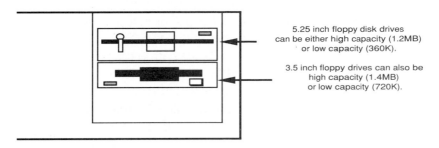

5.25 inch floppy disk drives can be either high capacity (1.2MB) or low capacity (360K).

3.5 inch floppy drives can also be high capacity (1.4MB) or low capacity (720K).

Figure 3: The chief problems on floppy drives are dirty drive heads and poor head alignment.

The next biggest cause of drive read and write errors is poor head alignment, which can also affect the drive's indexing and radial set. Alignment problems should normally be serviced by a computer repair shop, where technicians will also check the indexing and radial set. A floppy disk drive that has problems reading diskettes from other computers most likely has an alignment problem.

Checking for a misaligned floppy disk drive is not an exact science. A misaligned floppy disk drive can usually read and write its own diskettes, but has problems reading and writing to borrowed diskettes or diskettes formatted by another workstation. If workstation 1 is having difficulty reading and writing to a diskette from workstation 2, try reading that diskette on workstation 3; if workstations 1 and 3 find the diskette hard to read, workstation 2 may be out of alignment. If workstations 2 and 3 can read the diskette with no difficulty, the drive in workstation 1 may be out of alignment.

For random read and write errors, try a new diskette. When errors occur too frequently to be tolerated, replace the floppy disk drive and send the faulty disk drive for servicing.

Be sure as well to make boot diskettes from the correct type of disk drive. Many system supervisors have discovered that workstations with low-density drives have difficulty with boot diskettes created on a high-density drive. While the method for formatting a low-density diskette on a high-density drive is easy (FORMAT A:/S/4 <Enter>), many low-density drives cannot reliably read high-density drive formats; the result is read and write errors after a few months or sooner. To avoid problems, when you create your workstation boot diskettes, create high-density boot diskettes on a high-density drive and low-density boot diskettes on a low-density drive.

The disk controller card and the controller cable are other possible points of failure. When a disk controller card goes out, the failure normally prevents access to the floppy or hard disk drives. (When this happens, the disk drive light remains on and nothing appears on your screen.) Try replacing the controller card to see if that solves the problem. Intermittent problems are harder to analyze; the more the card does (for example, if it is controlling two floppy drives and a hard disk drive), the greater its chance for failure.

High-Density Diskettes

If you have a high-density drive, make sure that your diskettes have been tested for high-density use by looking for the label "HD" (High Density) on the diskette box. This is particularly true of 5 1/4" diskettes. For low-density drives using 5 1/4" diskettes, purchase diskettes with a "DS/DD" (Double Sided/Double Density). SS/DD (Single Sided/Double Density) diskettes have only been tested on one side of the diskette and were used for disk drives having one read/write head. Since disk drives have had read/write heads for both sides of the diskette since 1983, buy DS/DD diskettes to be sure the diskettes have been tested on both sides.

For 3 1/2" disks, this high-density specification is just as important. It is possible to use DD-type diskettes as high-density diskettes for 3 1/2" disks. However, you can have many failures if you use DD diskettes for high-density drives, for they have not been tested to handle high-density formatting. If a diskette does malfunction and you have stayed within the diskette limitations, you can sometimes send the faulty diskette back to the manufacturers for a replacement (read the warranty on the diskette box).

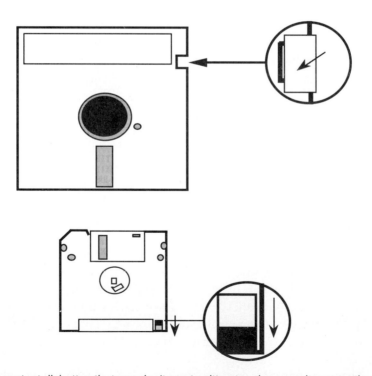

Figure 4: To protect diskettes that you don't want written to, place a write protection tab over the notch on 5.25 inch diskettes, or move the write protection switch down on 3.5 inch diskettes.

Low-Density Diskettes

Low-density diskettes are usually double-sided and double density (DS/DD). To be sure that your diskettes have been tested for double-density use, look for the label "DD" (double density) on the diskette box. Low-density 5 1/4" disk drive can't read high-density diskettes. So be sure to buy only low-density diskettes for a low-density drive.

Hard Disk Drives

Many personal computers come with internal hard disk drives, which were introduced into IBM's personal computer world with the IBM PC XT computer. With LANs, hard disks in each workstation are not really necessary, since workstations can use the hard drive capacity of the file server. But many workstations do have hard disk drives for personal files and for backups (usually for the peace of mind of the workstation operator).

Versions of DOS before v3.3 limited users to a 32MB hard disk (which actually formats to 33.4MB); even if you had a 40MB disk drive, you could access only 32MB of that drive. Even though you could divide the disk into smaller DOS partitions—four partitions of 8MB each, for example—you would still be limited to 32MB of total disk space.

However, DOS v3.3 allows you to create multiple DOS partitions above the initial 32MB range. If you have a 40MB drive, you can divide your drive into 32MB and 8MB partitions (the 8MB drive becoming your D: drive). Each 32MB drive size can also be partitioned into four logical drives; you can continue partitioning until you run out of partitions or letters in the alphabet. For example, you can divide a 32MB drive into C: (the active partition), D:, E:, and F: if you wish to have four 8MB-size logical drives. Or you can divide it into one 30MB partition and one 2MB partition.

DOS v4.0x allows you to make one DOS partition the size of the physical drive itself, no matter what size the physical drive. If you have an 80MB hard drive, the DOS partition can also be 80MB. With DOS v4.0x, you can create a primary partition (which you make active so you can boot from the hard disk) and you can create an extended partition to logically break up the disk drive. You can also assign logical drive letters within the extended DOS partition, so if the primary partition is C:, you can divide the extended partition into logical drives such as D:, E:, F:, and so forth. Consult the DOS manuals under FDISK for details.

Instead of a floppy boot diskette, you can use the workstation's hard disk to boot to the system. Once the hard disk has a low-level format (every hard disk comes with a low-level format; see page 36) and has in place an active partition (which you create through the FDISK utility), you can format the diskette to the DOS version you are currently using (FORMAT C:/S). (The /S parameter installs the system files and COMMAND.COM.) After you format the hard disk, you can create the CONFIG.SYS and AUTOEXEC.BAT files to load network files, such as IPX.COM, ANET3.COM, and NETBIOS.COM. (This procedure is explained in Chapter 4, "DOS and NetWare--Workstation Theory of Operations.")

Keyboard

There are several standard keyboard layouts, but the two basic keyboard layouts include the IBM PC keyboard, with ten function keys on the left-hand side, and the IBM AT extended keyboard, with 101 keys, including twelve function keys extending across the top.

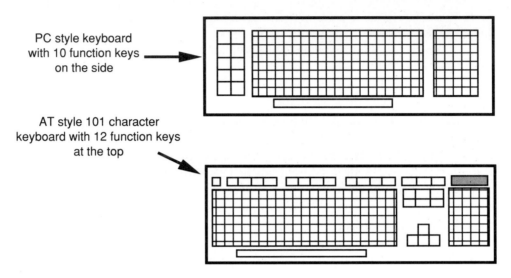

PC style keyboard
with 10 function keys
on the side

AT style 101 character
keyboard with 12 function keys
at the top

Figure 5: Keyboards come in all shapes and sizes, but the main difference is the 10 function keys on the side, like the IBM PC keyboard, or the 12 function keys across the top, like on the IBM AT extended keyboard.

For general keyboard maintenance, purchase a basic electronic cleaner such as Blue Shower at an electronics store to keep the keys clean. This solution also frees the keyboard from dust and light debris. To clean the tops of the keys, use alcohol or a pencil eraser. Spilling a drink onto a keyboard usually means replacing the keyboard, since it is barely more expensive to buy a new keyboard than to service one that has been spilled on.

You will frequently need to clean between the keys and the circuit board; you may even need to remove the top of the keyboard to get to the problem. (Since different keyboard manufacturers put their keyboards together differently, consult the owner's manual for disassembly instructions.) Then apply the electronic cleaner.

Sometimes a key sticks or the key signal doesn't display on the screen. This situation is usually caused by corroded connections that do not allow the metal connectors to touch one another, signalling that the key has been struck.

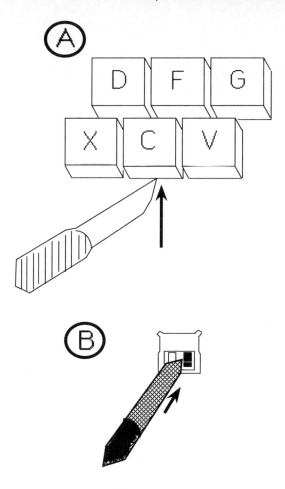

Figure 6A: Slip the blade beneath the sticking key and lift gently until the top of the key dislodges from the keyboard. B: Run a nail file between the two connectors to clean them. Then snap the top of the key back on.

Some keyboards let you pop off the keys and clean the connectors for better contact. You can check your keyboard with a flat instrument (such as a letter opener, screwdriver, or pocketknife). Slip the blade underneath the sticking key and lift gently until the key top dislodges from the keyboard. If you see two metal connectors, one on each side of the key depressor (which separates the connectors and prevents them from touching), run a fingernail file between the two connectors. Then depress the key again to see if the keystroke shows up on the screen. If it does, snap the key lid back on top of the key depressor; if it does not, give the user another keyboard and have the defective one serviced.

You can make a key cap remover from a paper clip. Simply unfold the paper clip into a straight piece of wire; with a pair of pliers, bend the wire into a U-shape with hooks. You can then slip the hooks under both sides of the key and pull up.

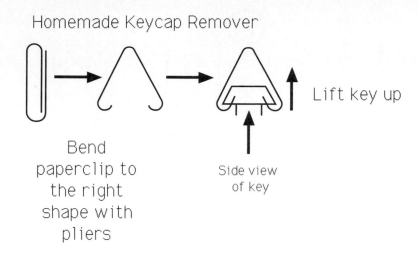

Figure 7: Creating and using a keycap remover tool.

A word of warning: A genuine IBM keyboard is the most difficult to take apart and put back together. If an IBM keyboard has sticky keys or if a key does not work, replace the keyboard and have it serviced.

Monitors

Monitors come in all shapes, sizes, and degrees of pixel resolution. The main thing to remember about monitors is that the graphic adapter must match the monitor type. For example, if you have a CGA (Color Graphics Adapter) monitor, you'll need a color graphics adapter. The same holds true with EGA (Enhanced Graphics Adapter), VGA (Virtual Graphics Adapter), and monochrome graphics. While some adapters will support both VGA and EGA, or EGA and CGA, not all of them do. Know your adapter card's limitations.

CGA color monitors provide up to 320 x 200 pixel resolution and up to four colors. Black-and-white monitors give you up to 640 x 200 pixel resolution and two colors. EGA color monitors provide up to 640 x 350 pixel resolution and up to 16 colors, while VGA color monitors provide 640 x 400 pixel resolution and up to 256 colors. The IBM PS/2 Models 25 and 30 have two selections for MCGA—640 x 350 pixel resolution with two colors, or 320 x 200 pixel resolution with 16 colors.

Monochrome graphics vary in pixel resolution because of the adapter cards used. One common monochrome adapter is the Hercules graphics adapter card, which has a 720 x 348 pixel resolution.

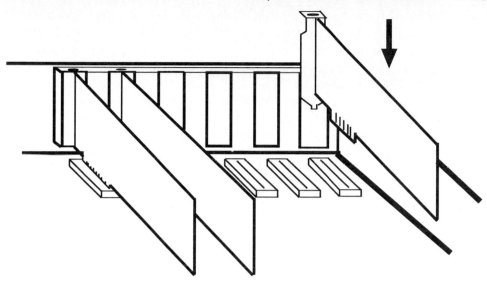

Figure 8: Place the adapter board firmly into the slot. Be sure to select the proper system board setting for color or monochrome monitors. Also, common blank monitor problems may result from turned down brightness or contrast knobs.

Common blank-monitor problems include someone having turned down the bright and contrast knobs so the screen is blank, having the cables become detached from the adapter, and (occasionally) having the wrong video card for the right monitor. Sometimes pushing the computer against the wall can knock the cable off the adapter. When replacing a color for a monochrome monitor, be sure to run SETUP and tell your computer what you have done; otherwise, you will receive a configuration error message and will be asked to run SETUP. Most computers have a jumper setting on the system board for monochrome and color monitors, so you will also need to reposition that jumper setting before running SETUP.

For cleaning the monitor screen, most cleanser and anti-static products work. Turn off your computer when cleaning the monitor; cleaning liquids can have an adverse effect on up-and-running workstations.

Power Supplies and Power Strips

A solid power source is paramount. You will chase more ghosts and have more intermittent network errors throughout your system because of a poor power supply than for any other reason.

On the workstation level, workstations with hard disk drives should have at least a power surge protector and a brownout protector to ensure data integrity. A poor power source can also affect workstations, causing undue stress on hard disk drive motors. An example of a power line testing tool is AC Monitor from Tasco.

Proper grounding of your office(s) is an important consideration to the network. Buildings that have more than one earth ground may not agree on the same zero voltage; networks that span these buildings can have server problems, resulting in servers going down periodically. Be sure there is only one ground point. Also, be sure workstations and cables are properly grounded.

Networks can have two kinds of power surges: external and internal. External power surges can be caused by lightning or poor power sources; lightning surges introduce large currents of electricity to powerline wiring, while utility load switching and power corrections can create irregularities in power quality.

Internal power surges are the result of workstations, disk subsystems, printers, and so forth, being turned on and off on the network during any given day. Conventional surge protectors send these power surges to the workstation's ground, where they are supposed to disappear. However, cabling systems use the ground circuit as a voltage reference, so power surges sent to ground can cause data loss. If you are having problems with periodic workstation failure, network failure, or corrupt data, take off surge protectors that send power surges to ground and look for surge protectors that send power surges to neutral rather than ground. (While ground and neutral do connect in the building's electrical service entrance, the distance to the entrance should isolate the neutral conductor from the ground conductor.) One surge protector specifically designed for this problem is Surge Eliminator by Zero Surge.

A related item worth mentioning is carpet static. You can attest to the shock strength of static electricity if you have ever had someone shuffle his feet on carpet and then touch your nose. Feet shufflers can send real static jolts through a workstation by not grounding themselves (touching wood or something that accepts the electrical charge) before touching the workstation's keyboard. Such static has been known to reset the workstation, equivalent to pressing the <Ctrl-Alt-Del> keys simultaneously.

Any type of anti-static carpet guard can help prevent carpet static (spray fabric softener also works well). If some of your network users have a knack for resetting their workstations by touch, purchase for each of them an anti-static pad which they can touch before working on the computer.

Network Interface Board

The PC, XT, or AT workstation needs only a few essentials to function on the network. The workstation itself includes the computer chassis, monitor, and keyboard; to make the workstation function on the network, the only additional physical components you need are a network interface board and a cable to connect the workstation to the network.

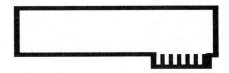

8-bit network interface board

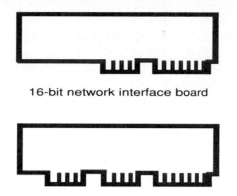

16-bit network interface board

32-bit EISA or MCA network interface board

Figure 9: Network interface boards come with 8-, 16-, and 32-bit communications capabilities. Many boards must be physically set for interrupt, I/O, base memory, DMA, and node addressing. Keep a running record of how your boards are set.

To connect to the LAN, each workstation contains a network interface board with a connected cable; the board/cable combination allows for network communications. The board, which fits into one of the workstation expansion slots, must be jumpered to the correct settings you choose when running GENSH or SHGEN.

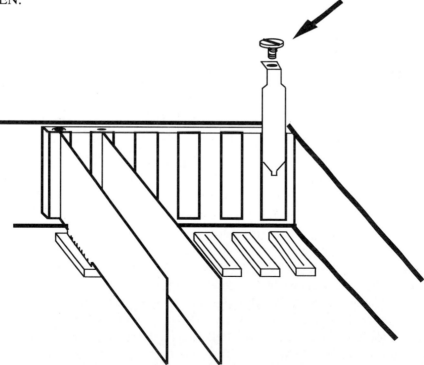

Figure 10: To install a network interface board, remove the screw from a metal slot that matches the board type you are installing, (8-, 16-, 32-bit) and place the board firmly in the slot. Add the screw and tighten it down.

When you generate the shell, you link a hardware-specific LAN driver into the IPX services. Your IPX.COM file or ANETx.COM file (for v2.0a) must be properly configured to the hardware configuration settings on your workstation network interface board. The GENSH utility uses setting 0 for the board's option number; you can check the network board setting against the NetWare Supplement manuals that come with NetWare, or against the supplement manual that came with the board. The supplement manuals that come with NetWare usually list the workstation default board settings in Appendix A or in the text of the manual.

For servers to send and receive requests to workstations, NetWare packets use specific network, node, and socket addresses for destination purposes. Workstations on the same network need different node addresses for the network to function properly. Some node addresses are set manually; for example, ARCnet boards must have the node address physically set on the board, while Ethernet boards come with a unique node address, so no jumper settings are necessary. Consult the supplement manual for your board to see how your board sets the node address.

NetWare v2.1x and v3.0 are not as restrictive as NetWare v2.0x; you have a choice of setting the I/O address, interrupt, RAM, and node address as well as DMA (when applicable) in the SHGEN utility. Whatever SHGEN option you choose, be sure jumper settings on the network interface board correspond with the selection. Otherwise, the shell driver will not be able to talk to the network board and you will receive network errors (see page 109). If you have problems with interrupt conflicts, go into SHGEN and choose the "Custom Configuration" option (see page 67 for instructions).

Keep a list of the board settings you are using for the network. These listings are invaluable when you must troubleshoot a problem or add new workstations to the network. Better yet, create a database in which you can list the board settings as well as a troubleshooting report for reference.

Cabling

Cabling is the physical element that connects workstations to servers, LANs, WANs, and dissimilar environments such as minicomputers and mainframes. Cabling includes coax, shielded twisted pair, unshielded twisted pair, and fiber optics. Cabling, topologies, and network interface boards define the physical layout or cabling scheme of your LAN.

In this text, the term "topologies" refer to the physical layout of the cable: for example, the star cluster, ring, linear bus, and star bus topologies. "Topologies" also refers to the access method of sending information across the cable. These methods include Carrier Sense Multiple Access with Collision Detection (CSMA/CD), polling, and token passing. CSMA/CD is most commonly used on an Ethernet linear bus topology; polling is most often used on the star cluster. Token passing is used on a ring, such as IBM Token-Ring, and on a star bus, such as ARCnet.

When dealing with copper cabling, such as coax and unshielded twisted pair, watch out for interference from lights, radios, and other objects that create interference (anything that generates an energy field). Shielded twisted pair is far less susceptible to interference than coax or unshielded twisted pair, and fiber optic is not susceptible to noise of this nature at all.

Cables exposed to walking and working areas are the most liable to fail. Keep cables from underfoot; spray the carpets with antistatic sprays or with a fabric softener solution to keep down the static that builds up when people walk around the office.

Do not push the computer against a wall; you might damage the cable or the connector on the network interface board. Keep within the physical constraints of the cable, and follow those constraints as outlined in the supplement manuals from Novell or from the board vendors. Cabling constraints listed in this manual include ARCnet, Ethernet, and Token-Ring.

ARCnet Constraints

ARCnet is a token bus topology which runs at 2.5Mbps. Cable specifications for Standard Microsystems' ARCnet and Novell's RX-Net are RG-62/U 93-Ohm coaxial, or duplex fiber optic (at 50, 62.5, 100, or 200 micron core).

For more than one workstation, networks need passive hubs and/or active hubs to relay the network token (active hubs also amplify the token). Passive hubs have four connectors (ports); an unused connector must be terminated with a 93-Ohm terminator. Cables connecting to a passive hub cannot exceed 100 feet. Active hubs, with eight or sixteen connectors, are self-terminating; they condition as well as amplify the token signal. This action allows 2,000-foot distances between workstations and active hubs or between other active hubs.

To avoid interference, twisted-pair ARCnet network interface boards must have a six-foot distance separating any two workstations. These network interface boards have unique addresses which you assign through an 8-pin dip switch. You can have 254 workstations on the same network—each node address must be unique on the network. (Available addresses are 1-255.) LANs with a different network address can have 254 workstations on them as well; so long as the network, node, and socket address is not duplicated, the internetwork will know to which server you are sending requests.

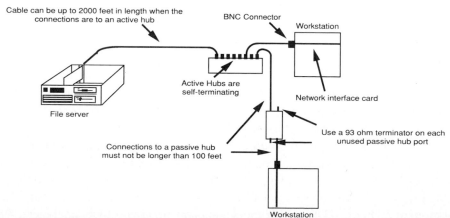

Figure 11: Most common errors on an ARCnet topology are in the lack of terminators and in duplicate node addresses. Consult the installation manual for setting IRQ, I/O base, base memory, and node addresses.

One common problem system supervisors encounter on ARCnet is the lack of terminators on passive hubs, at a T-connector, or at the end of a cable segment. Coax buses use 93-Ohm terminators; twisted-pair buses use 100-Ohm terminators. You can have a maximum of ten network interface boards on a twisted-pair segment when the bus length is less than 400 feet.

The second most common problem on ARCnet systems is duplicate node addresses. Again, a central database containing the workstation configurations can be very helpful. Another method for avoiding duplicate node addresses is marking in the supplement manual the addresses that are taken, and then placing the correct address number on each network interface board's metal bracket. Also, be sure to verify that the IRQ, I/O base address, and base memory selected on the network interface board match the option chosen in SHGEN.

Ethernet Constraints

Ethernet comes in two types: thick and thin. Thick Ethernet has a transceiver external to the network interface board, which is connected to the network interface board with the transceiver cable. Thick Ethernet cable is .4-inch coax cable; common thick Ethernet cable includes Belden 9880, Belden 89889, Montrose CBL5688, Montrose CBL5713, Malco 250-4315-0004, Malco 250-4314-0003, Inmac 1784, and Inmac 1785. For Novell thick Ethernet, you can use RG-59/U at 50 Ohms. Use the N-series 50 Ohm terminator for all thick Ethernet types (some terminators come with an attached grounding wire).

With thick Ethernet, you can have 100 workstations (transceivers) on a cable segment, and you can have five cable segments up to 500 meters each (1640 feet, for a combined total of 2,500 meters, or 8,200 feet). Workstation transceivers must be eight feet apart on the segment. The cable connecting the workstation to the external transceiver must not exceed 165 feet (50 meters). All cable segments must be terminated at each end with the 50-Ohm terminator, and one cable segment end must be grounded. Be sure to have the correct connectors, barrel connectors, and terminators for thick Ethernet.

Thin Ethernet has its transceiver on the board itself, so be sure the network board is set to use the internal transceiver (see installation guide for diagrams). Thin Ethernet uses RG-58A/U coax cable and BNC T-connectors to connect the cable to the Ethernet network interface board. You can have a maximum of five cable segments, with a maximum cable segment length of 607 feet (185 meters) and four repeaters connecting the segments. All five cable segments can amount to 3,035 feet (925 meters). Thin Ethernet cable segment ends must be terminated with 50-Ohm termination and grounded at one point. You can have thirty nodes per cable segment, and BNC T-connectors must be at least 1.5 feet (.5 meters) apart.

Good tools for troubleshooting Ethernet cables are Time Domain Reflectors, or TDRs. Through signal reflection, TDRs check for such cabling problems as short circuits caused by unexpected crimps, bad kinks, impedance problems, or cable breaks. Two examples of a TDR are MicroTest's Cable Scanner and Lanca Instruments' Digital TDR. Other tools that can help are protocol analyzers, which capture, monitor, and decipher packets on the network. Two examples include the Sniffer by Network General and the LANalyzer by Novell.

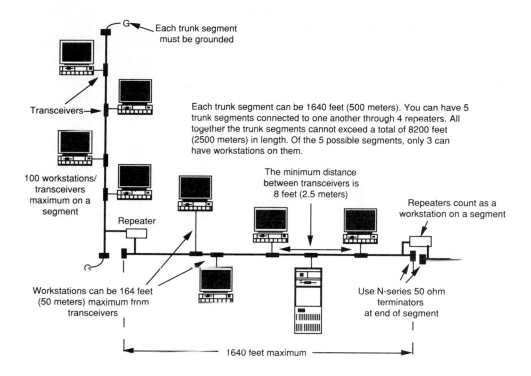

Each trunk segment
must be grounded

Transceivers

Each trunk segment can be 1640 feet (500 meters). You can have 5
trunk segments connected to one another through 4 repeaters. All
together the trunk segments cannot exceed a total of 8200 feet
(2500 meters) in length. Of the 5 possible segments, only 3 can
have workstations on them.

100 workstations/
transceivers
maximum on a
segment

Repeater

The minimum distance
between transceivers is
8 feet (2.5 meters)

Repeaters count as a
workstation on a segment

Workstations can be 164 feet
(50 meters) maximum from
transceivers

Use N-series 50 ohm
terminators
at end of segment

1640 feet maximum

Figure 12: Portrait of thick Ethernet cabling specifications.

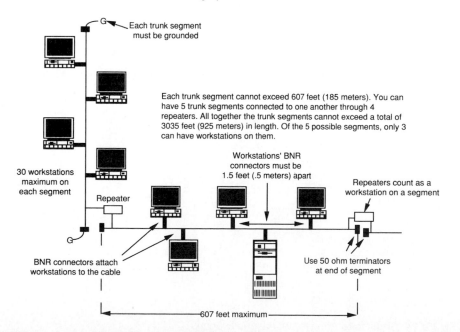

Each trunk segment
must be grounded

Each trunk segment cannot exceed 607 feet (185 meters). You can
have 5 trunk segments connected to one another through 4
repeaters. All together the trunk segments cannot exceed a total of
3035 feet (925 meters) in length. Of the 5 possible segments, only 3
can have workstations on them.

Workstations' BNR
connectors must be
1.5 feet (.5 meters) apart

Repeaters count as a
workstation on a segment

30 workstations
maximum on
each segment

Repeater

BNR connectors attach
workstations to the cable

Use 50 ohm terminators
at end of segment

607 feet maximum

Figure 13: Portrait of thin Ethernet specifications.

Token-Ring Constraints

The token-ring topology works electrically as a ring, with each workstation functioning as a repeater that passes the token around a circle of connected workstations. Only when a workstation has the token can it transmit its request. Token-ring uses shared memory and comes in two speeds: 4Mbps and 16 Mbps.

For large token-ring networks, the token-ring cable connecting workstation areas to a wiring closet or one wiring closet to another wiring closet is shielded twisted pair (Type 1) or unshielded twisted pair (Type 2). Type 1 can pass tokens at 16Mbps between 260 workstations; Type 2 adds four twisted pairs of solid AWG wires between the shield and cable sheath. Patch cables (which connect workstations and MAUs—multistation access units—together) is made of Type 6 cable, and must not exceed 150 feet (45 meters). Large token-ring networks can also contain distribution panels, equipment racks, cable brackets, and faceplates.

Small token-ring networks contain token-ring network interface boards, eight or sixteen port MAUs, a setup aid, adapter cables, and patch cables. Token-ring network interface boards connect to MAUs through Type 6 cable connected to adapter cables. Workstations within eight feet of a MAU use adapter cables that connect directly to one of the MAU ports; workstations more than eight feet (up to 150 feet, or 45 meters) distant from a MAU use patch cables that connect to the adapter cables. MAUs are connected to one another in a ring fashion through their Ring In/Ring Out (RI/RO) ports (a single MAU does not need such a connection); the cables connecting MAUs must also not exceed 150 feet (45 meters). The maximum number of stations is 96.

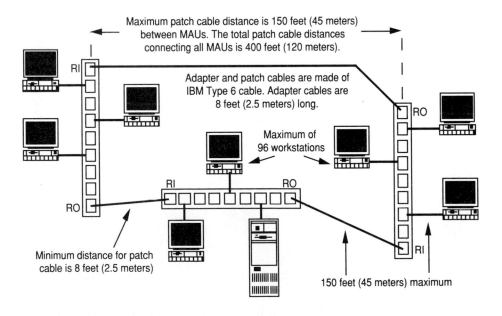

Figure 14: Small token-ring network specifications.

When troubleshooting a small token-ring topology, make sure the MAUs are plugged in and that you hear a distinct "click" when connecting cables to a MAU port. Also make sure there are no duplicate node addresses, and check the board settings against the option you chose in SHGEN. For IBM Token-Ring, you will receive software diskettes that you can use for troubleshooting the network interface board. This software will tell you if the network interface board is able to talk to the cable.

You should not splice patch cables, but you can make your own patch cable to the specified lengths. Patch cables should not run outside or be exposed to electric or magnetic fields created by fluorescent lights.

Workstation Memory

Most workstations have two types of memory: extended and expanded. Each memory type serves a purpose in the DOS environment, and some applications and utilities take advantage of one memory type but not the other.

Extended Memory

Extended memory is contiguous memory, which means there can be no holes in the memory extension. This memory goes from the address where memory ends in the workstation and extends into fields above DOS's 1MB (1024KB) limit. (There is also 64KB of memory beginning directly at 1024KB that is known as High memory and is addressable from real mode as well.) DOS's 1MB memory addressing limit is broken into two types: 640KB (known as main or RAM memory), which applications and utilities use, and 384KB (known as reserved memory), which the DOS operating system uses to store the addresses for its hardware drivers, monitor cards, LAN boards, and other devices.

Since applications can address only 640KB in DOS, most PC and XT computers have a 640KB maximum; many have only 512KB of memory (DOS reserved memory will work within the workstation's RAM constraints). But with the advent of the 80286-based AT computers, hardware technology expanded beyond the 640KB limit to 16MB. And with 80386-based computers, users can access up to 4GB (gigabytes) of physical memory. OS/2 is designed to take advantage of extended memory beyond the 640KB limit in 80286-, 80386-, and 80486-based machines. OS/2 takes advantage of these workstation's protected mode capabilities for memory access above 640KB. Other programs extend DOS itself to take advantage of a workstation's extended memory—programs such as Windows 386, and DESQview 286 and 386.

When adding memory to a workstation, be sure the memory board begins its addressing at the point where the workstation ends its memory (not including DOS's reserved memory). For example, whether the workstation has 512KB, 640KB, or 1MB (1024KB) of RAM, be sure the memory board begins at the proper memory address.

Depending on their hardware scheme, some computers include reserved memory and begin their extended memory at 1408 (1024 and 384). For example, Novell 286A and 386A workstations come with 1MB of memory and begin memory expansion at 1408. When buying additional memory, then, determine where the computer begins extended memory addressing and make sure the memory board you wish to purchase can begin at that address.

Some memory boards are hard-coded to begin at a certain memory address; if that memory address does not match the workstation, you cannot use it. Many memory boards, however, have configurable memory that you can set through hardware jumpers or software. These boards allow more flexibility.

DOS v4.0x comes with a HIMEM.SYS device driver that allows your workstation to access 64KB of extended memory. This driver allows other MS-DOS programs to store data in that extended memory. Placing this command in the CONFIG.SYS file (see the DOS 4.0x manual for details) will give your workstation 708KB of memory for applications rather than 640KB.

Expanded Memory

Expanded memory is a means of working with the reserved memory which usually lies above the 640KB limit, but below 1MB. Since 8086/8088, 80286, 80386, and 80486 microprocessors work within DOS's 1MB limit in real mode, they can access expanded memory by creating a window in reserved memory's physical address range. In order to access expanded memory, Lotus, Intel, and Microsoft collaborated to define the LIM EMS (Expanded Memory Specification) board. EMS is used to define an Expanded Memory Manager (EMM) which allows DOS to access expanded memory.

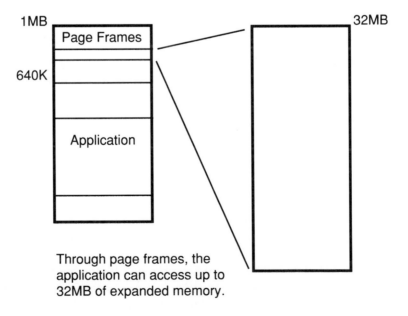

Figure 15: The Expanded Memory Specification (EMS) defines a page frame usually in Reserved Memory. The Expanded Memory Manager then allows an application running in DOS to use the page frames and map 16KB pages in and out of expanded memory. With EMS 4.0, you can have 8 pages in memory above 640KB.

Within reserved memory's 384KB range (between 768 and 960 memory address), the Expanded Memory Specification defines a page area, or frame, which maps to the LIM board's memory. There the workstation can access up to 32MB of expanded memory. The EMM allows applications to use eight 16KB physical page frames to access the LIM board's expanded memory banks for its use. Each page frame can access multiple physical pages by first mapping the address of the frame to its expanded memory location and then swapping in the pages (in 16KB chunks) as needed. This way, an application can access any area of expanded memory it allocates for use.

For best results, set up a full 64KB area in reserved memory for the LIM board. However, other devices, such as video cards and LAN boards, also use this area in reserved memory, so keep track of which boards you have installed and the memory address areas they occupy. If you have addressing conflict with any of your boards, those boards will not work. LAN boards, as NetWare is loaded, will overwrite other boards using conflicting addresses. A relatively safe address area is between E000h and F000h (see Figure 1 on page 4). Programs like System Sleuth show you if you have any reserved memory conflicts.

Expanded memory works differently than extended memory, principally because the EMM drivers which set up the page frame recognize how much expanded memory you have and where an application can access that memory. Install only LIM boards which meet LIM EMS 4.0 specifications; be sure the program you wish to run can take advantage of Expanded Memory Specification and therefore the Expanded Memory Manager.

3 Hardware Procedures

Adding Hardware to a Workstation: Running SETUP

Whenever you add a new hardware component or replace a component with a different kind of component in an 80286, an 80386, or an 80486 workstation, you must run a SETUP utility to tell the workstation of the change. When you start up the workstation, it runs through a checklist to confirm whether the setup is correct and to make sure that each ROM-designated component is in place. If for some reason the initial check finds inconsistencies, you will hear two beeps. If the monitor is functioning, an error message will usually indicate the problem.

SETUP allows you to manipulate the computer's installed memory, monitor type, floppy disk drives types, the date and time, and the disk type that most closely matches the hard disk drive. SETUP then writes the selected system configuration into the CMOS RAM, which contains some RAM and clock circuitry. CMOS does not use much electricity, so when the workstation is off, CMOS runs off the battery until you turn on the workstation again. The battery has a life of five years or longer, and recharges itself when the workstation is running. If the battery runs out, you will need to replace it; otherwise, you'll have to run SETUP every time you turn the workstation on so it can know its configuration.

Newer XT, 80286, and 80386 workstations have more sophisticated setup programs, showing what you designated in SETUP and what the program actually detects in the computer. If there are inconsistencies, the workstation will ask you to run SETUP and correct those inconsistencies. (That is, of course, if the monitor is functioning.)

Except for setting the CMOS RAM, there is nothing standard about how a SETUP program shows its information or how much information it provides. For example, you need to know the options in the ROM BIOS Drive Table when you add or replace the workstation's hard disk drive. Of six sample SETUP utilities, only two showed the ROM BIOS Drive Table with the drive head, cylinder, and sector counts as well as the precompensation values. AT Diagnostics, assuming you know the kind of hard disk installed in the workstation so you can match the drive type as it corresponds to the head/cylinder/sector and write precompensation values, does not provide a list of the drive types or their values.

Compaq takes a somewhat different approach, for its SETUP displays only the disk type and its corresponding drive size in megabytes:

Type 1 — 10 megabytes
Type 2 — 20 megabytes
Type 4 — 70 megabytes
Type 6 — 30 megabytes

and so forth. Compaq's SETUP also warns you that "other fixed disk drive suppliers may not supply types listed above." PS/2's SETUP also displays each disk type and its corresponding number of megabytes.

With this in mind, here is an example of one built-in SETUP utility. The information in the following figure is from a 386-based workstation.

```
┌─────────────────────────────────────────────────────────────────────┐
│  CMOS  SETUP  (C) Copyright 1985-1989,  American  Megatrends Inc.     │
├───────────────────────────────────┬─────────────────────────────────┤
│ Date (Mn/date/year) : Fri, July 30, 1990 │ Base Memory Size :    640KB    │
│ Time (hour/min/sec) : 18 : 15 : 18 │ Ext. Memory Size :    3072KB   │
│ Floppy drive A : 1.2MB, 5 1/2      │ Numeric Processor :  Not installed │
│ Floppy drive B : Not installed     │                                 │
│                                    │ Cyln Head WPcom LZone Sec Size  │
│ Hard disk C : Type : 35            │ 1024   9   65535  1024   17  77MB │
│ Hard disk C: Not installed         │                                 │
│ Primary display : VGA or EGA       │  Sun Mon Tue Wed Thu Fri Sat    │
│ Keyboard : Installed               │  27  28  29  30  31   1   2     │
│                                    │   3   4   5   6   7   8   9     │
│                                    │  10  11  12  13  14  15  16     │
│ Fixed Type = 01 . . .46, User defined type = 47, │ 17 18 19 20 21 22 23 │
│ For type 47 enter : Cyln, head, WPcom, LZone, sec, │ 24 25 26 27 28 29 30 │
│ (WPCom is 0 for all, 65535 for NONE) │                               │
│ ESC = Exit,        : Select, PgUp/PgDn = Modify │  1   2   3   4   5   6   7 │
└───────────────────────────────────┴─────────────────────────────────┘
```

Figure 16: By highlighting the drive type, you can thumb through the different disk drive settings or add one in by selecting type 47.

The upper right screen shows the date and time. To change these settings, first use the Up/Down-Left/Right arrow keys to highlight the time. The first entry highlighted shows the hours, followed by an entry for minutes and then an entry for seconds. Type in the correct numbers and press <Enter>. Then do the same for the date. Except for the memory option, the other entries have predefined selections.

Once you highlight a selection, press the PgDn key to see the next value and the PgUp key to see the previous value. When you find the desired value, simply leave that value on the screen; when you press Esc, you can then exit and save those settings to the CMOS RAM. The workstation then restarts with the new values.

Many new SETUP utilities display the discrepancies they detect. In the above example, if a workstation has a memory problem, SETUP shows you how much memory the workstation detects and how much memory the workstation has assigned. If there are discrepancies, you can change the "Extended Memory Size" values to match the memory detected.

The newer SETUPs also display the ROM BIOS Drive Table. This feature allows you to select the correct drive type for the hard drive you wish to install by allowing you to select the cylinder/head/sector values as well as the write precompensation values that matches the hard disk.

Some of the more generic SETUP programs do not include this list; they assume the workstation is an IBM AT and therefore follows the drive type table of IBM ATs. While IBM has established standard drive types for the AT line (see Appendix B), you cannot count on an AT clone counterpart to follow those rules. Since vendors can change a drive type to meet their particular needs, and since these drive types may even change with different ROM BIOS versions, you need a SETUP program that shows you the ROM BIOS Drive Table.

Adding a Hard Disk Drive

When adding a new hard disk drive to a workstation, keep the following steps in mind. (Appendix A gives you a workstation checklist that you can copy for each workstation; you can then keep a file or copy this information into a database for future reference.)

• Write down the name of the drive manufacturer;
• Set the drive jumper settings to the drive designation, such as C or D (this may or may not be necessary);
• Know the head/cylinder/sector and write precompensation values as well as the corresponding disk type;
• After installation, run the workstation's SETUP program to tell the workstation of its new addition;
• If necessary, run a low-level format;
• Run FDISK to install an active partition and divide the drive as desired;
• Run FORMAT /S, which formats the disk with a specific DOS COMMAND.COM file along with the hidden system files. You need to do this if you are planning to boot the workstation from the hard disk.

Most drives carry the drive's name and type, along with a bad disk table. All disk drives come with a list of the head/cylinder/sector and write precompensation values, as well as a list of the bad blocks the manufacturer found when performing a low-level format on the drive. The documentation also includes installation procedures and jumper settings.

If you find you have a drive without this documentation, but you know the drive name, call the vendor or a service center and ask the following questions:

1. Are there any jumper settings and/or terminators you should be aware of to run this drive as drive C:? As drive D:?

2. What is the number of heads, cylinders, sectors, and write precompensations for the drive?

3. Since workstations can have different ROM BIOS versions (and therefore different drive tables), which selection from the ROM BIOS drive table best matches the answer to question 2?   (If the vendor or service center does not have that answer, ask for the disk type for the IBM AT ROM BIOS.)

If you are installing a disk drive in a Compaq, you will need to check the Compaq-specific drive for C: and D: settings. Since the drive has only one connection cable (it combines the data and logical cable), you can use the drives only in other Compaqs. Disk drives for the IBM PC AT and compatibles are much more flexible and almost always come from the manufacturer already set to drive C:.

You must keep in mind a few things about the IBM PS/2 lines as well. If you have an ESDI controller, you will need an ESDI disk, and you can use software to designate the physical and logical drives. If you are using an MFM (Modified FM) controller in a Model 60 and above, you will probably need to physically set the disk drives to a different address.

When the drive type on the controller or in the ROM BIOS table does not match up with the head and cylinder count on your drive, choose the corresponding head count first, then the nearest cylinder count that is smaller than the cylinder count on the drive. Because the drive selection you chose is actually smaller than the disk drive itself, you will not get an exact match. Because you had to choose a smaller count (a larger one will not work), you will have to settle for having fewer available megabytes than you would have had with an exact match.

You must also keep in mind the sector count and the number of write precompensations from the specified track. If the write precompensation listing does not match the type of drive you have, you can receive read and write errors as the drive begins to fill and reach the area on the disk where the write precompensations take place. Because precompensation is not an exact science, you should fill your disk only three-quarters full to avoid read and write errors.

If you are losing valuable megabytes to non-matching drive types, you can get help from Vfeature Deluxe, a board and software program from Golden Bow Systems that gives you 250 different disk drive types to choose from. You will lose an expansion slot to the board, but for most workstations, this is not a problem.

Programs other than SETUP utilities that can show you the ROM BIOS table include LANSight by LAN Systems, Speed Store by Storage Dimensions, and California Ten Pack by Golden Bow, to name only a few.

Testing a Hardware Component

You will sometimes want to run tests on a particular hardware piece in a workstation. Several diagnostic tools can perform a low-level format; one diagnostic program that has been around since the IBM AT is the IBM Advanced Diagnostics. The software and manual walk you through the testing process. For example, suppose you want to make sure that the hard drive is connected correctly and runs well. Place the AT Diagnostics diskette into drive A: and reboot the machine (by simultaneously pressing <Ctrl-Alt-Del>). You will see a screen similar to this one:

```
The IBM Personal Computer
ADVANCED DIAGNOSTICS
Version 2.10
(C)Copyright IBM Corp. 1981, 1985


SELECT AN OPTION

0 - SYSTEM CHECKOUT
1 - FORMAT DISKETTE
2 - COPY DISKETTE
3 - PREPARE SYSTEM FOR MOVING
4 - SETUP
9 - END DIAGNOSTICS
```

To make sure that the drive is working properly, choose System Checkout (0) and press <Enter>. You will see a list of installed devices; if the list is correct, type Y <Enter>.

At the System Checkout screen, choose the "Run Tests One Time" option (0) <Enter>. You will then be asked which component you wish to test; choose the "Fixed Disk Drive and Adapter" option <Enter>.

At the Fixed Disk Diagnostic Menu, select "Run All Tests" (5) and the drive you wish to test—for example, 5,C—and press <Enter>. If at any time you choose the wrong selection, type <Ctrl-C>. You will either return to the previous menu or exit the program.

You will see a screen showing you which tests are being performed on which drive. The tests include seek, head, write/read/compare, error detection, and read verify. When the tests are finished, you will see the error codes for the errors each test has encountered (consult the diagnostics manual for each error code's explanation). If the tests encountered no errors, you will return to the System Checkout screen. Type 9 <Enter> to return to the "Select an Option" screen, then type 9 <Enter> again to end diagnostics.

Performing a Low-Level Format

For the most part, your service center will perform low-level formats on your hard disk drives. A low-level format checks for any bad cylinders on the disk drive and puts those cylinders into DOS's bad block table. You should run a low-level format on a hard disk drive:

• when track 0 is faltering and you can no longer boot from the hard drive, but you can still access the drive if you boot from a floppy diskette;

• when you are receiving a large number of abort/retry errors when writing to the drive (this can also mean a bad cable connection);

• when you have recovered the drive from an older workstation and you want to update the bad block table as well as ensure that the drive is still working.

To get the feel of a diagnostic program, look over these quick steps to setting up and running a low-level format on a drive. The following example also uses IBM Advanced Diagnostics v2.01. Before running a low-level format on a drive, be sure to back up the drive to floppy diskettes or the network.

To run a low-level format, insert the AT Diagnostics diskette into drive A: and reboot the machine. You'll see a screen similar to this one:

```
The IBM Personal Computer
ADVANCED DIAGNOSTICS
Version 2.10
(C)Copyright IBM Corp. 1981, 1985

SELECT AN OPTION

0 - SYSTEM CHECKOUT
1 - FORMAT DISKETTE
2 - COPY DISKETTE
3 - PREPARE SYSTEM FOR MOVING
4 - SETUP
9 - END DIAGNOSTICS
```

Choose System Checkout (0) and press <Enter>. You will see a list of installed devices; if the list is correct, type "Y" <Enter>. At the System Checkout screen, choose "Run Tests One Time" option (0) <Enter>. You will then be asked which component you wish to test; choose the "Fixed Disk Drive and Adapter" option <Enter>. At the Fixed Disk Diagnostic Menu, select the "Format Menu" option (5) <Enter>. The Format Selection Menu screen looks like this:

```
FORMAT SELECTION MENU
_____

1 - CONDITIONAL FORMAT
2 - UNCONDITIONAL FORMAT
3 - SURFACE ANALYSIS
4 - CHANGE INTERLEAVE
9 - RETURN TO FIXED DISK MENU
```

To perform a low-level format, select the "Unconditional Format" option (2) and the drive letter you are testing—for example, 2,C—and press <Enter>. You will receive a warning that all data on the fixed disk will be destroyed, and asking if you wish to continue. If you have not yet backed up your data, type "N" <Enter> and you'll return to the Format Selection Menu screen.

Typing "Y" <Enter> brings you another stern message that all data will be destroyed. Type "Y" <Enter> to continue. You next see the "Manufacturing Defect Entry" screen, where you can enter the defective blocks, just as manufacturers do when they run a similar test. These blocks are either listed on the disk drive or on a sheet of paper that you receive with the disk drive. If you have the bad block table, type "Y" <Enter> and enter the cylinder number, then head number for each of the bad blocks. Continue adding the head and cylinder numbers until you have no more to enter, then press "N" <Enter> at the "Any Defects To Enter? (Y/N)" prompt.

At the top of the screen you will see the heading "Formatting Is Being Performed On Drive C"; below that heading you will see the cylinders being counted down from the highest to the lowest. After the format completes, all defective cylinders are flagged as defective and written to DOS's bad block table so those cylinders will not be written to. You will then see a "Format Complete" message, to which you press <Enter> to return to the Format Selection Menu screen. Type 9 <Enter> until you exit the diagnostics program. At the "Prepare System for Desired Operation and Press Enter" prompt, place a DOS diskette into drive A: and prepare to run FDISK to create an active partition on drive C:.

Running FDISK

FDISK stands for "fixed disk setup." Once you run a low-level format on a disk, or when you buy a new disk drive, you will need to create DOS partitions and make one of those partitions "active" if you are going to boot from the hard disk. The active partition allows DOS to start automatically when you turn on the workstation; consequently, it is also the partition where you place the DOS system files.

Each DOS version performs FDISK somewhat differently, mainly because of the way each DOS version addresses hard disk drives. For example, DOS versions before 3.3 allowed you to access only 32MB of your disk drive, no matter how big the drive. DOS v3.3 allows you to have multiple 32MB partitions on the disk. DOS v4.0x allows you to have four partitions on the disk drive (no matter how big the drive) with only the primary partition marked as active. Use the DOS diskettes for the DOS version you wish to install. Follow the FDISK command in the correct DOS manual. This example will use IBM PC-DOS v3.3.

With a working copy of the DOS Startup (or Startup/Operation) diskette inserted, reboot the workstation so that it loads DOS, then type FDISK <Enter>.

You'll see a screen similar to the following:

```
IBM Personal Computer
Fixed Disk Setup Program Version 3.30
(C) Copyright IBM Corp. 1983, 1987

FDISK Options

Current Fixed Disk Drive: 1

Choose one of the following:

        1. Create DOS Partition
        2. Change Active Partition
        3. Delete DOS Partition
        4. Display Partition Information

Enter choice: [1]
```

Since the earlier example explained a low-level format on drive C:, choose "Create DOS Partition" (1) <Enter>. You'll then be asked to create a primary DOS partition. If the disk drive is 32MB or less and you want the drive to be one, active partition, press <Enter> and reboot the workstation.Consult your DOS manual for anything fancier than these basic steps.

Formatting the C: Drive

You next need to format the hard disk for the type of DOS you own. If you want to boot from the hard disk, you will also need to load the DOS system files. To do this, insert a working copy of the DOS Startup (or Startup/Operation) diskette into drive A: and type FORMAT C:/S/V <Enter>. (You can also use any diskette with COMMAND.COM and the system files, IBMBIO.COM and IBMDOS.COM.) The /S option loads COMMAND.COM and the two system files. DOS v4.0 also adds a *.COM system file. The /V option allows you to give the volume a name up to 11 characters long (DOS v4.0x gives you this option even if you do not use the parameter). You will be warned that formatting the disk will erase any data on the drive. Pressing "Y" <Enter> at the "Proceed with Format? (Y/N)" entry begins the formatting process. When the process is complete, you will see:

```
Format complete
System transferred

Volume label (11 characters, ENTER for none)?
```

To give the hard disk drive a name, you can type in the name of the person using the workstation, or the name and megabyte count of the hard disk itself, or whatever you choose to best keep track of the disk drive. After naming the volume, press <Enter> and you'll see the number of bytes of the total disk space, the number of bytes used by the system, and the number of bytes available on the disk. DOS v4.0x will also show the volume serial number.

At this point, set up the CONFIG.SYS and AUTOEXEC.BAT files so you can load the workstation's device and network drivers. Setting up CONFIG.SYS and AUTOEXEC.BAT files for network use are discussed in Chapter 4.

A good procedure with a newly formatted hard disk is to create directories for the data you wish to store. This helps unclutter the C: root directory, which will contain only the COMMAND.COM, CONFIG.SYS, and AUTOEXEC.BAT files, along with the directories you have created. It is a good idea to create a DOS directory that defines the DOS version you are using (MD DOS33 <Enter>, then CD DOS33 <Enter>) and load the files from the DOS diskettes into that directory (to see the DOS33 subdirectory path, type PROMPT PG <Enter>). To upload DOS diskettes, insert the DOS diskette(s) into drive A:, and at the C:\DOS33> prompt, type copy A:*.* <Enter>). You can then use this directory to format other diskettes with COMMAND.COM and system files.

Another good directory to create is a UTIL directory for the network files and other utilities or TSRs you want to load when the AUTOEXEC runs.

Formatting a Floppy Diskette

Formatting a floppy diskette is a relatively simple matter. With a working copy of the DOS Startup (or Startup/Operation) diskette inserted into drive A:, at the A: prompt type FORMAT B:/S/V <Enter>. (You can also use any diskette with COMMAND.COM and the two system files, IBMBIO.COM and IBMDOS.COM, to perform a system transfer.) If you have only one floppy disk drive, place the unformatted diskette into drive A:, which is substituting for drive B:, and press <Enter>. Be prepared to do a number of disk swaps with the Startup diskette.

If you have two floppy disk drives, place the unformatted diskette into drive B: before pressing <Enter>. Again, formatting with the /S option loads COMMAND.COM and the system files, and the /V option allows you to give the diskette a volume name up to 11 characters long, which is a good way of keeping track of diskettes.

As a special note, if you have created a DOS directory on the network (such as SYS:PUBLIC/MSDOS/V3.30) and try to format a diskette in A: drive with the system files, you will be asked to insert a diskette that has the system files (and COMMAND.COM). If you happen to have a boot diskette that contains the correct DOS version, use that diskette to format the new diskette with COMMAND.COM and the system files. Or you can go to the DOS directory on the hard drive and format the diskettes.

Another special note: when you format diskettes for file storage or transfer, use the FORMAT command without the /S parameter. These diskettes will be formatted according to the disk drive format but will be generic enough to allow other DOS versions to read the files from the diskette. Some exceptions are high-density diskettes being read by low-density disk drives, or double-sided diskettes being read by single-sided disk drives, but these exceptions are based on drive types, not DOS versions.

Upgrading the DOS Version on a Diskette and Disk

When upgrading the DOS version on a workstation, you need not reformat the diskettes or hard disk. To copy a different version of the system files to a floppy diskette, place the working copy of the DOS Startup (or Startup/Operation) diskette into drive A: and the diskette that needs upgrading in drive B:, and at the A: prompt, type A:SYS B: <Enter>. If you have only one disk drive, you will be prompted to insert the startup diskette periodically, so plan on doing disk swaps. You must also copy over the new version of COMMAND.COM from the Startup diskette by typing A:COPY COMMAND.COM B: <Enter>.

To copy a different version of the system files to the hard drive—for example, drive C:—place the working copy of the DOS Startup (or Startup/Operation) diskette in drive A: and at the A: prompt, type SYS C: <Enter>. Then copy over the new version of COMMAND.COM from the Startup diskette. If you ever decide to down grade from a DOS 4.0x diskette to a DOS 3.x, follow the same procedure. If you are down grading hard disk drives, however, run 4.0x FDISK first and remove any active partitions before attempting to reformat the hard disk to DOS 3.x.

4 DOS and NetWare-- Workstation Theory of Operations

Local area networks use the processing power of each workstation to perform tasks. While the file server handles security by restricting access privileges to certain files, and also handles file locking, printing, and updating the data on the server disks (among a number of other operations), the workstation takes care of the data processing. Here's how it works:

When you turn on the workstation, it sets up the DOS environment from the boot diskette or hard disk by loading the device drivers (such as a mouse driver) and other environmental variables (such as creating a virtual disk out of extended memory) from the CONFIG.SYS file. The workstation then loads COMMAND.COM and looks for an AUTOEXEC.BAT file to load any other workstation parameters, such as PROMPT and PATH commands, or any TSRs you cannot live without (see page 52 about TSRs). With the DOS environment established, the AUTOEXEC also loads the network files, which consist of IPX (IPX.COM) and the NetWare shell (NETx.COM) for NetWare v2.1x and above. For NetWare v2.0a workstations, the NetWare shell (ANETx.COM) contains IPX.

IPX stands for Internetwork Packet eXchange protocol, a derivative of XNS, the Xerox protocol. When you generate a NetWare shell through the GENSH or SHGEN utility (see page 62 or 64 respectively), you tell that utility which avenues it can use to communicate through the network interface board to the network. Network interface boards use the I/O address, interrupt, IRQ, and DMA channels (when necessary) as their avenues for communication. GENSH/SHGEN then links IPX to these specifications, creating a hardware-specific LAN driver which can handle all the hardware-specific tasks, such as formatting data for transmission over the network cable.

Getting Connected

The basic commands required for establishing a network connection from the AUTOEXEC.BAT include:

IPX   (v2.0a simply has ANETx for these first two commands)
NETx
F: (default network LOGIN drive)
LOGIN <servername/username>

When the IPX driver loads, it establishes an avenue for communication with the network interface board and attached cable, allowing access to attached workstations and servers. Then the NetWare shell loads (the NetWare shell is the generic portion of the network connection and runs on top of IPX). As the shell loads, it first establishes a connection to a network server by using IPX to broadcast "Get Nearest Server." The first server to respond to the request establishes a connection with that workstation. When you initially log in, you will see "Attached to server <servername>" after the shell parameters.

As the shell connects to a server, it gains access to that server's bindery, allowing you to attach to any server that appears in the connected server's routing table. The AUTOEXEC file then changes to the SYS:LOGIN directory, which DOS v3.x designates as drive F:. (You can, however, change this default in the CONFIG.SYS file—see page 56.)

With a drive at the LOGIN directory, you are able to initiate a LOGIN command to a designated server if the server you are connected to can communicate with the server you wish to log in to. The NetWare shell sends a "Get Local Target" call to the designated server and queries for the best route to that server. If you are physically attached to the targeted server and the server answers to the "Get Nearest Server" call, you will have a direct connection to the server; all NetWare requests will use that connection.

If you are not physically attached to the designated server, NetWare will route the request to that server, giving you a logical connection. As the designated server responds to the call, it answers through the best route available at the time of connection. The NetWare shell then drops the connection to its initial server and establishes a connection with the designated server.

Newer versions of the NetWare shell since the release of the NetWare 386 v3.01 shell version allow you to designate a "preferred server" with the shell command. For example, you can place the command NETx PS=OBIWON in the AUTOEXEC.BAT file and the NetWare shell will try to first connect with the server OBIWON. This option cuts out the logistics of first attaching to an initial server, then connecting to the designated server. However, if the shell cannot attach to the specified server (in this case OBIWON), the shell will establish a connection to another server if it can.

With the connection in place, the LOGIN command checks to make sure the name you typed is a bindery entity with bindery properties such as a password, a login script, and directory designations, along with their security equivalences. If you have a password, you will be asked to "Enter your password." The correct response places your bindery information into the server's memory and runs your login script or a default login script. (You will not see a login script if you attach to a server instead of log in to a server.)

DOS and the NetWare Shell

When an application or utility at the workstation wants DOS to perform a specific task, it issues an Int 21h command to get DOS's attention, then passes the necessary information to perform that task. DOS then looks up the function in its function table, executes the specified function, and returns the necessary information or procedure back to the application. When the application or utility needs another task, it issues another Int 21h call to DOS, and the whole process begins again.

This is where the NetWare shell comes in. The NetWare shell acts as a redirector that takes over Int 21h and watches for all DOS Int 21h calls. When an application or utility makes an Int 21h call to awaken DOS, the shell determines if that call should be serviced at the server or at the workstation. If the request belongs to a network drive, the shell translates the DOS request into a NetWare Core Protocol (NCP) request packet and sends the packet to the designated server. The server answers the request and sends back a response to the application or utility. This transaction is transparent to the application.

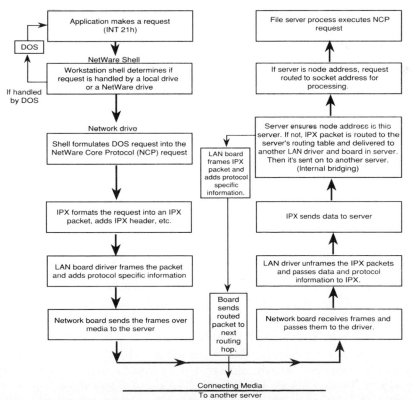

Figure 17: What happens when an application makes a request.

If the request belongs to a local drive, the NetWare shell passes the request to DOS; DOS answers the request and sends back a response to the application. This way, DOS takes care of its responsibilities, and NetWare takes care of its responsibilities.

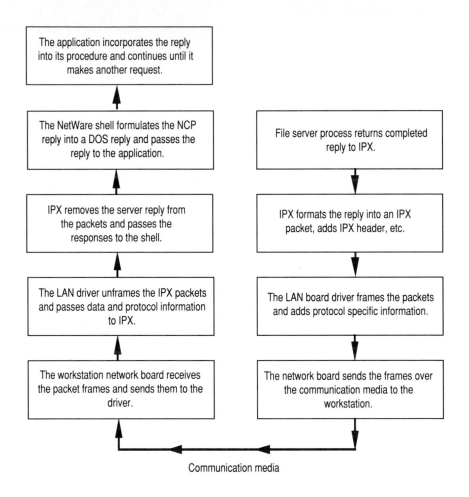

Figure 18: What happens when a server replies to an application's request.

NetWare Commands That Function Similarly to DOS Commands

Since NetWare and DOS are both operating systems, each offers utilities to make computing a little easier. And since DOS is a standalone environment, NetWare often expands upon DOS's utilities to incorporate the network environment. Still, there is some overlap. Below is a list of DOS and NetWare commands that have similar functions. For the most part, both sets of commands work from the network (DOS) prompt. Noted exceptions are listed under the heading, "DOS Utilities That Do *Not* Work the Same in NetWare."

DOS Utilities	*NetWare Utilities*
APPEND (/PATH:ON /X:ON /E)	SMODE (options 1-7, see page 86)
ASSIGN (A=C B=C)	MAP (*1:= or S1:=)
ATTRIB (+A -A, +R -R)	FLAG (Shareable ReadOnly, etc.)
BACKUP (/D: /T: /F:)	LARCHIVE, NARCHIVE, NBACKUP
BREAK (ON OFF)	SET BREAK (system or user login scripts)
CHDIR (CD)	SESSION (Current Drive Mappings & F3)
CHDIR (CD)	FILER (Select Current Directory option)
CHKDSK (workstation stats)	CHKVOL, VOLINFO (server stats)
COPY (/A /B /V)	NCOPY, FILER (Copy File option)
DEL, ERASE (* or ?)	FILER (File Info option & press Del)
DATE (mm-dd-yy, etc.)	SYSTIME (shows date and time)
MKDIR (MD)	FILER (Subdirectory option & press Ins)
PATH (;)	MAP (*1:= or S1:=)
PRINT (/D /B /U etc.)	NPRINT (S= P= Q= J= etc.)
RECOVER (* or ?)	LRESTORE, NRESTORE, NBACKUP
RENAME (files)	RENDIR (directories)
RESTORE (* or ?)	LRESTORE, NRESTORE, NBACKUP
RMDIR (RD)	FILER (Subdirectory option & Del)
SET (name=[parameter])	SET (system and user login scripts)
SORT (/R /+n)	NDIR (using the SORT option)
SUBST	MAP (*1:= S1:=)
TIME (hh:mm:ss)	SYSTIME (shows date and time)
TREE (/A /F)	LISTDIR (/R /D /S /A)
TYPE	FILER (View File option in File Info)
VER (DOS version)	NVER (NetBIOS, IPX, LAN driver, etc.)
VOL (HD and diskette names)	CHKVOL, VOLINFO (server volumes)

DOS Commands That Do *Not* Work the Same in NetWare

While DOS commands always work normally in the local drive environment, some commands behave differently when asked to execute in a NetWare networking environment. You may also find DOS commands other than the ones listed here that behave differently. For example, XCOPY from DOS versions 3.1 and 3.3 work well with NetWare, but some supervisors have experienced problems with DOS v3.2's XCOPY.

When DOS sees the colon (:) after the server and volume names, it associates that colon with the root directory. Because DOS sees this as the root, you can use the backslash (\) key to designate a volume root. For example, entering the "CD\" command at network directory prompt will always return you to the root directory.

In any case, here are the DOS commands that behave differently in the NetWare environment (versions 2.0x to 3.01) than in a local drive environment at the workstation.

ASSIGN. ASSIGN allows one drive to be equivalent to another drive. When working on the network, use the MAP utility to assign drive equivalences. For example, if you want drive K: to be equivalent to drive F:, type MAP K:=F: <Enter> at the command line. Use the ASSIGN command for local drives only.

BACKUP. This command applies particularly to NetWare v2.15 running NetWare for Macintosh. In such an instance, the DOS BACKUP command is unable to recognize Macintosh files. Use the MACBACK utility for backing up Macintosh files.

CHKDSK. This internal DOS command cannot be used on network drives, since it looks for 512-byte DOS blocks and not for NetWare's file format. Use CHKDSK for local drives and CHKVOL for network drives. To see how much memory the workstation has left after loading the NetWare shell, go to A:, then type CHKDSK <Enter>. You can also use CHKDSK to see how many bad sectors the diskette contains.

COMP. This command compares the contents of a file or group of files to the contents of another file or group of files. When using this command, remember that DOS commands do not recognize server and volume names in a DOS directory path. Therefore, you must use NetWare's MAP command to designate the server and volume in a directory path.

    For example, if you want to compare the JAN.RPT file from ADMIN/ SYS:REPORTS to the JAN.RPT file in ADMIN/VOL1:1990/REPORTS, first map drives to both directory paths; for example, MAP G:=ADMIN/SYS:REPORTS <Enter> and MAP H:=ADMIN/VOL1:1990/REPORTS <Enter>. Then you can type COMP G:JAN.RPT H:JAN.RPT <Enter>.

COMSPEC=C:COMMAND.COM or A:COMMAND.COM. The COMSPEC command tells DOS where to find COMMAND.COM when DOS needs to initiate a command process (allowing the workstation to run applications). If you have set up the COMSPEC command in the system login script, take out the COMSPEC command in any AUTOEXEC.BAT file on the network. Otherwise, the resulting conflicts will cause workstations to hang when you exit applications.

COPY. You will not be able to specify the server or volume name in the directory path when using the COPY command. To copy files from one volume to another, use the MAP command to set up the drive mappings. Then use the drive letters in the COPY command. For example, if you want to copy all the *.RPT files from ADMIN/SYS:REPORTS to ADMIN/VOL1:1990/REPORTS, first map drives to both directory paths, such as MAP G:=ADMIN/SYS:REPORTS <Enter> and MAP H:=ADMIN/VOL1:1990/REPORTS <Enter>. Then you type COPY G:*.RPT H: <Enter>.

    You can also use NCOPY. COPY will not copy a Macintosh resource fork; NCOPY for NetWare v2.15 and above will.

DIR. You will not be able to specify the server or volume name in the directory path. To see a directory on a different volume, use the MAP command to set up the drive mappings. Then use the drive letter in your DIR command: for example, DIR H: <Enter>. For NetWare v2.1x and above, you can also use NetWare's NDIR command. For NetWare v2.0a, you can use NetWare's UDIR.

DISKCOMP. Because NetWare creates blocks of 4096 bytes or more when formatting its disk drives, the DISKCOMP command will not function on the network. Even with NetWare v2.0a, this command will not be able to compare NetWare drives. Use DISKCOMP only on local disk drives.

DISKCOPY. Because NetWare creates blocks of 4096 bytes or more when formatting its disk drives, the DISKCOPY command will not function on the network. Even with NetWare v2.0a, this command is unable to copy NetWare disks. Use DISKCOPY only on local disk drives.

ERASE and **DEL**. You will not be able to specify the server or volume name in the directory path. To erase a file or files on a different volume, use the MAP command to set up the drive mappings, then use the drive letter in your ERASE command. The DEL command works the same way. For example, after you copy all the *.RPT files from G:\ADMIN\SYS:REPORTS to H:\ADMIN\VOL1:1990\REPORTS, to delete the *.RPT files from a directory mapped to G:, type DEL G:*.RPT <Enter>. You may wish to go to the G: directory before using the DEL or ERASE command; in that case, simply type DEL *.RPT <Enter> from the G: command line prompt.

If you erase something you did not mean to erase, use the SALVAGE command to get back the files. But there are some stipulations to using SALVAGE in NetWare versions before 3.0:

• Any file modification, such as running DEL or ERASE or creating any files since you performed the deletion, makes it impossible to retrieve those files.

• You cannot log out, log in again, and then run SALVAGE to retrieve files you deleted in your previous server connection. Since you need the same server connection, you must also run SALVAGE from the same workstation from which you performed the deletion.

• You cannot run PURGE after you delete the file and before you run SALVAGE.

With NetWare v3.0, SALVAGE lets you view your deleted files, purge or recover deleted files, or restore files to your directory or a DELETED.SAV directory. Files deleted from a server running NetWare 386 remain on the server disks until the server needs that disk space for other files. NetWare 386 also gives deleted files a deletion date, so if you have multiple deleted files with the same name, you can salvage the most current deleted version. Like undeleted files, deleted files are controlled by a user's security rights.

As a supervisor, you can limit how long deleted files exist on NetWare drives through the console SET command—see the SET command in the *NetWare 386 System Administration* manual.

FORMAT. Because NetWare creates blocks of 4096 bytes or more with a good deal of security information built into each block, the FORMAT command will not work on a network drive. You must use COMPSURF instead. Use the FORMAT command only on local disk drives. FORMAT is an external DOS command; you will need access to the directory where you store FORMAT when you format a diskette. To add the system files (FORMAT /S) from a network drive, you must have a diskette containing the system files when transferring the COMMAND.COM, IBMBIO.SYS, and IBMDOS.SYS files to a newly formatted diskette. Otherwise, you can use the DOS directory on a C: drive, as explained earlier.

Also, be sure to make boot diskettes from the same type of disk drive that the diskette will run on (see page 12).

LABEL. Do not use the LABEL command on the network; it tries to delete all the files in the root directory of the volume. If this happens and you have a version of NetWare prior to NetWare 386, try SALVAGE to see if you can recover the lost files. The same principles apply to SALVAGE here as they are explained in DEL and ERASE (page 47). If SALVAGE does not work, you will have to restore those files through your regular restore methods.

MKDIR (can also be **MD**). You will not be able to specify the server or volume name in the directory path. To make a directory on a different volume than the volume you are presently in, use the MAP command to set up the drive mappings, then use the drive letter in your MKDIR command. For example, if you want to make a CHARGE directory beneath the H:\ADMIN\VOL1:1990\REPORTS directory, either go to the H: directory and type MD CHARGE <Enter>, or type MD H:\CHARGE <Enter> if you are in another directory path. You can also create directories in the NetWare FILER utility.

PATH. While the PATH command works normally in a NetWare environment, it works best on your local paths. Use MAP's search drive capabilities for the network environment. You can set up a MAP command to include local drives as search drives: for example, MAP S5:=C:\UTILS. Because of how the NetWare shell works, local drives are only searched for executable files (such as *.COM, *.BAT, and *.EXE files) that you invoke from the command line, or the drives are searched by an application that specifically looks at the DOS path variable. If you have a PATH command in your AUTOEXEC.BAT file, the drives listed in the PATH command will show up as search drives when you type MAP.

PRINT. The PRINT command will not function on the network unless you have a local printer attached and you have issued an ENDCAP command to nullify the CAPTURE command in NetWare v2.1x and above (for NetWare v2.0a, it's the

ENDSPOOL command to nullify SPOOL). If you have SPOOL or CAPTURE in effect, the <Shift-PrtSc> combination will either work fine, or give the impression that the workstation has hung. Use the DOS PRINT command only when you have local printers attached and you have designated in the application where you want to print. PRINT works the same as SPOOL and CAPTURE do for the network, so only use PRINT with a local printer.

You can prevent a workstation from appearing to hang when you press the <Shift-PrtSc> combination by placing the Local Printers = 0 parameter in the SHELL.CFG file for NetWare v2.1x and above. (See page 77.) The workstation doesn't always hang—it just sometimes takes the application a long time to detect the printer is off-line.

RECOVER. Since RECOVER is a DOS command, it will not function on the network; use it only on local disk drives. Use NetWare's SALVAGE command for the network if you typed DEL or ERASE at the wrong time and you have not created or deleted anything since you did type DEL or ERASE (see page 47).

RENAME. Be sure to conform to standard DOS conventions when you use this command, or RENAME will not work. DOS naming conventions include an eight-character filename (maximum) along with an optional three-character extension. Acceptable characters include any letter of the alphabet, as well as certain other symbols: ~ ! @ # $ % ^ & ( ) - _ { } '.

RESTORE. To use the DOS RESTORE utility, you must be in the same directory from which you back up files. Use NRESTORE in conjunction with the NARCHIVE utility, or LRESTORE in conjunction with the LARCHIVE utility. In some versions of NetWare, you must use the restoring features in the NBACKUP utility.

RMDIR (can also be **RD**). You will not be able to specify the server or volume name in the directory path. To remove a directory on a different volume than the volume you are presently in, use the MAP command to set up the drive mappings, then use the drive letter in your RMDIR command. But you must be in the directory above the directory you wish to remove, and there cannot be any files in the directory or you will get an error message. You can remove both files and directories together through the FILER utility. But if another workstation has a drive mapped to one of the directories you wish to delete, you will not be able to delete that directory.

SUBST. The SUBST command works only on your local disk drives. Use the MAP command for mapping network drives. If you wish to have several local drive mappings using the SUBST command, go into your CONFIG.SYS file and designate the last drive to correspond to your last local drive. For example, if you use your local disk drive extensively, and if you use the SUBST command for local drives through drive H:, put LAST DRIVE = H: <Enter> in your CONFIG.SYS file. Then NetWare will know to begin the network drives at I:. Otherwise, NetWare will default to F: and your local drive substitutions will be overwritten.

XCOPY. You will not be able to specify the server or volume name in the directory path. To copy files from one volume to another, use the MAP command to set up the drive mappings. Then use the drive letters in the XCOPY command. For example, if you want to copy all the *.RPT files from ADMIN/SYS:REPORTS to ADMIN/VOL1:1990/REPORTS, first map drives to both directory paths: for example, MAP G:=ADMIN/SYS:REPORTS <Enter> and MAP H:=ADMIN/VOL1:1990/REPORTS <Enter>. Then type XCOPY G:*.RPT H: <Enter>.

If you use XCOPY in a batch file, you must be in the directory from which you are copying. You can also use NetWare's NCOPY command. Keep in mind that XCOPY will not copy a Macintosh resource fork, and NCOPY will. But XCOPY will copy your subdirectory structure (XCOPY /S), and versions of NCOPY before NetWare 386 cannot do that. XCOPY also has a /Modify parameter (XCOPY /M) that allows you to copy only the files that have been modified since the last time you backed up; NCOPY does not have that capability.

By using the /M parameter, you can use XCOPY to back up to multiple diskettes. When one diskette is full, XCOPY stops running. You then place another diskette in drive A: and retype the same XCOPY command (such as XCOPY F:*.* /M /S). The /M parameter turns off the archive bit on all the files that are copied up to that point and begins backing up unmodified files at the point where the first diskette filled up. You can repeat this procedure until you have backed up all modified files in the current F: directory and all subdirectories beneath the current directory.

Network Software for the Workstation

With a few TSR exceptions, almost every standalone application will work in the NetWare environment. (The exceptions are applications that require more memory than is left after the IPX and/or the NetWare shell have loaded.) And there are network versions of almost every application you use.

Network applications are designed to limit the number of users who can access an application; single-user applications have no such protection and can therefore be used beyond their licensing agreement. However, there are some schemes you can set up to protect against such license violations.

One method is to establish groups in order to control access to an application. For example, if you have four standalone copies of Microsoft Excel in the office, place one copy of the application in a directory called EXCEL, create a group in SYSCON named EXCEL, and assign that group directory rights to use the program. Users who are not members of that group will have no rights in the EXCEL directory, and therefore cannot use the program.

Some programs allow single-user access for each manual bought. This means that anyone who has a manual can access the program. If you have only four manuals, but seven users need periodic access to the program, put all seven users in the group and assign that group the rights they need to access the application. Then use a program such as Integrity Software's Sitelock or Connect Computer's Turnstyle to limit the number of active sessions an application can have. With such a program in operation, when four users are actively using the application, any other user will have to wait until one of the four exits the program.

But for the most part, your network users should be using network versions of their applications. If you are logged in as supervisor or equivalent on a NetWare v2.1x server or above, and you want to see all the *.EXE and *.COM files on your network as well as the directory (or directories) they are in, go to the root of a volume such as SYS: (CD\ <Enter>), and type NDIR * FN=*.EXE FN=*.COM SUB >APPS <Enter>.

The ensuing process can take a while, but eventually you will have a file called APPS in the current directory. You can then print that ASCII file through NPRINT or view it in any word processor. The printout will tell you the total number of files and how much disk space they use. You can then police your network for pirated or redundant software.

Applications Interpreting NetWare Messages

To better understand how applications interpret error messages, here is a brief repeat explanation on how DOS applications and the NetWare shell work together, first in the DOS environment and then in the NetWare environment.

When an application wants DOS to perform a function, the application issues an Int 21h command to get DOS's attention, then passes the necessary information that performs a specific task. DOS then looks up the function in its function table, executes the specified function, and returns the requested information or process back to the application. The application repeats this process for each interrupt the application generates.

As stated before, the NetWare shell acts as a redirector that takes over Int 21h and watches for all DOS Int 21h calls. When an application makes an Int 21h call and the request belongs to a network drive, the shell translates the DOS request into a NetWare Core Protocol (NCP) request packet and sends the packet to the designated server. The server answers the request and sends back a response to the application.

Since the application thinks DOS is handling the function, it also expects DOS to return an error message to the application when something goes amiss. An application will often waylay the error message that DOS sends and present on the screen its own message instead of the DOS message. Such messages are usually specific to what the application was trying to perform when the error occurred.

The application does not know that it is running on a server; it therefore does not know how to interpret error messages resulting from server maladies. For example, if the server goes down while you are in an application like WordPerfect and you try to update a file on the server, you will see a "Disk Error 88: error writing to disk" message, which usually indicates that the server has gone down or that you have lost your connection to the server. Fortunately, if you receive this error message in WordPerfect v4.2, you can return to the document, place a diskette in drive A:, and press <F10>, a procedure which will (after several tries) save the file to the floppy diskette. This procedure has had spotted success with WordPerfect 5.0 and 5.1.

Since each application can interpret the DOS error message to mean something specific to that application, it becomes all but impossible to anticipate the way these error messages will appear in NetWare. If you want to better understand what an error message means on the DOS and application levels, and if you are a bit adventurous, buy a DOS Technical Reference Manual and familiarize yourself with DOS error messages and what they mean. Then read about error messages in the manual to the application in question. Then try to equate certain application error messages to a NetWare situation.

Another useful book for supervisors of NetWare v2.0a, v2.1x, and v3.0 networks is the Novell System Messages manual (#100-000372-001, 100-000584-001 for NetWare 386). Although the manual does not explain all the error messages for v2.1x or NetWare 386, it is still a good reference for better understanding the error messages that glare cryptically at you from the screen.

TSRs and DOS

Terminate-and-stay-resident (TSR) programs add convenience to the DOS environment. These programs load into the workstation's RAM and take up residence until you turn off the workstation. You normally invoke these programs by using a hot key or a hot-key combination. Depending on how well-behaved the TSR is, you can invoke the TSR while still in another application, or any time you return to the DOS shell from within an application.

You can have a number of TSRs loaded into your workstation. The AUTOEXEC example on page 59 shows three memory-resident programs loaded: HotKey, CED (a command editor), and then the network TSRs, IPX and NET3. To load TSRs from an AUTOEXEC.BAT file, put the program files either on the boot diskette or in a C: directory where the AUTOEXEC can find them.

In making decisions about using TSRs on the network, remember that they can conflict with each other, they can cancel each other out, and they can take up so much memory that you will not have enough memory left to load a particular application.

If you are installing a number of TSRs on the network, you will need to experiment to make sure they do not conflict with each other. When two TSRs conflict, the workstation hangs when it tries to load them or when you try to invoke one of them. If you encounter this problem, try loading the TSRs in a different order, or try taking out the least-used TSR to see if the others will load and work correctly.

If two TSRs cancel each other out, nothing happens when you try to invoke one of them. In this case, you must find out which TSRs are conflicting and then get a product like TurboPower Software's MARK and RELEASE to release one TSR when you use another TSR that conflicts with it. The third problem—taking up too much memory—can also be solved through a product like MARK and RELEASE.

Terminating TSRs

Since TSRs are resident in RAM even when not in use, terminating a TSR usually requires rebooting the workstation and not loading that program. However, programs such as MARK and RELEASE allow you to remove TSRs from memory without rebooting the workstation.

The principle is simple. You type MARK <Enter> to place a Mark in memory before loading a string of TSRs. Then when you need the memory taken up by those TSRs, type RELEASE <Enter> to remove the TSRs up to the place marked in memory. If you are running programs (such as Action Technology's The Coordinator) that require a lot of memory, you can release any TSRs that take up memory.

You can also set up a batch file to mark memory, load a number of TSRs and applications that work together (for example, a word processor and a thesaurus TSR), and then release the TSR when you exit the program and finish the batch file. Here's an example of such a batch file:

```
@ECHO OFF
C:
CD\
MARK
CD\WS4
WF                      (WordFinder)
WS                      (WordStar)
C:
CD\
RELEASE
```

This batch file sets up a mark before loading the WordFinder TSR, then releases the TSR after exiting WordStar. RELEASE will not function until the batch file is over; therefore, you should place RELEASE at the end of the batch file instead of at the beginning.

Sometimes when you leave an application, DOS loads another command processor which does not know about the batch file and therefore does not run RELEASE. If you find this to be the case, you can create a generic batch file (for example, R.BAT) that simply runs RELEASE. Turbo Software also has a utility called MAPMEM which shows you which programs are presently taking up workstation memory.

While IPX and NETx are considered TSRs, they do not work well with normal TSR mark-and-release programs. The end result is that you usually have to reboot the workstation and run a different batch file in the AUTOEXEC to accommodate a different LAN board. However, Turbo Software also has a program called NMARK and NRELEASE which can mark and release IPX and NETx files.

TSRs and NetWare

To run TSRs at the workstation, do not install them from your login script or from the MENU utility. Instead, load them from the AUTOEXEC.BAT file, after the login script executes, or before going into the MENU utility. These utilities invoke a copy of COMMAND.COM and then load themselves into memory, which means that TSRs will load into memory beyond these other programs.

As you exit MENU or the login script, these utilities also exit the memory where they ran. But because the TSR is locked into memory above the location MENU or the login script used to occupy, there is a hole in memory that cannot be used by other programs or utilities. Depending on the size of your login script or MENU, the 4KB TSR you loaded can take up anywhere from 12KB to 50KB.

Here again, utilities such as MARK and RELEASE are useful for releasing memory holes if they occur. Another handy product is LANSpace from LANSystems. LANSpace runs as a 4KB TSR and performs some excellent memory swapping that allows you to run memory-intensive programs like The Coordinator while you are in a large application like WordPerfect. LANSystems also has programs that will load IPX into extended memory.

You will have to experiment to learn how much liberty you can take with NetWare utilities and TSRs.

Creating a Boot Diskette for the DOS Workstation

The basic steps in creating a boot diskette include formatting a floppy diskette (see page 12), setting up the CONFIG.SYS and AUTOEXEC.BAT files, and (optionally) modifying the shell commands in SHELL.CFG if you are running NetWare v2.1x and above. Supervisors also need to run GENSH or SHGEN in order to place the proper NetWare files on the diskette. These files include ANETx.COM (for NetWare v2.0a), IPX.COM, NETx.COM, and, when applicable, NETBIOS.EXE and INT2F.COM. This section describes how to make a floppy diskette into a workstation boot diskette, as well as explaining the particulars of using the workstation C: drive from which to boot.

The first step in creating a boot diskette is to include the DOS version you wish the user to have. A boot diskette contains COMMAND.COM and the system files, IBMBIO.COM and IBMDOS.COM. With a working copy of the DOS Startup (or Startup/Operation) diskette inserted into drive A:, at the A: prompt type FORMAT B:/S/V <Enter>. If you have only one floppy disk drive, place the unformatted diskette into drive A:, which is substituting for drive B:, and press <Enter>. For those supervisors with a DOS directory on their workstation's hard disk, go to that DOS directory and type FORMAT A:/S/V <Enter>. You will not need any other diskettes to perform the system file transfer.

Copyright law requires that each network DOS user have his or her own DOS manual.

DOS Versions and Corresponding NetWare Versions

When you generate NetWare shells, be sure your version of NetWare supports the DOS type the computer uses. Here is a list of NetWare versions and the DOS versions they support:

NetWare Versions	DOS Versions
NetWare 68	2.0, 2.1, 3.0, 3.1, 3.2
NetWare 86	2.0, 2.1, 3.0, 3.1, 3.2
ELS NetWare (run as 86)	2.0, 2.1, 3.0, 3.1, 3.2, 3.3
ELS NetWare (run as 286)	2.0, 2.1, 3.0, 3.1, 3.2, 3.3, 4.0x
NetWare 286 v2.0a	2.0, 2.1, 3.0, 3.1, 3.2, 3.3

NetWare 286 v2.1 and v2.11	2.0, 2.1, 3.0, 3.1, 3.2, 3.3, 4.0x
NetWare 286 v2.12	2.0, 2.1, 3.0, 3.1, 3.2, 3.3, 4.0x
NetWare 286 v2.15	2.0, 2.1, 3.0, 3.1, 3.2, 3.3, 4.0x
NetWare 386 v1.0	2.0, 2.1, 3.0, 3.1, 3.2, 3.3, 4.0x

Setting Up the CONFIG.SYS File

The CONFIG.SYS file is a list of configuration commands that help set up the DOS workstation environment. The commands in the CONFIG.SYS file are for setting up the workstation's DOS environment; when you want to adjust the NetWare environment for your workstations (with NetWare v2.1x and above), use the SHELL.CFG file (see page 77).

When you turn on the workstation, DOS searches for the CONFIG.SYS file in the root directory of the diskette found in drive A:, or, in the case of a hard disk, the root directory of the active partition. If DOS cannot find such a file, DOS assigns default configuration values.

DOS v4.0x takes this process one step further. When you run SELECT on a hard drive installation, DOS creates a CONFIG.SYS file for you with the following parameters:

```
BREAK=ON
BUFFERS=20
FILES=8
LASTDRIVE=E
SHELL=C:\DOS\COMMAND.COM /P /E:256
DEVICE=C:\DOS\ANSI.SYS
INSTALL=C:\DOS\FASTOPEN.EXE C:=(50,25)
```

If you already have a CONFIG.SYS file, DOS will create a CONFIG.400 file containing these parameters. If you want these parameters to appear in the original CONFIG.SYS file, either add them to that file or simply delete the old CONFIG.SYS file and rename the CONFIG.400 file to CONFIG.SYS.

DOS v3.3 allows for 11 different CONFIG.SYS commands; DOS v4.0x allows for 17. For details about these commands, consult your DOS manual. This discussion will focus on the commands that are most useful for networking purposes. The following CONFIG.SYS batch file assumes an installed hard disk drive with a UTIL directory; for diskettes, be sure the filenames and drivers that CONFIG.SYS calls for are located on the diskette.

```
COPY CON CONFIG.SYS

BREAK=OFF
FILES=30
LASTDRIVE=D
SHELL=C:COMMAND.COM /P /E:512
DEVICE=C:\UTIL\ANSI.SYS
DEVICE=C:\UTIL\VDISK.SYS 384 512 128 /E
DEVICE=C:\UTIL\MSMOUSE.SYS
LASTDRIVE=D
^Z
```

BREAK=ON/OFF. BREAK OFF (the default) prevents you from breaking out of a program (Ctrl+Break, or Ctrl+C) until the executing program writes to the screen or printer. BREAK ON means you can break out whenever you press Ctrl+Break. To prevent users from breaking out of batch files, use the BREAK OFF default.

FILES=30. This command shows the number of files (between eight and 255) the workstation can have open at once. If you are running programs such as DESQview 386 or Microsoft's Windows—that is to say, programs which extend DOS's functionality—you may need to increase the number of open files to cover the extra DOS sessions you are running. A good rule of thumb is twenty open files per session. However, the FILE command in CONFIG.SYS does not affect network files; to adjust NetWare's network FILE parameter, use SHELL.CFG (see page 83).

DEVICE=ANSI.SYS. While not really necessary for networking, the ANSI.SYS file does allow you to readdress your function keys and add color to the DOS prompt (see page 75). Put the ANSI.SYS file on the diskette or ensure a path to the file if you are using a hard disk drive: for example, DEVICE=C:\UTIL\ANSI.SYS.

SHELL=C:COMMAND.COM /P /E:512. This command tells the DOS shell where to find the COMMAND processor file. (The command also reflects a hard drive environment—C:; if you are using diskettes, you would type A:COMMAND.COM.) The /P parameter tells DOS to run AUTOEXEC (the default); the /E parameter expands memory for the DOS environment to 512 bytes. You may need to expand the DOS environment from its default of 160 bytes if you need more memory for some of the environmental commands in NetWare's MENU utility, or if you plan to run an application that acquires such an expansion.

DEVICE=C:\UTIL\VDISK.SYS 384 512 128 /E. This command allows you to set up a virtual disk out of the memory above DOS's 640KB limit. (The preceding example is for a workstation with 1MB of memory, or 384KB above DOS's 640KB.) The 512 parameter signifies the byte sector size, and the 128 parameter specifies the number of directory entries allowed. The /E parameter designates extended memory beyond 640KB. DOS v4.0x adds a /X:x parameter, allowing you to designate the number of data sector transfers DOS can perform at a time (the default is 8).

      The virtual disk becomes the next available drive after the hard disk(s); do not forget to factor it in when designating the LASTDRIVE= parameter.

DEVICE=C:\UTIL\MSMOUSE.SYS. This command installs the mouse driver for an installed mouse. More and more programs are using mouse features.

LASTDRIVE=D. This command changes the DOS v3.x default from LAST-DRIVE = E in order to make another drive available to network mappings. In this instance, the parameter takes into account two floppy disk drives, a hard disk drive (C:), and a virtual disk drive (D:), making E: the first network drive. If you have two floppy disk drives and no hard or virtual drives, you can set LASTDRIVE=B. Changing the default last drive in CONFIG.SYS also eliminates the message you see when a MAP command overwrites a local drive designation (originally reserved for a local disk).

When you change the LASTDRIVE parameter, be sure that you have a MAP designated to that spot (in this instance, E:). Otherwise, NetWare will fill the first spot with SYS:LOGIN, an area to which users usually have no rights. You can get around this problem by placing the following commands in the system login script:

```
IF MEMBER OF "PERSONAL" THEN BEGIN
MAP *1:=servername/volumename:PERSONAL/%LOGIN_NAME
END
```

This login parameter means that whatever CONFIG.SYS's LASTDRIVE parameter is, map the first drive (*1) to the directory whose login name matches that directory name. For example, if the workstation user's name is BOB and his login name is BOB, create a BOB subdirectory under the PERSONAL directory. (The servername/volumename corresponds to the server and volume that you create the PERSONAL directory.) Then when BOB logs in, he will automatically have a personal directory where he can store his personal notes and files.

The above example also means you have to be a member of the PERSONAL group to have this drive mapping. You can use the EVERYONE group instead of creating a PERSONAL group, but you must think through how you wish to allot the GUEST login parameter.

Remember that the CONFIG.SYS file sets up the workstation environment. If you have NetWare v2.1x or greater, use the SHELL.CFG file to make changes in the way the workstation functions on the network. (See page 77.)

Creating the AUTOEXEC.BAT File

After DOS reads the information from the CONFIG.SYS file and begins setting up the workstation environment, DOS loads the COMMAND processor (which is COMMAND.COM) and then looks for the AUTOEXEC.BAT file to run the commands found there. DOS searches for the AUTOEXEC.BAT file in the directory where it stores the COMMAND.COM file—for example, the boot diskette or the root directory of the hard drive—and initiates the COMMAND processor.

Where you store COMMAND.COM actually depends on where DOS begins creating the workstation environment. Sometimes DOS stores COMMAND .COM in two places (the active partition area on the hard disk and the DOS subdirectory) and references these two places. For example, when DOS v4.0x creates its AUTOEXEC.BAT file, it sets up its COMSPEC (a special path that DOS uses to find COMMAND.COM) to find the COMMAND.COM file in the C:\DOS directory. That way, DOS will be able to find the COMMAND processor whenever it needs to initiate a command.

If DOS cannot find an AUTOEXEC.BAT file, it assumes that initial batch processing is finished and awaits a command. For DOS v4.0x, when you run the SELECT utility on a hard disk, DOS creates an AUTOEXEC.BAT file which may include the following parameters:

```
@ECHO OFF
SET COMPSEC=C:\DOS\COMMAND.COM
VERIFY OFF
PATH C:\DOS
APPEND /E
APPEND C:\DOS
PROMPT $P$G
C:\DOS\GRAPHICS
VER
DOSSHELL
```

Like CONFIG.SYS, the AUTOEXEC.BAT file is also contains a series of commands to customize the workstation environment. For network communication, you will need the following commands in your AUTOEXEC.BAT. (To create a batch file, begin the process by typing COPY CON followed by the batch file name.)

```
COPY CON AUTOEXEC.BAT
@ECHO OFF
PROMPT $P$G              (not necessary, but helpful)
IPX                      (NetWare v2.0 will not have this command)
NET2, NET3, or NET4      (NetWare v2.0 will have ANETx)
NETBIOS                  (when running NetBIOS applications)
INT2F                    (when applications need a network sign)
F:                       (depends on DOS version and CONFIG.SYS)
LOGIN servername/username
^Z
```

In DOS v3.3 and greater, the "at" sign (@) hides the command from view while the ECHO OFF command prevents the commands from being displayed. Again, the PROMPT command (which causes the directory path to display at the network prompt) is not mandatory, but it does help users to understand at a glance where they are in the directory structure. The IPX command loads the IPX driver for NetWare v2.1x and greater. (For NetWare v2.0x, you will not need this command.) The DOS version you are running determines which NETx.COM or ANETx.COM command you enter.

If your network is running applications and utilities that use the NetBIOS communications protocol, you must also add NETBIOS and INT2F commands to the AUTOEXEC and copy the NETBIOS.COM and INT2F.COM files onto the boot diskette. The NETBIOS command loads NetWare's NETBIOS.COM file, which emulates a NetBIOS connector. Some poorly written applications running on NetBIOS look to see if you have the PC LAN program loaded. INT2F.COM lies to these applications and assures the applications that they are running on a network.

The F: command brings you to the default network drive letter if you have DOS v3.x and v4.x; for DOS v2.x, the drive is C:. The drive letter you choose for the network prompt also depends on which drive letter you entered at the LAST-DRIVE= parameter in the CONFIG.SYS file (see page 56).

If you are running DOS v4.0x, place the network commands before the DOSSHELL command. Then place the appropriate DOS and network files on the boot diskette. Another example of a workstation AUTOEXEC.BAT file follows:

```
@ECHO OFF
VERIFY ON
C:\UTIL\QUICKKEY
C:\UTIL\CED
CLS
PATH=C:\DOS;C:\UTIL
PROMPT $P $T  $D$ $G
IPX
NET3
D:
LOGIN OBIWAN/BOB
```

In this AUTOEXEC, the ECHO OFF command prevents the commands from being displayed, and the "at" (@) sign prevents the ECHO OFF sign from being displayed. VERIFY ON is a DOS command that verifies that all fles are written correctly to disk. The next two commands are TSRs: QUICKKEY affects the keyboard buffers to provide greater cursor speed, and CED is a command line editor. The AUTOEXEC.BAT file is a good place to load TSRs (see page 52). The CLS command clears the screen. The network commands have already been explained.

You should load all of your TSRs before you set any DOS environment variables, such as the PATH and PROMPT commands. DOS assigns a copy of the DOS environment with every TSR you load after setting the variables, which takes up more bytes of the workstation's 640KB memory. By setting the environmental variables after the workstation loads TSRs, you will reduce the memory space that each TSR uses. Be sure to designate the directory path where the TSRs can be found.

The PATH command gives access to applications and utilities stored in the designated directories without having to go into the directory itself: for example, through the PATH command, you can access the files in both C:\DOS and C:\UTIL directories. The PATH command affects only the DOS environment, so you can enter as many directory designations as needed.

The PROMPT command in the above example changes the command line prompt to display the subdirectory structure, the time and date, and a "greater than" sign (>). Consult the DOS manual or page 75 to learn about possible variations to the PROMPT command. You can also place the PROMPT command in the system login script, such as SET PROMPT = "$P $T $D $G" if you wish every user to share the same PROMPT command. Of course, users can change the PROMPT command to anything they like in their own personal login script or at the network prompt.

The AUTOEXEC gives you flexibility in setting up different workstation environments. With large installations, however, you will find it simplest to establish, and use exclusively, a few boot diskette formulas. So for the sake of convenience, standardize on a DOS version, a network interface board, a cabling topology, and your major applications. Otherwise, you compound your maintenance efforts.

5 Running the Shell Generation Utilities

When you generate a NetWare shell, you are linking a LAN driver specific to the network interface board you are installing into the IPX services. Not only are IPX services linked specifically to the network interface board, the services are also specific to the board's I/O, interrupt, and DMA settings. So matching the board settings to the LAN driver you choose in GENSH or SHGEN is very important.

Another aspect to shell generation is the NetWare shell itself. Actually, the NetWare shell is the same no matter which network interface board you are running. This is especially true for NetWare v2.1x and above, for you create only an IPX.COM file—all the other *.COM files are on the SHGEN-1 (or SHGEN-2) diskette. But for NetWare v2.0a, IPX was integrated into the shell, so when you link IPX to the LAN driver, you also create ANET2.COM and ANET3.COM files.

The Ways of Running GENSH or SHGEN

You can run SHGEN in three ways: from a working diskette copy, from a hard disk drive, or from a network drive. For NetWare v2.0a's GENSH utility, you can generate your shell files only with the floppy drive method, so make working copies of the diskettes you use before you generate the workstation shell.

Here is a list of the diskettes you will need for the different NetWare versions. Be sure to have on hand a working copy of DOS's COMMAND.COM that matches the DOS version you boot the workstation with:

For v2.0a
GENSH-1
GENSH-2

For v2.1x on 5.25" Diskettes
SHGEN-1
SHGEN-2
LAN_DRV_001
LAN_DRV_002

For v2.1x on 3.5" Diskettes
SHGEN-1
LAN_DRV_001

For v3.0 on High-density 5.25" Diskettes
SHGEN-1
LAN_DRV_??? (optional)

First of all, make working copies of the diskette by inserting SHGEN-1 into drive A:, typing DISKCOPY A: B: <Enter> or DISKCOPY A: A: <Enter>, and following the directions. Then make working copies of all the shell generation diskettes.

With a working copy in hand, place the *-1 diskette into drive A: and type the respective command. For v2.0a, place the GENSH-1 diskette in drive A: and type GENSH <Enter>; for NetWare v2.1x, place the SHGEN-1 diskette into drive A: and type SHGEN <Enter>; for NetWare 386 v3.0, place the SHGEN-1 diskette into a high-density drive and type SHGEN <Enter>.

For maintenance purposes, it is a simple matter to create a directory on your local hard drive or network drive and copy the files from the shell generation diskette(s) into that directory. You also place into the directory any third-party LAN drivers.

The NetWare manuals suggest that you create two directories: NETWORK and SHGEN-1. At the C: or network prompt, create a NETWORK directory and go into that directory (MD NETWORK <Enter> and CD NETWORK <Enter>). Copy in the SHGEN.EXE file (NCOPY A:SHGEN.EXE <Enter>). Create the SHGEN-1 subdirectory (MD SHGEN-1 <Enter>), go into that directory (CD SHGEN-1 <Enter>), and copy the files from the other diskettes into that directory (NCOPY A:*.* <Enter>). To run SHGEN, go back into the NETWORK directory (CD.. <Enter>) and type SHGEN <Enter>.

Running GENSH For NetWare v2.0a

NetWare 2.0a comes with GENSH-1 and GENSH-2 diskettes. First, boot your computer with DOS, place a working copy of the GENSH-1 diskette into drive A:, and type GENSH <Enter>. You will see the "Available Shell Options" window, along with a list of supported network interface boards. The options include:

3COM EtherLink
Allen-Bradley VistaLAN/PC
AT&T StarLAN

> Corvus Omninet
> Corvus Omninet (no interrupts)
> Davong MultiLink
> Gateway G-Net
> IBM ASYNC Remote Workstation Dial In
> IBM PC Cluster
> IBM PC Cluster (no interrupts)
> IBM PC Network
> IBM Token-Ring
> Nestar PLAN 2000
> Novell Star
> Novell Star Intelligent NIC
> Novell Star Intelligent NIC (no interrupts)
> Orchid / Santa Clara / AST PCnet
> Proteon ProNET with Checksum
> Standard Microsystems ARCNET

Each of these options is using setting 0, the default board setting. Make sure the setting on the board matches the default; unless customized, all boards comes with the default setting already in place. Select the option that matches your board by pressing <Enter> on the highlighted option, and you will see:

```
Copying Selected driver to disk GENSH-2.
Insert disk GENSH-2.
Strike a key when ready . . .
```

Insert the GENSH-2 diskette and press <Enter>. The GENSH-2 diskette will link a LAN driver for the board type you chose into the IPX services of the NetWare shell, allowing IPX to take care of hardware tasks specific to the board you are installing. On the screen, you will see:

```
Linking DOS 2.x shell.
Linking DOS 3.x shell.
Linking NETBIOS emulator.
Shell generation complete.
```

The GENSH-2 diskette contains three additional files: ANET2.COM, ANET3.COM, and NETBIOS.COM (a good reason to make working copies of the GENSH diskettes). For workstations running DOS 2.x, copy the AET2.COM file onto the workstation's boot diskette; for workstations running DOS 3.x, copy the ANET3.COM file. If you have applications running NetBIOS as the communications protocol, copy the NETBIOS.COM file to the boot diskette as well.

If you are installing more than one type of network interface board in the workstations, save the *.COM files you have just created to another diskette and label that diskette to indicate which network interface board those *.COM files belong to. For future reference, write the board's settings on the label.

Running SHGEN for NetWare v2.1 to v2.15

Running SHGEN for NetWare v2.1x is more complicated than running NetWare v2.0a's GENSH. The main reason is that SHGEN allows you to choose a different board setting than the default setting on the network interface board. You can reset the network interface board if it has an address conflict with an already installed board.

SHGEN comes with three methods of linking IPX to the LAN driver: default, intermediate, and advanced. The default method takes option 0 as the board setting; the intermediate method allows you to choose the board setting option you wish. You will use the advanced option if you need to avoid hardware conflicts within a workstation, or if you are adding a LAN driver not contained on the LAN_DRV_001 and LAN_DRV_002 diskettes.

You can also choose where to run SHGEN from: diskettes, the hard drive, or a network drive. If you made working copies of the NetWare diskettes and you wish to run SHGEN from a floppy drive, place the working copy of the SHGEN-1 diskette into drive A: and type SHGEN <Enter> at the network prompt. If you know which option you wish to choose (default, intermediate, or custom), you can designate that choice by typing SHGEN -D (default) or -I (intermediate) or -C (custom). You must perform a number of disk swaps during this process, but you will be prompted as to which diskette to insert at the which stage of the process.

For maintenance purposes, you can create a directory on either a hard disk or a network drive and copy the files from the shell generation diskette(s) into that directory. To create a directory on a hard drive, go to the C: root (CD\<Enter>), place the SHGEN-1 diskette into drive A:, and type A:SHGEN <Enter>. When you select the configuration option you wish and press <Enter>, you will see the "SHGEN Run Options" listed; highlight "Hard Disk" and press <Enter>. Then in the "Drive:" window, type C <Enter>. SHGEN will create a NETWARE directory at the root directory as well as SHGEN subdirectories, and copy the files from the diskettes into the respective directories. Simply swap out the diskettes when prompted.

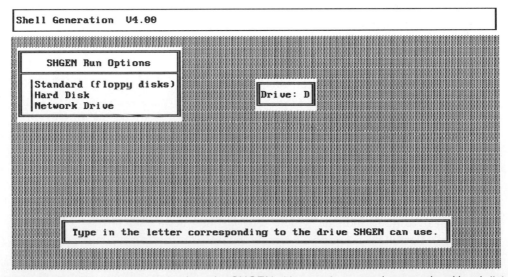

Figure 19: NetWare allows you to place the SHGEN either on the network or on a local hard disk.

Once you upload SHGEN-1, SHGEN-2, and LAN_DRV_.001 diskettes, you will be asked to upload any additional diskettes, such as third-party driver diskettes. If you have such diskettes, load them here. When you are finished, highlight "No" and press <Enter> to go to the "Available LAN Drivers" window. After you create the shell files using the hard-drive method, you will be prompted to download the shell files to a diskette. Answering "Yes," inserting the boot diskette, and pressing <Esc> will download IPX.COM, NET3.COM, and NET4.COM to the diskette.

Having SHGEN create network directories works the same way as the local hard disk method, except that SHGEN creates the directories at the end of whichever directory path you designate in the "Drive" window. SHGEN will create the NETWARE directory at the end of the directory path.

Choose your method of generating the shell files, and at the appropriate directory, type SHGEN <Enter>. SHGEN comes with three options: default, intermediate, and advanced. If you type in the option incorrectly when calling up SHGEN, you will see:

```
>shgen n-c
Usage: shgen [-[n][c|i|d][s]]
        where n = New Shell Generation
                    c = Custom Generation
                    i = Intermediate Generation
                    d = Default Generation
                    s = Standard Drive Usage
```

Using the Default SHGEN Option

The default configuration option gives you the same ease as v2.0a's GENSH utility; you simply choose the LAN board from the "Available LAN Drivers" window, and SHGEN assumes the board is on setting 0 and creates an IPX driver for you.

After typing SHGEN, highlight the "Default Configuration" option and press <Enter>. You'll see the "SHGEN Run Options" window with the "Standard (Floppy Disks)" option highlighted. Press <Enter>, and you will see a list of the supported LAN drivers appear in the "Available LAN Drivers" window. Highlight the name of the supported driver and press <Enter>. You will then see the "Selected Configurations" window with the default board settings (option 0). Press <Enter>; SHGEN then links the IPX.OBJ file on the SHGEN-2 diskette with the selected LAN *.OBJ file on the LAN_DRV_001 diskette.

The utility then will copy the IPX.COM file to the SHGEN-2 diskette, display a message confirming this fact, and ask you to press <Esc> to continue. Pressing <Esc> returns you to the A: prompt. You can then copy the IPX.COM, NETx.COM, and the NetBIOS files (if necessary) to the boot diskette and move to the next step of preparing a boot diskette (this step is described on page 58).

If you do not choose the correct settings, IPX will be trying to talk down one interrupt and I/O port and the board will not have those communication avenues open. When this happens, you will most likely be unable to load IPX and the workstation will hang. Make doubly sure the board settings match the driver configuration option you choose. The easiest way to select board settings and driver options is to use the default board setting, which corresponds to option 0 in the "Available LAN Driver Configurations" window. But check the network interface board supplement to make sure that is the case.

Using the Intermediate SHGEN Option

The "Intermediate Configuration" option is essentially the same as the "Default" option, but it allows you to select a board configuration other than the default board configuration. This allows you to prevent IRQ, or interrupt, conflicts with other boards in the workstation.

To select the intermediate method, choose the "Intermediate Configuration" option from the "Shell Generation Level" window—or, to select this method at the command line, add the -I parameter (SHGEN -I <Enter>). Then choose whether you wish to generate the network files from diskettes, a hard drive, or a network drive, and press <Enter>. At the "Available LAN Drivers" window, select the correct board type and press <Enter>.

You will see the "Available LAN Driver Configurations" window, which lists the IRQ, I/O Base address, DMA, and/or RAM options available for that board. Select the option that matches the board settings and press <Enter>. The SFT/ Advanced NetWare 286 Installation manual suggests that you keep the following considerations in mind when selecting the board settings:

• Use the default configuration option if the workstation is using remote reset.

• Boards from the factory are set at the 0 option—use the default to eliminate the need to reset the boards.

• Pay attention to information that comes with the boards; some configurations may be valid only for certain boards, or certain boards may need to be inserted into certain slots (8-bit vs. 16-bit slots).

• Choose the type of bus for the appropriate board (do this in the "Custom Configuration" option).

• Choose only a configuration option for IBM Token-Ring primary adapters.

• When installing adapters for the PS/2 Model 30 and above, set the configuration through the software on the IBM REFERENCE diskette; then match the settings in SHGEN to those selected settings. Run the REFERENCE diskette first; if you have hardware conflicts within the workstation, you can resolve them before running SHGEN.

Once you select an option, you will see the selected option's configuration, along with the LAN board/driver specification. You will also see a screen asking if you wish to "Continue Shell Generation Using Selected Configurations?" with the "Yes" option highlighted.

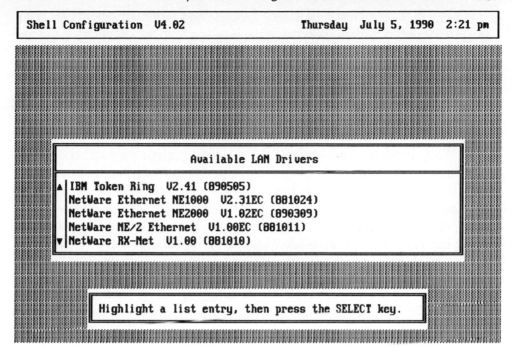

Available LAN Drivers

IBM Token Ring V2.41 (890505)
NetWare Ethernet NE1000 V2.31EC (881024)
NetWare Ethernet NE2000 V1.02EC (890309)
NetWare NE/2 Ethernet V1.00EC (881011)
NetWare RX-Net V1.00 (881010)

Highlight a list entry, then press the SELECT key.

Figure 20: Once you select the LAN board and driver, press yes to configure the IPX file.

Pressing <Enter> again begins the linking process; SHGEN copies the IPX.COM file to the SHGEN-2 diskette or directory, displays a message confirming this fact, and asks you to press <Esc> to continue. Pressing <Esc> either returns you to the A: prompt or brings up a window asking if you wish to download the generated files to a diskette. Pressing <Enter> on the "Yes" option will download the IPX.COM, NET3.COM, and NET4.COM files. You can then copy the NetBIOS files (if necessary) to the boot diskette.

Selecting the Custom Option

The Custom Configuration option allows you to specify the kind of hardware the workstation contains. It also allows you to add any third-party drivers you need. After typing SHGEN, highlight the Custom Configuration option and press <Enter>. You will see the "SHGEN Run Options" window with the Standard (Floppy Disks) option highlighted. Choose the method by which you plan to run SHGEN and press <Enter>. For example, if you are running SHGEN on the hard drive, select that option, type in the drive letter specification, and press <Enter>.

Choose the Select Shell Configuration option from the "Shell Generation Options" window. If you already have a valid shell in the SHGEN-2 directory, you will see a message to that effect. You will see the "Available Options" window with such options as Select Resource Sets (optional), Select LAN Driver, Configure Driver/Resources, Edit Resource List, Edit Resource Sets, and Save Selections and Continue.

If the workstation contains optional resources, such as the AST clock and calendar card, choose the Select Resource Sets option; select those options by highlighting them and pressing <Enter>. As you select an item, other items with settings that conflict with the selection will disappear from the selection area. This will tell you that there is conflict within the initial selections. You must then decide which resource you wish to keep in the workstation, or see if resources with conflicting IRQs can be set differently. (PS/2s with Micro Channel buses will automatically configure themselves to their internal resource sets.) To unselect an item, choose the Deselect option from the "Resource Set Options" window, highlight the offending option, and press <Enter>.

To add an item not in the resource selections, choose the Load and Select option from the "Resource Set Options" window. You will see three options in the "Resource Set Definitions Already Exist" window: Do Not Load New Resource Set Definitions, Merge New With Existing Resource Set Definitions, and Replace Existing Resource Set Definitions. The merge option brings an item into the list of existing definitions, but you must label the diskette SHGEN-1, call the new item file SUBSYS.SYS, and place the diskette in drive A: when you choose the option. If you want this new item to overwrite an existing resource definition, choose the Replace option rather than the Merge option. Otherwise, the Merge option will simply present you with two resource definitions with the same name (the bottom definition is the newly added definition).

Steps for Adding LAN Drivers

Once you have selected the optional resources in a workstation, press <Esc> and choose the Select LAN Driver option. If you did not add any additional LAN drivers when you first installed SHGEN, or if you have added other drivers since the initial installation, first complete the following steps:

• Go to the network prompt under the NETWARE directory and create a directory for the additional driver—for example, MD LAN_DRV_.003. It is usual to name the directory after the driver label; however, since you are creating a DOS directory, you will have to put a period before the 003 extension.

• Go into the directory (CD LAN_DRV_.003 <Enter>), place the diskette with the additional drivers in drive A:, and copy the driver(s) over to the directory (COPY A:*.* <Enter>).

• Reenter SHGEN; type SHGEN -C <Enter>. The "Load and Select" option in SHGEN will look for additional drivers from the LAN_DRV_.* directories, load them into memory, and cause them to appear in the "Available LAN Drivers" window.

Select the LAN driver and press <Enter>. To deselect a driver, highlight the selection and press <Enter>. Then you can make a different selection if you like.

Once you have selected the drivers and resource sets, choose the Configure Driver/Resource option to select the options referring to the resources and drivers that will not conflict with other hardware settings. When you choose a resource, you must choose its configuration so it will not conflict with the LAN driver selection.

Select the Choose Resource Configuration first; this option will narrow the selection of LAN drivers from which to choose. Once you select the resource option, you will see those resources that need to be configured listed in the "Resource Sets With Unconfigured Resource" window. Pressing <Enter> on the name of a resource displays the "Unconfigured Resources" window; highlight the option and press <Enter> to see the selections available to be configured. When you select an item from the "Unconfigured Resources" window, you will see the "Available Resource Configurations" window, with the settings that you can use for a particular resource.

For example, if you choose the LPT1 port as a resource item, you will see two options from which to choose. While most LPT1 ports come set to IRQ 7 and I/O Base 378-37Fh, you can also (usually through software) set LPT1 to IRQ 7 and I/O Base 3BCh. Whichever setting you choose, LAN driver options that use IRQ 7 and I/O Base 3BCh will disappear from the "Available Resource Configurations" window as well as other (as yet unconfigured) resource sets if they have conflicting settings.

Once you configure all the resources, select the "Choose LAN Configuration" option. Press <Enter> and you will see the LAN driver you selected listed in the "Select LAN Driver" option. Press <Enter> again, and you will see which available LAN drivers will not conflict with other hardware selections. (This information is available here because you selected the workstation resources first.) If you have no LAN driver options from which to choose, you will need to unconfigure a hardware piece until you free up a LAN driver option. You will not be able to use the conflicting hardware device together with the LAN board specified.

Once you select a LAN driver specification, be sure the network interface board is set to those settings, or you will receive error messages (see page 109) and the board may not work at all. After selecting the hardware settings for resource sets and LAN drivers, you can review the consequences by choosing the Review Select Configurations option that now appears in the "Configure Driver/Resource" window. This option shows your current configurations for LAN driver and resource sets. If the list of resource sets is longer than one page, you can press the Up/Down arrow keys to see the other selections. Pressing <Esc> brings you back to the "Configure Driver/Resource" window; pressing <Esc> again brings you to the "Available Options" window.

If a workstation has an undefined hardware resource and you want to add a resource set to SHGEN—for example, a CD ROM device that uses Interrupt 5 and I/O base 386h—you can choose the "Edit Resource List" and "Edit Resource Set" options from the "Available Options" window. These are covered in detail in Appendix A of the NetWare 286 Installation manual.

To finish the shell generation process, choose the "Save Selections and Continue" option and press <Enter>. This option saves all the work you have done so far and brings you to the "Continue Shell generation Using Selected Configurations?" window; pressing <Enter> brings up the "Save New Resource Set Definitions?" window with the Yes option highlighted. Pressing <Enter> saves the new definitions; pressing <Esc> discards them.

Once you have saved everything up to this point, you will return to the "Shell Generation Options" window with a new option highlighted—Link NetWare Shell. Pressing <Enter> links the NetWare IPX to the hardware settings. You will then return to the "Shell Generation Options" window with yet another new option—Configure NetWare Shell. Pressing <Enter> on this option creates a valid shell for the specified hardware and displays "Valid Shell Exists on SHGEN-2" window on the screen.

The "Shell Generation Options" window now displays only two options, one of which is to exit SHGEN. Pressing <Enter> on the Exit SHGEN option brings up a window asking if you wish to exit SHGEN. Pressing <Enter> again brings up the "Download Shell files to Floppy Disk?" window. If you wish to put the IPX.COM, NET3.COM, and NET4.COM files on a boot diskette, place the boot diskette into drive A: and press <Enter>. You will see a window instructing you to "Insert a floppy disk to receive the shell files in drive 'A.' <Press <Esc> to Continue>." Follow the directions and press <Esc>. The files will copy to the boot diskette, and you will return to the NETWARE directory. If you do not wish to place the *.COM files on a boot diskette, highlight the No option and press <Enter>; you will return to the NETWARE directory.

Running SHGEN for NetWare 386

NetWare 386 installation is easier than NetWare 286 v2.1x installation. It takes one high-density SHGEN-1 diskette containing all the drivers that Novell ships with NetWare 386. Other drivers are available from third parties and can be installed as well.

First of all, from a running workstation, place a working copy of the SHGEN-1 diskette into drive A: and type SHGEN <Enter>. You will see the "LAN Driver Options" window with two choices: Select LAN Driver From List and Load into List from LAN_DRV_??? Disk.

If the driver you need is on a diskette supplied with the network interface board, select the Load Into List from LAN_DRV_??? Disk option. You will be asked to place that LAN_DRV_??? diskette in any drive and press <Esc>. This action loads the driver(s) into the listing in the "Available LAN Drivers" window.

The LAN drivers available through NetWare v3.0 include:

> IBM PC II & Baseband V1.10 (880526)
> IBM Token-Ring V2.41 (890505)
> NetWare Ethernet NE1000 V2.31EC (881024)
> NetWare Ethernet NE2000 V1.02EC (880309)
> NetWare NE/2 Ethernet V1.00EC (881011)
> NetWare RX-Net V1.00 (881010)
> NetWare RX-Net/2 — SMC PS110 V1.00 (880817)

Choose a LAN driver by matching the driver to the board you have either installed or intend to install, highlighting the option, and pressing <Enter>. That option will be entered in the "Selected LAN Driver" window and you will see a

Change Selection option in the "LAN Driver Options" window. If you like the selection, press <Esc> and save your selection; otherwise, press <Enter> and you will return to the "LAN Driver Options" window with the original two choices.

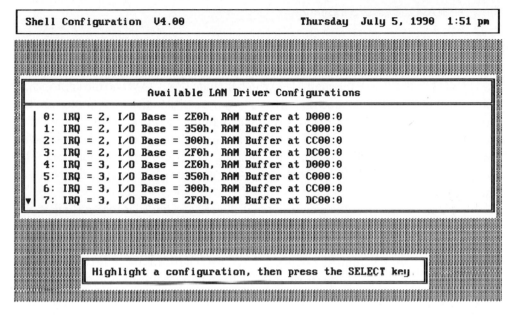

```
┌──────────────────────────────────────────────────────────────────────────┐
│ Shell Configuration   V4.00                    Thursday  July 5, 1990  1:51 pm │
└──────────────────────────────────────────────────────────────────────────┘

        ┌──────────────────────────────────────────────────────────────┐
        │           Available LAN Driver Configurations                │
        │                                                              │
        │  0:  IRQ = 2,  I/O Base = 2E0h,  RAM Buffer at D000:0         │
        │  1:  IRQ = 2,  I/O Base = 350h,  RAM Buffer at C000:0         │
        │  2:  IRQ = 2,  I/O Base = 300h,  RAM Buffer at CC00:0         │
        │  3:  IRQ = 2,  I/O Base = 2F0h,  RAM Buffer at DC00:0         │
        │  4:  IRQ = 3,  I/O Base = 2E0h,  RAM Buffer at D000:0         │
        │  5:  IRQ = 3,  I/O Base = 350h,  RAM Buffer at C000:0         │
        │  6:  IRQ = 3,  I/O Base = 300h,  RAM Buffer at CC00:0         │
        │▼ 7:  IRQ = 3,  I/O Base = 2F0h,  RAM Buffer at DC00:0         │
        └──────────────────────────────────────────────────────────────┘

        ┌──────────────────────────────────────────────────────────────┐
        │  Highlight a configuration, then press the SELECT key        │
        └──────────────────────────────────────────────────────────────┘
```

Figure 21: Although you can choose a number of board settings, if possible choose option 0 for consistency.

Once you press <Esc>, you will see the "Available LAN Driver Configurations" window, containing all the I/O, interrupts, DMA, and RAM settings that the board you selected can use. Choose the settings that match the way you have the board jumpered (boards come defaulted to option 0). Press <Enter> on the desired driver and you will see the "Selected Configurations" window with the selected driver and settings together. You will also see a window saying, "Continue Shell Generation Using Selected Configuration?" If your selection is correct, press <Enter>; if not, type "N" and press <Enter>. You must then reselect the driver and board settings.

When you choose Yes, you will see:

```
Linking SHGEN-1:IPX.COM.
Configuring SHGEN-1:IPX.
```

After the information about linking and configuring, you will see the "Valid shell have been placed on SHGEN-1 <Press ESCAPE to Continue>" message. Press <Esc> to return to the network prompt. You will see the IPX.COM file added to the SHGEN-1 diskette. For workstations running DOS 3.x, copy the NET3.COM and IPX.COM files onto the workstation's boot diskette; for workstations running DOS 4.x, copy the NET4.COM and IPX.COM files. If you have applications running on NetBIOS as their transport mechanism, copy the NETBIOS.EXE and INT2F.COM files as well. The NetBIOS files are not generated during SHGEN.

If you are installing more than one type of network interface board in workstations and you need to rerun SHGEN, save the IPX.COM file you just created to another diskette and label that diskette to remind you which network interface board the *.COM files belong to. Also include the board's settings so you will know how the LAN driver is configured.

Finishing Up the Boot Diskette

The necessary files for a workstation boot diskette include CONFIG.SYS, AUTOEXEC.BAT, and the shell files, which include IPX.COM and the appropriate NETx.COM file for NetWare v2.1x. If you have created a SHELL.CFG file, include this as well (see page 77 for details). For NetWare v2.0a, the shell file you need to include is the appropriate ANETx.COM file (depending on the DOS version the workstation is running). If you are running NetBIOS applications, add the NETBIOS.COM and INT2F.COM files as well, and be sure to include their calls in the AUTOEXEC.BAT file.

You must also include on the boot diskette the other files that you call in the CONFIG.SYS and AUTOEXEC.BAT files. These files include mouse drivers, the ANSI.SYS file, and any TSRs you call from the AUTOEXEC.BAT file.

If you are installing the network interface boards in the workstations, refer to the manuals that come from Novell or with the boards themselves and follow their instructions. You can also use the operations manual that comes with the workstation. These manuals contain illustrations demonstrating how to change the board's factory settings (if necessary) and how to install and remove the boards from a workstation. The manuals also explain cabling and connecting the cable to the workstation; follow the cabling instruction closely, obeying the cable specifications as you go.

With the board installed, the cable connected, and the boot diskette finished, turn off the workstation, place the boot diskette in drive A:, and turn the workstation back on. The workstation should load the DOS environment, then load the NetWare drivers to set up the network connection. What you see on the screen depends on what you included in the AUTOEXEC.BAT file. If you include no LASTDRIVE command in CONFIG.SYS, the ECHO OFF command as well as the server and user name in the AUTOEXEC.BAT on a boot diskette, you will see a screen similar to this one:

```
A:> IPX
Novell IPX/SPX v2.15
(C) Copyright 1985, 1988 Novell Inc.  All Rights Reserved.

LAN Option: NetWare Ethernet NE-1000 v2.31EC (881024)
Hardware Configuration: IRQ = 3, I/O Base = 300h, no DMA or ROM

A:> NET3
NetWare v2.15 rev C - Workstation Shell for PC DOS v3.x
(C) Copyright 1983, 1988 Novell Inc.  All Rights Reserved.

Attached to server OBIWAN
Friday, March 23, 1990 1:21:34 pm
```

```
A:> F:
F:\LOGIN> LOGIN OBIWAN/BOB
Enter your password:
```

At this point, users can enter their passwords and see the drive mappings set up for them in the system login script or in their personal login scripts. Either way, they are successfully logged in.

6 Optional Enhancements

Adding Color to the DOS Prompt

For workstations with color monitors, you will probably want to set different colors than DOS's default of white characters on a black background. Through the ANSI.SYS file, you can set the color and graphics attributes of a color monitor screen. Be sure the ANSI.SYS file is on the boot diskette or in a path that DOS recognizes and from which DOS can execute the file. Also, be sure to add the DEVICE = (path)ANSI.SYS parameter in the CONFIG.SYS file so you can invoke ANSI.SYS. Examples of this type of parameter would be DEVICE=A:ANSI.SYS, or DEVICE=C:\DOS\ANSI.SYS.

With ANSI.SYS in place, use the PROMPT command to set the foreground and background colors. But first, in order to get around better with the color schemes, familiarize yourself with the following list of parameters (in alphabet order) you can perform in the PROMPT command. Be sure to precede each character you use with a dollar sign "$" in the string.

PROMPT Character	What You See on the Screen
_ (underline)	Brings you to the beginning of a new line
b	Displays the | character
d	Displays the current date
e	A hexadecimal escape sequence that allows you to add the color to the prompt; the "e" character is followed by "[" and the sequence ends with "m": for example, $e[36m
g	Displays the greater-than sign (>)

h	Creates a backspace, allowing you to erase preceding characters
l	Displays the less-than sign (<)
n	Displays the default drive
p	Displays the directory path
q	Displays the equal-to sign (=)
s	Displays a leading space only
t	Displays the current time
v	Displays the DOS version number

Use the PROMPT command to display subdirectories (PROMPT PG), date and time (PROMPT $D $T), list messages (PROMPT DON'T FORGET 3PM MEETING$G), and add color to the prompt. For example:

```
PROMPT $P$G$E[#;#m
```

The dollar sign P parameter tells DOS to display the directory path, and the dollar sign G parameter displays the greater-than sign. The $E[parameters set up the escape sequence for ANSI.SYS to change colors. The first pound sign (#) sets the foreground color, while the second pound sign sets the background color. The m parameter ends that color sequence. The color code selection that takes the place of the pound sign is:

30	black foreground	40	black background
31	red foreground	41	red background
32	green foreground	42	green background
33	yellow foreground	43	yellow background
34	blue foreground	44	blue background
35	magenta foreground	45	magenta background
36	cyan foreground	46	cyan background
37	white foreground	47	white background

For example, to display the directory path and make DOS display yellow characters on a blue background, add the PROMPT PE[33;44m <Enter> parameter to the AUTOEXEC.BAT file or in the network login script.

You can also set graphics attributes, such as a blinking cursor and reverse video colors. Set graphics attributes the same way you set a color sequence (PROMPT $E[#M), but with one-digit instead of two-digit numbers to select the attribute code. The selections and their attributes include:

0	all attributes off (white on black)
1	bold (high intensity) on
4	underscore on (IBM Monochrome Display only)
5	blink on
7	reverse video on
8	canceled on (invisible text)

You can combine color and graphics attributes in the same PROMPT command, as well as add other PROMPT parameters—for example, PG. (See the DOS manual for greater detail.) The following PROMPT command sets the DOS prompt to display the directory path, along with the time and date, in bold white letters enclosed by red brackets ([ ]), then sets the foreground color to cyan:

```
PROMPT=$e[1;31m[$e[37m$p $t $d$e[31m]$e[0m$e[36m
```

To make certain you are absolutely clear on this process, go through the example command item by item. The first $e[1; sets the color to bold and the 31m sets the [bracket to red. The next $e[37m resets the foreground color to white; the $p which follows requires the DOS prompt to display the directory path. The $p is followed by $t, which requires the prompt to display the time, and $d, which requires the prompt to display the workstation's current date. The next $e[31m sets the adjacent bracket] to red, followed by the $e[0m to turn all the attributes off. The last $e[36m sets the color for the return commands (for example, what you see when you type DIR <Enter>) to cyan—a light blue color.

Sometimes playing around with the PROMPT command can make you run out of environment space. But you can increase the environment space in the CONFIG.SYS file through the DOS SHELL command: for example, SHELL–C:COMMAND.COM /E:512 <Enter>. This example expands the environment table to 512 bytes. If you need yet more space, you can type /E:1024 <Enter>—all the way up to 3000 bytes for DOS v4.01. Experiment to find out what you need.

Modifying Workstation Environment through the v.21x SHELL.CFG File

For NetWare v2.1x and NetWare 386 supervisors, NetWare offers greater flexibility in assigning initial network settings; the SHELL.CFG file is useful in adding performance and flexibility to IPX/SPX, the NetWare shell, and NetBIOS to enable them to work better on your network. However, some of these parameters may not work in textbook fashion; you may need to experiment to adapt these parameters to your particular environment.

While the network defaults are usually adequate, it is sometimes necessary to adjust network settings. The following section contains a list of the SHELL.CFG parameters and what they mean, along with examples of their use.

Creating the SHELL.CFG File

SHELL.CFG is a specialized text file that you can create at the command line or with any ASCII text editor. The SHELL.CFG file is similar to the CONFIG.SYS file in that the SHELL.CFG file contains configuration values that IPX.COM, NETBIOS.COM, and NETx.COM read and interpret when your workstation starts up. However, these values are network-specific; they adjust the operating parameters of the NetWare shell, IPX, or NetBIOS.

You create the SHELL.CFG file in the same way you create any other text file—by typing COPY CON SHELL.CFG <Enter>, entering the value parameters, and ending the batch file with ^Z (which you create by pressing the <F6> key or by pressing the Ctrl and Z keys simultaneously). An example SHELL.CFG file would look like this:

```
COPY CON SHELL.CFG
IPX SOCKETS = 32
SPX CONNECTIONS = 20
CACHE BUFFERS = 6
FILE HANDLES = 100
PRINT HEADER = 32
PRINT TAIL = 32
READ ONLY COMPATIBILITY = ON
LOCAL PRINTERS = 0
^Z
```

The Options IPX.COM Uses

Here's a list of the values (along with their default parameters) that IPX.COM uses:

```
IPX SOCKETS = 20
IPX RETRY COUNT = 20
SPX CONNECTIONS = 15
SPX ABORT TIMEOUT = 540
SPX VERIFY TIMEOUT = 108
SPX LISTEN TIMEOUT = 54
IPATCH = <byte offset><value>
```

The maintenance release of NetWare v2.15 (Rev C) and NetWare 386 added three new options. These options and their defaults include:

```
INT64 = ON
INT7A = ON
CONFIG OPTION = <n>
```

When you want to modify IPX's functionality, add the modified parameter to the SHELL.CFG file. The default parameters are tried and true, and you will gain little by making the parameters smaller than the default. Here's a brief explanation of the IPX options and what they mean:

IPX SOCKETS = <number>. A socket is an internal destination (address); it is the third element in the network/node/socket header that IPX uses to route communications on the internet. Sockets work well for background operations that send packets to an area for processing without tying up normal communications channels for their operations.

Sockets are numbers that IPX recognizes; shell processes tell IPX which sockets they need to send its request to, and IPX then stamps that socket number on any packets the shell sends to that process. IPX also uses socket numbers for packets your workstations receive; IPX can therefore deliver packets directly to a process that is listening to a specific socket number. The process then performs its designated request and sends information back, using the socket number. Socket numbers are very specific; if you send packets to one socket, processes using other sockets will not receive those packets.

The IPX socket number specification allows IPX sockets in your workstation to service different communications functions. The default of twenty is more than even IPX-specific applications can use. NetWare currently uses six sockets; the NetWare shell uses three sockets—one for the NetWare's watchdog algorithm, one for message broadcasts, and one for the shell itself. The SPX diagnostic routine uses two sockets, and NetBIOS uses one socket.

A few programs are written specifically to use IPX; those applications or utilities that require more IPX sockets than the default will include that information in their documentation. You can drop the socket number to seven and still have plenty of sockets in almost all occasions. Each socket is between 6 to 8 bytes in size.

IPX RETRY COUNT = < number>. This number determines how many times the NetWare shell, SPX, or NetBIOS will send a retry to a communications partner if a request is not answered. (In the case of the shell, the communications partner is the server.)

The default is twenty, but you can vary this number with each installation. If you select a smaller number—ten, for example—IPX will drop the connection faster than the normal thirty seconds it takes to terminate a connection. When a workstation legitimately loses its connection, a smaller number such as three means that you will receive a connection error in less time than the normal thirty or forty seconds.

If your server is reliable and you have relatively few servers—five or so—attached on a network, you may wish to lower the retry count. However, if you do change the count and you start having connection problems, go back to the default.

For larger installations, first go into FCONSOLE, choose the Statistics option, then choose the LAN I/O Statistics option and see if the following entries have a number of retries: Reexecuted Requests, Duplicate Replies Sent, and Positive Acknowledgement Sent. Two aspects most often affect these entries: how well workstations are communicating with the server, and the network's cabling scheme.

If these numbers go into the hundreds shortly after the server comes up, you are having slight cabling and routing problems, and you will probably need the full 20 count in your retries. If you lower the retry count, you may unnecessarily cut off a connection when a simple retry would suffice. (It would also be a good idea to run a point-to-point test to other workstations with programs like NetWare Care or Thomas-Conrad's TXD to narrow down the problem cable or network interface boards.)

But increasing the retry count for a busy LAN can have the unfortunate side effect of causing NetBIOS and SPX to run more slowly. NetBIOS is heavily influenced by the "IPX Retry Count" and the "NetBIOS Retry Delay" options because you are actually estimating how long it takes a packet to reach the farthest node on the farthest network. The numbers in these two options depend on the applications the server(s) is running, the speed of the workstations and servers, the bandwidth (8-, 16-, or 32-bit) of the network interface boards, and the activity on the internet.

SPX Connections

SPX CONNECTIONS = <number>. This option is similar to the IPX sockets; it determines how many SPX connections (the default is 15) the workstation can use at the same time. Only a handful of programs take full advantage of IPX, and fewer still use SPX, such as the SPX SNA Gateway. Applications and utilities that need more SPX connections will have that information in their installation documentation.

Each SPX connection slot takes 90 bytes, so if you need memory space and you are not running SPX-specific programs, you can drop the connections number to three. An obvious sign that you allocated too few connections is when an application consistently dies that never did before you changed the connection number. If this happens, change the connection number back to the default and run the application again.

SPX ABORT TIMEOUT = <number>. When an SPX program sends a packet to a communications partner (such as a server) and the partner does not answer, SPX sends a number of retries. If thirty seconds elapse during these retries, SPX concludes that the communications partner or the network has failed and terminates the connection on the workstation side. The NetWare Supervisor Reference manual states that the SPX Abort Timeout, the SPX Verify Timeout, and the SPX Listen Timeout all work on a "tick" basis (there are 18.21 ticks per second for IBM PCs and compatibles). Thirty seconds is roughly 540 ticks.

You should leave the Abort Timeout option at 30 seconds, because if a communications partner does not respond in 30 seconds, that partner is probably unable to respond. If you do change this option to something like ten seconds (182.1 ticks) and you have uncommon network traffic (caused, most likely, by a bad network interface board or faulty cable segment), you may not be giving your communication partner time to respond to the request.

SPX VERIFY TIMEOUT = <number>. This option is used in conjunction with the SPX Abort Timeout and SPX Listen Timeout options. SPX sends a verify timeout packet every three seconds to ensure that the SPX session is still open at the other end of the connection. If SPX does not hear from the opposite connection end, it will start sending "Are you there?" (listen timeout) packets.

If SPX does not hear from the connection partner for the default thirty seconds, SPX stops trying and initiates the "Abort Timeout" sequence, thereby dropping the session. The session will be like carrying on a telephone conversation with someone, waiting six seconds, hanging up, and then asking if he is still there. Unless Novell tells you differently, don't change this number; Novell technical support personnel work from the assumption that the SPX Abort Timeout, SPX Verify Timeout, and SPX Listen Timeout have not been changed. Unless instructed, go with the defaults.

SPX LISTEN TIMEOUT = <number>. The Listen Timeout option is the "Are you alive?" packet that SPX sends every six seconds to ensure that the SPX session is still open at the other end of the connection.

   If you have an SPX-specific application sending packets over a slow link, such as a modem or an X.25 link, you may sometimes lose your connection. You can increase these three timeout options to avoid this problem. However, the program will take longer to discover connection problems when the connection really is lost.

IPATCH = <byte offset><value>. The Ipatch option puts patches into the IPX.COM program. When IPX loads, it looks for any Ipatch address locations and values to incorporate into IPX. If it finds any, IPX loads the Ipatch information. You will seldom need the Ipatch option; Novell IPX patches are in .EXE files that load themselves into the proper offsets, saving you from having to enter the changes by hand. Only use this option if you are told to by Novell technical support personnel.

INT64 = ON/OFF and INT7A = ON/OFF. These options are for compatibility purposes. In the early days of NetWare, the standard way to access IPX services was through Int 64h. But an IBM office application was also using Int 64h, so Novell adopted Int 7Ah. This call, too, was used by another company, so Novell now recommends that applications accessing IPX services do so through Int 2Fh. Int 2Fh returns the "far call" address of IPX services and then make the request through that address.

   The INT options offer a way for programs written for earlier NetWare versions to function on the network. For better or worse, these options are set to "On," which means you will have problems with any applications using an Int 64h or 7Ah. The reason for the "On" setting is that some applications may require that Int 64h or 7Ah be there for IPX; these applications will not work without the call.

   However, if an application that uses Int 64h or Int 7Ah keeps blowing up, try loading IPX and NETx.COM, then the program. If the program malfunctions or dies, that program is probably conflicting with one of these interrupts. Set the interrupt options to "Off" and try the program again. Or call the vendor and ask if the application uses Int 64h or Int 7Ah.

CONFIG OPTION = <n>. This option allows you to set the network interface board configuration to any valid SHGEN option without having to go in and rerun SHGEN. For example, if your NE-1000 configuration option is set to option 0 (IRQ=3, I/O 300h, no DMA) and you want to change it to option 2 (IRQ=4, I/O 340h, no DMA), type "CONFIG OPTION = 2" in the SHELL.CFG file (be sure the board also reflects those settings or the change will not work). You can find the options in the NetWare board supplements or in the third-party documentation.

Config Option presently defaults to whatever configuration option you set up during SHGEN or in DCONFIG. If you enter an invalid setting, the "Config Option" will revert to the configuration option you set up during SHGEN.

NETx.COM Options

Replace the default parameters in the NETx.COM file when you want to change their functionality. Here is a list of the NETx.COM file values you may change, along with their default parameters:

```
CACHE BUFFERS = 5
EOJ = ON
FILE HANDLES = 40
HOLD = OFF
SHARE = ON
LONG MACHINE TYPE = IBM_PC
SHORT MACHINE = IBM
LOCK RETRIES = 3
LOCK DELAY = 1
READ ONLY COMPATIBILITY = OFF
SEARCH MODE = 1
MAXIMUM TASKS = 31
PRINT HEADER = 64
PRINT TAIL = 16
LOCAL PRINTERS = number of ports
PATCH = <byte offset> <value>
TASK MODE = 2
```

Newer releases of the NetWare shell (since NetWare 386 v3.01 release) add eight more options:

```
ALL SERVERS = OFF
MAX CUR DIR = 64
MAX PATH LENGTH = 255
SHOW DOTS = OFF
SET STATION TIME = ON
SPECIAL UPPERCASE = OFF
PREFERRED SERVER = servername
ENTRY STACK SIZE = 10
```

CACHE BUFFERS = <number>. Workstation caching is similar to file server caching. The file server uses caching as a place to store applications, utilities, and data that are accessed most often. Eliminating the need to access the hard disk for information speeds server operations immensely. Workstations use caching to handle data requests and replies more efficiently. Through caching, the NetWare shell provides a place to store data for files the workstation has open.

Workstation caching also lessens network traffic because workstations require less time to get data on and off the wire. Cache buffers store incoming data, move data off the cables, and cut down on lost packet retries. Workstation cache buffers are 512 bytes in size; the default is five (2.5KB). When applications perform sequential I/O reads, performance improves because applications are reading 512 bytes each time, rather than just one or two bytes. However, reads that are not sequential (random I/O reads from database fields that are less than 512 bytes in size) will not benefit from the cache buffers.

Memory is rare and precious to a user working under DOS's 640KB limitation; still, caching buffers can enhance network performance if the workstation performs a good deal of sequential I/O reading. If workstations are using word processors or spreadsheets only, try increasing the cache size and see if network or workstation performance improves.

EOJ = ON/OFF (default is ON). The End Of Job request automatically closes files, locks, and semaphores after a particular task is terminated. The default is ON, but only as a precautionary measure. EOJ = OFF applies to those few applications written to the DOS platform before DOS version 3.0. Other applications take advantage of DOS EOJ capabilities, making this option unnecessary.

FILE HANDLES = <number>. The file handles you set in DOS's CONFIG.SYS affect only local devices. For DOS 3.3 and below, this number defaults to 8 (DOS 4.01 defaults to 20) and signifies all the files that DOS's entire operating system can have open at one time on the workstation. Within DOS's open file arena, the file handle table has room for twenty entries, of which five are already taken for standard input, output, error, auxiliary, and printer.

NetWare and DOS do not share open files between the two environments. The SHELL.CFG file comes with a default of forty file handles—the number of files a workstation on the network can have open at one time. Forty is sufficient for most applications and environments; however, it, too, can be technically (but not practically) extended to 255.

One file handle is 32 bytes in size; the shell default is forty file handles (1.2KB). Increase this number only if a network application gives you an error message saying you do not have enough file handles. Applications use extra file handles to access information not found in their .EXE files—for example, when you run a spelling program from within a word processor. Future applications will undoubtedly have more files open at a time as well.

Some applications (such as WordPerfect) determine the number of files they can open by opening a local device and then duplicating the file opening procedure until reaching the number of open files the application specifies. This procedure means you will need to place OPEN FILES = 20 in the workstation's CONFIG.SYS file, even though the application will not open any files at the local level other than this initial check. Thus, you must configure both DOS and the NetWare shell to handle the application's file requirements.

You also need to take into account DOS-extendable operating systems, such as Windows 386, DESQview 386, Double-DOS, and so forth. These operating systems can have twenty file handles open per application. Because they can also have several applications open at a time, they can quickly reach the NetWare shell's file handle limit. Then the next application request to open a file will not be able to complete that request. When you begin receiving such error messages as "no file handles" or "unable to open file," increase the number of file handles in the SHELL.CFG file.

HOLD = ON/OFF (default is OFF). Leave this default to OFF. Some early applications (written to DOS versions before v3.0) did not use file handles, so they did not keep their files open the entire time someone was using them. One person could open a file and make changes to it while another person was using it.

However, most current applications are written to take advantage of DOS file handles, and most older software programs have been rewritten to avoid allowing more than one person to access a file at the same time. But if you have a pre-DOS v3.0 program, you may need to use the HOLDON utility. Better yet, buy its network upgrade (since HOLDON is no longer being shipped with the most current releases of NetWare).

Do not use the HOLD = ON option in SHELL.CFG (use the HOLDON command utility instead); the HOLDON option keeps files open for the entire network session. Another major disadvantage for setting the SHELL.CFG option to HOLD = ON is that this option also keeps printers from accessing files, leaving you unable to print. To print, you must exit the application, type HOLDOFF <Enter>, reenter the application, and run the printing command. Again, buy the program's network upgrade.

SHARE = ON/OFF (defaults to ON). The Share option allows other (child) processes that an application creates to use the same file handles as the application itself. Otherwise, SHARE = OFF will return a different file handle when a child process initiates. Usually the application will take care of file handles, so there is little reason to change the default. This option affects only files that reside on network drives, leaving local drives to be handled by the applications themselves.

LONG MACHINE TYPE = IBM_PC. Use the long machine name when you set up the %MACHINE variable in the system login script, or when you have a workstation that does not go by the IBM_PC machine name (most clones do, however). To use the %MACHINE variable with a brand of workstation, such as AT&T or Compaq, which does not use the IBM_PC machine name, type LONG MACHINE TYPE = AT&T or COMPAQ <Enter> in your SHELL.CFG file.

To use the machine name in the system login script for the DOS version path specification, type the following:

```
MAP INS S2:=SYS:PUBLIC\%MACHINE\%OS\%OS_VERSION
```

If you create the directories along the path designation, the above example translates into SYS:PUBLIC\IBM_PC\MSDOS\V3.30. Then if you create a directory path for Compaqs, and use COMPAQ in the long machine name on Compaq workstations, you will see SYS:PUBLIC\COMPAQ\MSDOS\V3.30.

You use this DOS version path in the system login script to designate the DOS type a particular workstation uses. If you create the full directory path, the previous MAP example will map the workstation to the version of DOS it uses when it boots up. You then add COMSPEC=Y:\COMMAND.COM to the system login script to enable DOS to find a command processor while the workstation is logged into the network.

SHORT MACHINE TYPE = IBM. Some monitors from Compaq and AT&T emulate color monitors by using gray scales instead of actual colors. These monitors must use the CMPQ$RUN.OVL file located in SYS:PUBLIC; this file sets up a black-and-white default palette for NetWare menu utilities. Otherwise, the grey scales may not show against the background. In your SHELL.CFG file, type SHORT MACHINE TYPE = CMPQ as the short machine name parameter. This will call the CMPQ$RUN.OVL file when you access a menu utility.

LOCK RETRIES = <number>. When you ask for a file lock on a file that is already locked, the Lock Retries option will try again to lock the file. If the file is already locked, the shell retries a certain number of times (the default is 3) with a certain amount of delay time in between (Lock Delay).

LOCK DELAY = <number> (set to 1). The Lock Delay option establishes how long the shell waits before retrying to lock a file. The Lock Delay option works on a "tick" basis (18.21 ticks per second for IBM PCs and compatibles). The option is set to 1, which means the shell will retry every .0556 seconds until it uses up its three lock retries in .15 seconds.

Change the default only when someone is in an application, such as a database, that does not offer a retry threshold of its own and that person is performing a lot of file locking activity. In such a case, the record lock is being held slightly longer than the last retry count, causing an error message such as "File is locked," or "Abort, Retry, or Fail?" These messages could simply mean that someone is already in the file, and the user must wait for the file to be released. However, if the user chooses "Retry" after the "Abort, Retry, or Fail?" message and can consistently open the file, that could mean you need to increase the retry count.

Fortunately, most applications written today do their own lock retries.

READ ONLY COMPATIBILITY = ON/OFF (default is OFF). In versions of NetWare before v2.1x, you could open a file with Read-Write access even though the file was flagged Read/Only. But when you tried to write to the file, you received an error message. With NetWare v2.1 and above, however, you cannot access a file flagged Read/Only when you have requested Read-Write access. Instead of trying (and failing) to save your modifications, you cannot open the file. When you set the

Read Only Compatibility to ON, you allow the shell to open a Read/Only file with the intention to write to that file. Do this only when the program asks for Read/Write access even when it intends to only read the file—for example, in an application such as the earlier versions of ATC's The Coordinator. If you run a version of The Coordinator previous to v2.0, set the Read Only Compatibility to ON; otherwise, leave this option to the default.

SEARCH MODE = <number>. The Search Mode option helps applications to find the auxiliary files they need in order to perform their tasks. When started, many applications open a number of other files (such as overlay files and data files) as a resource to the application. The Search Mode option determines when applications can look in the NetWare search drives to find these auxiliary files.

Normally, when an application requires auxiliary files, it specifies a path to that file as part of its setup menu or routine. If the application does not specify a path, the NetWare shell will search any directories specified in the PATH command. The Search Mode option can tell the shell exactly how and when to use the search drives.

Some applications open their auxiliary files and read the files' contents; other applications read and write to their auxiliary files. You may need to consult the documentation for each application to determine if the application just reads its auxiliary files or reads and writes to them.

Search Mode has five settings: Mode 1, Mode 2, Mode 3, Mode 5, and Mode 7. Each mode specifies a different way of using search drives. Here are the current mode settings:

Mode 1. This is the default mode for the SHELL.CFG file. With this setting, the shell looks in the search drives only when the application specifies no path and the file is not in the default directory. Mode 1 is for both read-only and read-write requests; NetWare displays "search on all opens with no path" on the screen when you specify this mode.

Mode 2. This mode prevents the shell from looking in any search drives for auxiliary files. NetWare calls this mode "do not search."

Mode 3. This search mode works like Mode 1, except that the shell looks in search drives for read-only requests. NetWare displays "search on read-only opens with no path" on the screen when you specify this mode.

Mode 5. This mode allows the shell to look in the search drives you or a user specifies, even if the application also specifies a path. NetWare displays "search on all opens."

Mode 7. This search mode works like Mode 5, except that the shell looks in the search drives for read-only requests. NetWare displays "search on all read-only opens."

SHELL.CFG settings apply to all applications on a global basis, so choose the mode (usually the default search mode) that works for most your programs. If applications are unable to find their auxiliary files through the shell's default search mode, use the SMODE command to flag the executable file with the proper mode (see the *Utilities Reference* manual for details). You might initially try the default mode.

MAXIMUM TASKS = <number> (default is 31). This option establishes the maximum number of tasks a workstation can actively maintain at a time. Normally, the default of 31 tasks is more than enough. However, applications that extend DOS's capabilities (for example, Microsoft Windows and DESQview 386) may need a larger number. You can set this option to any number from 8 to 128.

PRINT HEADER = <number>. Use this option in conjunction with the way you set up certain printer options in the PRINTDEF and PRINTCON utilities. The three circumstances under which you would use PRINTDEF are when one print job is affected by previous print jobs, when an application does not have the driver capability to take full advantage of the printer, or when you need to define specific paper forms.

With the PRINTDEF utility, you define the functionality of the printer (known as a device) itself and therefore how the printer will print. Once you define the printer's functions, you also define the "mode" of operation that tells the printer how to print a particular job. Some print modes are small, involving two or three functions only; others can be quite large.

The Print Header option can change the header buffer's byte size to accommodate the larger mode functions. To find out your mode sizes and the buffer size you need you must go into PRINTDEF, thumb through printer modes and find the mode with the most functions, then count every character in each of the functions of that mode. Resize your buffer by allowing for one byte per character.

When counting that setting's characters, keep in mind that all the characters within a pair of delimiter brackets (< >) are considered as one character, and each character outside the brackets is also considered as one character. For example, <0x1b>3<ETX> is three characters long—one character for <0x1b>, one character for 3, and one character for <ETX>. If you have not set up any printer definitions in PRINTDEF, use the default buffer size, which is 64 bytes (characters) long. If you are using the PRINTCON (Printer Configuration) utility with PRINTDEF's defaults, count the function characters in the biggest defined mode and use that as the Print Header default.

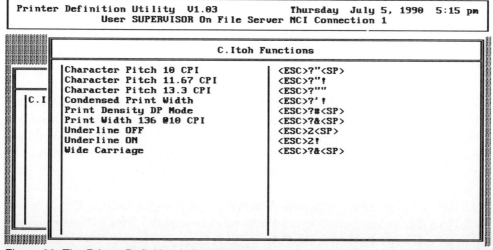

Figure 22: The Printer Definition Utility window.

PRINT TAIL = <number>. This option contains the Re-initialize Mode for network printers as they are defined in PRINTDEF. The default size of this option is 16 bytes; since most Re-initialize Modes are short, you will need to do nothing. For example, Hewlett-Packard uses two characters (<ESC>E) for its re-initialization sequence. However, to re-initialize the IBM ProPrinter, you must turn off every function you defined in the Proprinter Mode, which can make for quite a large re-initialization mode.

To see how the re-initialization modes are presently defined, go into PRINTDEF, choose Print Devices, then Edit Print Devices. Next, select the printers, the Device Modes, and then look at the Re-initialize Modes for all defined devices; choose the largest re-initialize setting. Use the same rules for counting characters that you used for the Print Header option. Once you have counted the characters in the different Re-initialization modes, choose the largest one and set your Print Tail option accordingly. If you are not using PRINTDEF, use the default.

LOCAL PRINTERS = <number>. Use this option to indicate how many local printers are on the workstation. If the workstations on the network do not have local printers attached (except for those workstations running network printers locally), set this option to 0. The 0 setting prevents workstations from hanging when users accidentally press <Shift>-<Print Screen> and the CAPTURE utility has not been run, or if the workstation does not have a local printer attached. Accidently pressing <Shift>-<Print Screen> is a common problem with the older IBM PC keyboards, whose <Shift> and <PrtSc> keys are scrunched together. (The workstation does not actually hang; it just takes a long time to discover there is no attached printer.)

Along this line, many supervisors forget that the Local Printer option is set to 0 when users add a local or network printer to a workstation. You can waste time troubleshooting cables and ports when what you really need to do is reset this option to 1.

TASK MODE = <number> (defaults to 2). When a workstation uses programs like Microsoft's Windows 386 operating system (OS), the 386 OS creates a series of virtual machine modes for each 640KB of memory and designates these memory groups into other machine modes. Each virtual machine mode expects certain environment parameters to exist. When you initiate another mode by changing over to another window, the shell copies the environment parameters from VM0 (the default) to the next mode.

Sometimes the VM0 environment intrudes on the other virtual machine modes, giving you problems with changing drive mappings, such as CD.., MAP, and MAP or DEL in the other environments. If you experience these intrusions when running Windows 386, set the Task Mode parameter to 0. The NetWare shell then creates a new DOS environment for each new VM. If you are running Windows 3.0, be sure you have a default of 2 (which should be left alone).

PATCH = <byte offset> <value>. The Patch option works like the IPatch option in IPX.COM, except that it instead puts patches into the NETx.COM program. Normally, you need not enter the Patch option changes by hand. Any shell patches from Novell are in .EXE files that load themselves into the proper offsets. Only use this option if you are told to do so by Novell technical support personnel. Then have Novell send you the updated *.COM or *.EXE version.

Newer versions of the NetWare shell since the release of the NetWare 386 v3.01 shell version have eight new additional options. The options and their definitions are discussed below.

ALL SERVERS = OFF. In shell versions before the release of v3.01, when you pressed <Enter> after performing a task, the NetWare shell sent an "End of Task" to every server the workstation was attached to. For the newer NetWare shell versions, the All Servers option defaults to OFF, which limits sending the "End of Task" to only those servers involved with the current task. When you change the option to equal ON, then every server a workstation is attached to will receive the "End of Task" request. For most uses, it is best to leave this option OFF.

MAX CUR DIR LENGTH = 64 (bytes). When you type <Enter> and you have set up PROMPT $P to see the full directory path, DOS allows you to see only 64 bytes of directory path information. However, some network paths may exceed 64 bytes, making it impossible for DOS to handle the path display.

With the new shell versions since the release of v3.01, you can configure the exact number of characters you need the directory path to display. NetWare shell versions prior to v3.01 defaulted to 128 bytes; thus, directory paths longer than 128 bytes would end abruptly in mid character. If you are using NetWare shell versions since v3.01 and find that a workstation's full directory path is truncating (ending abruptly), add more bytes to this option. The Max Cur Dir Length option can be set from 64 to 255 bytes long.

MAX PATH LENGTH = 255 (bytes). DOS defines a valid ASCII string at 128 bytes, allowing you to use 128 bytes of directory path information in a file name. With the new shell versions since the release of v3.01, you may find this number too limiting for some directory path lengths. The newer shell versions default to 255 bytes. This option can also be set from 64 to 255 bytes long, and the path length does not include any file or server names.

SHOW DOTS = ON. Certain programs (such as Windows) allow you to move up directories in the directory path by highlighting "." and ".." entries and pressing <Enter> or by clicking on these path entries. With shell versions prior to the release of v3.01, however, NetWare had no way to let you do this. The Show Dots option allows these programs to use the "." and ".." options to change directories.

As a point of interest, it is best to set this option to OFF if you are not running programs that use dots to transverse directories. If you are using programs such as Windows on NetWare v2.1x networks, update your shell version to add this capability. Without the dot capability, programs like Windows assume it is in the root directory, which may not be the case.

SET STATION TIME = ON. When you load the NetWare shell on a workstation, the shell sets the workstation's internal clock to the same time as the network server. If you don't want workstations set to the server time, place this option in the SHELL.CFG file and set the option to OFF. However, the login process also sets the workstation's internal clock, as does the SYSTIME command if you type SYSTIME <Enter> at the network prompt.

SPECIAL UPPERCASE = OFF. You would set this option to ON when you wish DOS to translate ASCII values (characters) that are above 127h to uppercase. You would set this option to ON if you are running a foreign version of DOS as well as NetWare. The foreign DOS versions will know how to interpret the keyboard with different language keys, and by setting this option to ON, NetWare will defer to DOS. Otherwise, you can leave this option to OFF and DOS will not translate these characters to uppercase.

PREFERRED SERVER = servername. The IPX driver establishes an avenue for communication with the network interface board and attached cable, allowing access to attached workstations and servers. Then as the NetWare shell loads, it first establishes a connection to a network server by using IPX to broadcast "Get Nearest Server." The first server to respond to the request establishes a connection with that workstation. When you initially load the NetWare shell, you will see "Attached to server <servername>" after the shell parameters, which may or may not be the server you wish to log in to.

The preferred server option allows you to specify the server you wish to attach to; the shell then attempts to connect the workstation to the specified server rather than the first server that responds to the "Get Nearest Server" broadcast. The server name can be up to 48 characters long. Be sure to use a valid server name when you use this option. The shell will also attempt up to five other server connections in case it cannot establish a connection with the specified server. That way, you will receive a server connection even though it won't be with the server you specified. If the shell cannot connect to the first five servers, you will see "Server has no available slots" message on the screen.

ENTRY STACK SIZE = 10. This option is used in conjunction with the Expanded Memory Specification (EMS) shell, which is the EMS version of the NETx file (EMSNETx.EXE). The EMS version allows workstations to load the NetWare shell (except for 7KB) into expanded memory, thus giving the workstation 32KB more of DOS's 640KB available for application use. You must also load an EMS 4.0 driver through the CONFIG.SYS file.

When the shell receives another shell request while it is busy doing something else, the shell must save the memory page mappings it is busy with. The Entry Stack option allows the workstation to configure the internal page mapping stack size that the shell will use. The stack size can be 5 to 40, and defaults to 10. If you see the message "Entry stack size too small," increment the default value by five.

Defaults of NETBIOS.EXE

NetBIOS is a peer-to-peer communications protocol, which means that any NetBIOS node can talk to any other node. In a Novell environment, then, a file server, workstation, or bridge can talk to other workstations, bridges, or servers through the NetBIOS API (Application Programmers Interface). Programmers can write applications using NetBIOS as a communications mechanism that can share information with other nodes running the same NetBIOS applications.

When using NetBIOS in the NetWare environment, you first load IPX to set up its environment. NetBIOS then communicates on IPX socket 455h. The procedure is not unlike a radio transmission: only those radios tuned to a certain frequency will receive a station call. Similarly, only those nodes listening on NetBIOS will receive information from NetBIOS.

Once you install NetBIOS, an application that wants to communicate with another node must first inform other NetBIOS nodes of the name it will be known by. The application must first add a name to the residing NetBIOS node's local name table. The calling node does this by sending a name claim request to all the other nodes speaking NetBIOS in order to get the name registered. If another node says it is using that name, the requesting node must try other names until it finds a name that no other node is using.

With NetWare v2.15 revision B, each local node has a name table of twenty-six names (NetWare prior to revision B has sixteen); if no other node claims the name, the requesting node registers the name in the name table.

If the network includes bridges connecting multiple networks, the name claim is first broadcast on the local network. The claim is then propagated at the bridge, where it is sent to the next network. If there is another bridge, the claim is propagated there to the network connected to the bridge. This continues until all the bridges and networks are covered.

Once the name is registered, each requesting node writes the new name in its local name table where it can find the names quickly. Applications using NetBIOS can then use names from the name table when they wish to communicate.

With the name registered, applications can create a NetBIOS session (a guaranteed delivery method, like SPX). As a session begins, the calling node looks for a node with the designated name and sends a connect request packet to that node, who then sends an answer back. The request and answer contain each other's node addresses, making it possible for the application to sends packets to the appropriate address.

Since sessions are "guaranteed-delivery" communications, they acknowledge in-bound data packets and send verifications on idle sessions every three seconds. If one node does not hear anything from its partner for six seconds, the node sends request for verification packets every three seconds until it hears from the other connection side. If the other side does not respond in thirty seconds, the querying connection side assumes the session has gone away and tears down the connection.

With NetBIOS in place, applications can send information back and forth, using the established session. Some types of applications that can use NetBIOS are diagnostics, messaging systems such as E-mail, and gateways into dissimilar environments. The box that the application comes in, or the documentation to the application, will tell you if it is using NetBIOS as its communication protocol.

With this in mind, here is a list of the values (along with their default parameters) used by NETBIOS.EXE. If your version of NetBIOS supports a particular option and you place that option in the SHELL.CFG, you will see that option display on the workstation's screen when the workstation load NetBIOS.

```
NETBIOS SESSIONS = 10
NETBIOS SEND BUFFERS = 6
NETBIOS RECEİVE BUFFERS = 6
NETBIOS RETRY DELAY = 10
NETBIOS ABORT TIMEOUT = 540
NETBIOS VERIFY TIMEOUT = 54
NETBIOS LISTEN TIMEOUT = 108
NPATCH = <byte offset><value>
```

With the revision B version of the 2.15 shell and NetWare 386, the default number of NetBIOS Sessions has increased from 10 to 32. Revision B and NetWare 386 also add:

```
NETBIOS RETRY COUNT = 20
NETBIOS INTERNET = ON
NETBIOS COMMANDS = 12
```

NETBIOS SESSIONS = <number> (default is 10). This value indicates how many NetBIOS sessions the workstation can support at one time. You can have as few as 4 sessions, or as many as 100. Revision B and NetWare 386 shells can have 250 sessions but default to 32 sessions.

Each session entry you add takes about 90 bytes per session. Depending on the NetBIOS applications you have purchased, unless you are going through gateways (which might need more sessions), the 10-session default is sufficient. If you do not run NetBIOS-specific applications, do not load NETBIOS.EXE.

The session table is not the same as the NetBIOS name table, but the two tables are related. The vendor of the NetBIOS application should tell you how to set up your environment in terms of your NetBIOS Session value and your NetBIOS Command value. If the application uses more than the NETBIOS.EXE defaults, set up the session table and name table accordingly.

If, while you are running NetBIOS, you receive "No more available NetBIOS sessions" messages, add more sessions by changing the default value in the SHELL.CFG file. Usually this number will depend on how many NetBIOS applications you are running, how many sessions (and commands) those applications need, and whether your system has peak usage times for those applications.

NETBIOS SEND AND RECEIVE BUFFERS = <number> (defaults are 6).
Send and receive buffers manage IPX resources at a lower level. NetBIOS allocates
an ECB (Event Control Block—NetWare's means of getting requests and replies
around on the network) for each of these buffers. Typical ECBs for NetBIOS are
about 64 bytes in length. Each receive buffer also includes space for the largest
packet the LAN driver can receive.

Increase these numbers only if you have extensive NetBIOS traffic. Or, if
you have a server/client application running on a workstation, you may need to increase the receive buffers on the server side to better handle the increased incoming
traffic. (You might also increase the receive buffers to see if the application's performance improves.) Start with an additional five buffers.

NETBIOS RETRY DELAY = <number> (defaults to 10). This entry shows how
long NetBIOS will delay before sending a retry to a communications partner if a
request is not answered. The delay works on a "tick" basis. (There are 18.21 ticks
per second for IBM PCs and compatibles.) Ten ticks is roughly 1/2 second.

The NetBIOS Retry Delay is intimately tied to the IPX Retry Count; the two
numbers multiplied together give you the total timeout value. For example, the
default for the IPX Retry Count is twenty and the NetBIOS Retry Delay is 1/2
second. That gives NetBIOS ten seconds to retry sending its broadcasts when an application attempts to register or find a network name. (Rev B and 386 use the
NetBIOS Retry Count option instead of the IPX Retry Count option.)

You can definitely see a performance difference between different retry
counts when registering or finding a NetBIOS name. And you can change the per-
ceived time difference by changing the IPX Retry Count. For example, changing
the IPX Retry Count to ten drops your total timeout value to five seconds. If you
drop the NetBIOS Retry Count to 5, the delay will be only 2 1/2 seconds, which
seems much faster to the user.

But keep in mind several factors, including network size, network performance, network layout (including bridges), and protocol type. For example, if you
have eight networks, but only one has NetBIOS activity, you can decrease the
NetBIOS Retry Count to 5 without affecting the other networks. If a user needs to
talk to NetBIOS on a network that is eight networks away, you should leave the IPX
Retry Count at 20 or even higher.

As a rule of thumb, the IPX Retry Count is affected by the quality of your
cabling system. If the system is reliable, with relatively few servers (five, for
example) attached to each other, you can lower the IPX Retry Count. (See page 79
for further explanation.)

Another factor affecting NetBIOS applications is your cabling scheme; for
example, whether your system is doing internal bridging through each file server,
or using a backbone. With internal bridging, the number of hops an application must
travel can be significantly greater than on a backbone.

Internal bridging affects NetBIOS in particular, because each bridge
rebroadcasts NetBIOS queries to the LANs attached to it. If retry intervals are too
short, you will unnecessarily hamper your NetBIOS services. You might end up

with duplicated NetBIOS names because you did not give the query packets enough time to respond to the initial name claim.

Another matter to consider is the cabling type and the relative protocol speed you are using: for example, ARCnet sends packets at 2.5Mbps, Ethernet sends packets at 10Mbps, and token-ring sends packets at 4 or 16 Mbps. You must also take into account the network management in the protocols as well. For instance, token-ring will seem slower simply because of its network management overhead.

The Verify, Listen, and Abort Entries

The NetBIOS Verify Timeout, the NetBIOS Listen Timeout, and the NetBIOS Abort Timeout are set up the same way as the SPX timeouts. These option values apply after NetBIOS creates a session, and deal with how NetBIOS maintains the session itself.

The *NetWare Supervisor Reference* manual states that the NetBIOS Verify Timeout, the NetBIOS Listen Timeout, and the NetBIOS Abort Timeout all work on a "tick" basis; there are 18.21 ticks per second for IBM PCs and compatibles. Thirty seconds is roughly 540 ticks.

NETBIOS VERIFY TIMEOUT = <number> (default is 54 ticks, or 3 seconds). This option is used in conjunction with NetBIOS Abort Timeout and NetBIOS Listen Timeout options. NetBIOS sends an "I'm still alive" (verify timeout) packet every three seconds to ensure that the NetBIOS session is still open. If no packets are being exchanged within the NetBIOS session, it will start sending "Are you there?" (listen timeout) packets to ensure that the session is still working.

NETBIOS LISTEN TIMEOUT = <number> (default is 108 ticks, or 6 seconds). The Listen Timeout entry is the amount of time NetBIOS waits before it sends an "Are you alive?" packet to the other side of the session connection. If NetBIOS does not hear from the other connection partner end for a specified time (defaulted to 30 seconds), NetBIOS will stop trying and initiate the Abort Timeout sequence, thereby dropping the session.

NETBIOS ABORT TIMEOUT = <number> (default is 540 ticks, or 30 seconds). When a NetBIOS program sends a packet to a communications partner and the partner does not answer, NetBIOS performs a number of retries. If thirty seconds elapse, NetBIOS concludes that the communication partner or the network has failed and tears down the session.

It is best to leave the Abort Timeout option at thirty seconds, because if you do not hear from a communications partner in thirty seconds, it is probably unable to respond. If you change the option to something like ten seconds (182.1 ticks) and your network slows down, you may cut off your session unnecessarily.

Taking too many seconds off the Abort Timeout interval can give the session partner insufficient time to respond to the original request. This mistake could create a problem if the session partner is a number of network bridges away or if the packet is lost along the way. Unless Novell tells you differently, don't change this number; Novell technical support personnel work from the assumption that the NetBIOS Abort Timeout, NetBIOS Verify Timeout, and NetBIOS Listen Timeout have not been changed. Unless instructed, go with the defaults.

NPATCH = <byte offset><value>. The Npatch option, equivalent to NETx.COM's Patch option, is used for putting patches into the NETBIOS.EXE data segment. When NetBIOS loads, it looks for any Npatch byte offset locations and values to incorporate into NetBIOS. If NetBIOS finds any, it loads the Npatch information. You will seldom need the Npatch option; Novell NetBIOS patches come in an executable form that load themselves into the proper offsets, saving you from having to enter the changes by hand. Only use this option if you are told to by Novell technical support personnel. The engineer passing along the information by phone will walk you through the procedure.

Revision B and NetWare 386 NetBIOS Commands

With the revision B version of NetWare v2.15 shell and NetWare 386, Novell adds three more NetBIOS SHELL.CFG options to its repertoire: NetBIOS Retry Count – 20, NetBIOS Internet = On, and NetBIOS Commands = 12.

NETBIOS RETRY COUNT = 20. The revision B version of NetWare v2.15 shell and NetWare 386 use this NetBIOS option instead of the IPX Retry Count. This number determines how many times NetBIOS will send a retry to a communications partner if a request is not answered.

The default is twenty, but you can vary this number with each installation. If you select a smaller number—ten, for example—NetBIOS will drop the connection faster than the normal thirty seconds it takes to terminate a connection. When a workstation legitimately loses its connection, a smaller number such as three means that you will receive a connection error in less time than the normal thirty or forty seconds.

If your server is reliable and you have relatively few servers—five or so— attached on a network, you may wish to lower the retry count. However, if you do change the count and you start having connection problems, go back to the default.

But increasing the retry count for a busy LAN can have the unfortunate side effect of causing NetBIOS to run more slowly. NetBIOS is heavily influenced by the "NetBIOS Retry Count" and the "NetBIOS Retry Delay" options because you are actually estimating how long it takes a packet to reach the farthest node on the farthest network. The numbers in these two options depend on the nodes the application is running, the speed of the nodes, the bandwidth (8-, 16-, or 32-bit) of the network interface boards, and the activity on the internet. You will have to experiment to see how your network handles its packets.

NETBIOS INTERNET = ON/OFF (defaults to ON). If you are running NetBIOS applications on only one network and are not accessing workstations on other networks, you can set this option to OFF. Setting the entry to OFF means that NetBIOS will not send a broadcast over a bridge; rather, it will broadcast only on its own local network. This setup improves performance when NetBIOS is establishing sessions. It also reduces the number of broadcast retries.

NETBIOS COMMANDS = NUMBER (default is 12). The Commands option establishes the number of simultaneous commands that NetBIOS can process at a given time. Possible choices for this entry range from four to 250 commands. Depending on your NetBIOS activity, applications can submit a number of events to NetBIOS for sending. If your network runs many sessions using NetBIOS, commands may fail because you have reached the limit on pending commands.

The NetBIOS Command option does relate to the NetBIOS Sessions entry. The vendor of the NetBIOS application will tell you how to set up your environment in terms of NetBIOS Sessions and NetBIOS Command entries. If your application uses more than the SHELL.CFG defaults (10 and 12 respectively), set up these two entries accordingly; if the application does not, use the default unless you start getting errors.

7 Troubleshooting Workstation Problems

Aside from a user's initial gut reaction (usually a primal scream) to a workstation problem, the system supervisor is the first line of defense for network management and maintenance. Diagnosing and troubleshooting workstations often takes a Zen approach; you start with what the problem is not and, through the process of elimination, find out what the problem is. Some problems are readily apparent—for example, when error messages on the screen steer you in the direction of the problem. But often, you find yourself with a malfunctioning workstation and no clue as to where to begin to fix it.

With this in mind, here are some steps to help you narrow the troubleshooting field at the workstation level. The general questions will help you isolate a particular situation; the steps that follow the lettered statements will help you to isolate the problem still further until you find a solution.

GENERAL QUESTIONS
A) Is the workstation having problems loading DOS?
B) Is the workstation having problems loading NetWare or logging in?
C) Is more than one workstation affected?
D) Did the workstation run properly before this problem occurred?
E) Is this workstation a new installation?

A) *Workstation has problems loading DOS*:
    1.   Check for physical problems.
    2.   Check the workstation with a new DOS diskette.
    3.   If necessary, run the PS/2's Reference Diskette.

1. Check for physical workstation problems.

Physical workstation problems can be a source of endless frustration. Unfortunately, when something goes wrong physically with a PC, you usually receive no error messages (or any other useful indication of what the problem might be). In such a case, here is a list of checkpoints to look at when diagnosing physical problems.

• Check the power cord connection between the back of the workstation and the wall socket.

• Check the power cable to the monitor as well.

• Do not push the workstation tightly against the wall, where cord or cable damage can occur.

• Turn on the workstation and listen for the fan. If the fan is not running, you may have a power problem within the workstation, a faulty cable, or a faulty socket. Replace the power cord first, or try a new power socket. If the workstation still does not work, place a different workstation at the problem location and see if it has the same problem.

• If nothing appears on the screen, but the monitor light is on, be sure the monitor's brightness and contrast knobs are not simply turned down. If the monitor's power is not connected to an AT-clone workstation, turn off the workstation only and see if you get a screen full of wavy lines. If you do, replace the monitor board, then the monitor. (However, this trick does not always work, especially on the newer PCs and monitors that shut off automatically when the workstation is not on.)

• See if the computer goes through its internal RAM and ROM testing procedures. You will see a memory check in the upper left-hand corner of the screen (if the screen is working). The IBM PC/AT, PS/2, and most compatibles will display an error message indicating the configuration error.

• Faulty power can knock out the CMOS RAM storage area that contains workstation setup parameters. If messages (such as memory, CMOS, or drive errors) appear on the screen when you first turn on the workstation, run SETUP or diagnostics.

• Check the keyboard connection for possible problems. Type a few characters and see if they appear on the screen (be sure the screen is working first). Be sure the keyboard is not locked through a hardware key or loaded software. If nothing happens when you type on the keyboard, connect a different keyboard and try typing on that keyboard. Some AT-type keyboards do not have extended or expanded capabilities and therefore do not work with the newer 286- and 386-based computers.

When swapping keyboards (a natural tendency for users who dislike the AT-style keyboard), be sure the swapped keyboard can function properly with the computer. Also, be sure to shut down the workstation before swapping keyboards— this is a good practice, for you may damage the keyboard ROM.

Be sure the hard drive or drive A: light comes on when the workstation performs its internal testing. If it does not, place a diskette in drive A: and type DIR

<Enter>, or transfer to the hard disk drive (usually by typing C:) and type DIR <Enter>. Faulty disk controllers will sometimes leave the drive light on and you without drive access. If you have added any new hardware to the workstation, run SETUP and tell the workstation it has new hardware. The workstation cannot use the new hardware until you add the necessary information to its CMOS RAM; you must then restart the workstation to initiate the new configuration.

2. Check the workstation with a new DOS diskette.

If the workstation checks out physically, create two boot diskettes: one diskette containing nothing but COMMAND.COM (and DOS's system files), and another diskette with CONFIG.SYS and the NetWare connection/shell files (ANETx.COM for v2.0a and IPX.COM and NETx.COM for v2.15 and above). The diskette with CONFIG.SYS and shell files should not be the workstation's boot diskette; if the boot diskette is the problem, you will not be able to isolate it as a probable failure point.

First see if the workstation can load DOS, leaving you with prompts to change the current date and time, followed by the DOS version, copyright, and DOS prompt on the screen. If you do not see this, you may have a physical drive error with drive A:. A good place to start looking is with the disk drive, the controller, or the cable connecting the two. You will not get much response from the disk drive if you put a high-density diskette in a drive that needs a 360KB format (for 5.25" diskettes, or 720KB for 3.5" diskettes). Be sure you have the correct diskette.

3.   For token-ring networks with PS/2 workstations, check TOKREUI.COM, NETBEUI.COM or DXMAID programs.

If you are running PS/2s on a token-ring network, and if you are running IBM's version of NetBIOS (rather than Novell's version), the performance of certain programs depends on when you bought the token-ring boards. For example, IBM Token-Ring boards purchased before April 1987 came with an IBM Token-Ring Network PC Adapter diskette containing TOKREUI.COM and NETBEUI.COM files. If you are using IBM's NetBIOS, you must use NETBEUI.COM. Whether or not you are running NetBIOS, you need to run TOKREUI before IPX.COM in the AUTOEXEC.BAT, for TOKREUI gives the network interface board its base memory address. (Be sure to copy the TOKREUI.COM file from the PC Adapter diskette to the boot diskette.)

IBM Token-Ring boards purchased after April 1987 come with a LAN Support Program diskette, containing the DXMAID program. This program creates three files for IBM's NetBIOS emulator program; you need it only if you are running IBM's version of NetBIOS. (For more information, consult Novell's NetWare Installation Supplement for IBM Token-Ring Network manual.)

Token-Ring topologies from IBM come with a setup aid which checks the ports. If only one workstation is affected, check the port with the setup aid, then check the patch cable for possible problems.

B. *Workstation is having problems loading NetWare or logging in.*

      1.   See if the workstation can load CONFIG.SYS.

      2.   See if the workstation can load NetWare shell files.

1. See if the workstation can load CONFIG.SYS.

If the workstation can boot DOS, next try the diskette with CONFIG.SYS and the shell files. The CONFIG.SYS file should contain whatever drivers/ parameters are common across your network.

Workstations that cannot find a particular driver or parameter in the CONFIG.SYS file will display a message to that effect before going to the AUTOEXEC.BAT file. This message flashes on and off the screen quickly—but there is a way to call up the message so that you can read it. If you think the workstation's regular boot diskette is fine, rename the AUTOEXEC to a different name, such as RENAME A:AUTOEXEC.BAT A:A.BAT <Enter>. Then type A to begin the A.BAT file. The file will stay put on the screen so you can see if there are any CONFIG.SYS errors.

If the workstation does not hang while you run a watered-down CONFIG.SYS file, but does hang during the workstation's regular CONFIG.SYS process, try checking the device parameters against the DOS manual or against the instruction manual that comes with the device, making sure they are correctly set up. Then reload the device drivers onto the boot diskette. If this does not work, try the process of elimination; take out one of the device drivers in your CONFIG.SYS and see if the file can load the other device drivers. Try one device driver at a time until you discover the problem.

2. See if the workstation can load NetWare shell files.

The main reason for not using an AUTOEXEC.BAT is to avoid loading any TSRs before establishing a connection with the server. CONFIG.SYS errors and their solutions can be found in the DOS manual. If you see no errors loading CONFIG.SYS and DOS, next type ANET2 <Enter> or ANET3 <Enter> for NetWare v2.0a, or IPX <Enter> for NetWare v2.1x and NetWare v3.0.

As the IPX driver for NetWare v2.1x and above establishes communications with the network interface board and consequently with the network, you will see messages which tell you the interrupt and addressing option you chose in SHGEN:

```
Novell IPX/SPX <version number>
(C) Copyright 1985, 1988 Novell Inc.  All Rights Reserved.

LAN Option: NetWare RX-Net V1.00 (881010)
Hardware Configuration: IRQ = 2, I/O Base = 2EOh, RAM Buffer at
D000:0
```

If there is a conflict with the board settings and the option you select in SHGEN (GENSH uses the default board settings), the process of loading IPX may hang and you may not see an error message. Be sure the board settings for I/O, IRQ, and DMA match the option you chose during SHGEN, or that the network interface board is set to the default setting if you are running NetWare v2.0a. If the problem still persists, replace the IPX.COM file (or ANETx.COM file for NetWare v2.0a), then the network interface board.

Also be sure you have not mixed NetWare shell configurations with network interface boards. For example, you will receive an error if you run an NE-1000 shell with an NE-2000 board, even though you used the same configuration settings. Because the boards are different enough (in this case, the buffers), you will receive an error message.

Sometimes a 16-bit board will not run in a workstation configuration, but an 8-bit board will. If the network board is new, or if this is a new installation, consult the Independent Product Testing bulletins from Novell to ensure that the network interface board you are using has been tested with the kind of workstation you have. The bulletins also note any limitations for that workstation discovered in testing. Your reseller or dealer should have these bulletins, or you can call Novell.

Once you have established a connection with the network, type NETx <Enter> (x signifies your particular DOS version). With NetWare v2.0a, the NetWare shell loads after the IPX driver. If the server cannot be found and other workstations are fine, the problem lies in the cable connection. (If more than one workstation is affected, see C, below.) You will also see error messages if the network interface board does not work with that workstation, as in the problem described above.

If the workstation makes it through the above scenario and allows you to type F: <Enter> (default network letter) and LOGIN servername/supervisor <Enter>, the problem is most likely a faulty workstation boot diskette. Make sure that the user has not added any extraneous commands or TSRs to the AUTOEXEC.BAT or CONFIG.SYS files that are conflicting with the NetWare shell files. Then recopy the NetWare shell files to a new boot diskette.

C. *More than one workstation is affected.*
  1.   Find out whether the condition is isolated or network-wide.
  2.   Check the cabling specifications.
  3.   Check the bridges, hubs, and terminators.

1. Find out whether the condition is isolated or network-wide.

When the condition affects more than one workstation, the most likely place to look for the problem is the cabling system or the server itself. If everyone is affected, start with the server, the server connection to a hub or port, the server cable, or the server's network interface board.

First, make sure the server is still running by checking the screen for a network error message, or by running TRACK ON at the server console to see if the routing tables are sending and receiving routing information. If the server is running and is sending but not receiving information, you are having problems with the server cable, cable connection to the network interface board, the network interface board, or the cable connection or connection port to the first cable repeater. (TRACK OFF gets you out of the router tracking program.)

If you are running Ethernet, you might need to use a Time Domain Reflector (TDR) to check the cable's signal reflection for short circuits caused by crimps, kinks, cable bends, and breaks. Two useful TDRs are Cable Scanner by MicroTest and Digital TDR by Lanca Instruments. For impedance problems, make sure your tester can check for impedances.

For problems that affect only a small group of workstations, start with the workstations' most commonly shared elements, such as signal repeaters (hubs and MAUs), terminators, or a common cable segment. Most often, grouped problems result from faulty hubs or cabling. When using passive hubs on an ARCnet topology, be sure unused hub ports are terminated (active hubs are self-terminating).

Token-Ring topologies from IBM come with a setup aid which checks the ports. If a MAU is not working, check the RO (Ring-Out) cable port on the connecting MAU and the RI (Ring-In) port on the suspected MAU. Then check the patch cables for possible problems by replacing the cable and trying again. If the cable and RI/RO ports work, check the other cable ports on the suspected MAU, one at a time, with the setup aid. When placing patch cables in the cable ports, be sure you hear a distinctive click when the connectors snap into place.

For thin Ethernet cabling systems, check the BNC T-connector/workstation connection that is nearest the server on the cable route. If this connector or connection is bad, workstations that follow on the cable route will not be able to communicate with the server. Also, be sure you have a BNC terminator attached to both ends of every trunk segment you have installed, and have each cable segment grounded. For short circuits caused by crimps, kinks, cable bends, and breaking problems, you may wish to use a TDR (Time Domain Reflector).

For thick Ethernet, be sure transceivers are securely fastened to the cable segment. Also, be sure you have a terminator attached to both ends of every trunk segment you have installed, and have each cable segment grounded. For short circuits caused by crimps, kinks, cable bends, and breaking problems, you may wish to use a TDR (Time Domain Reflector).

For twisted pair cabling, you can use a twisted pair scanner for troubleshooting the actual physical line. Microtest and Nevada Western make twisted pair scanners.

Sometimes the problem is network-wide; servers that have a bad network interface board can play "peek-a-boo" with the other servers. This game happens when the network interface board connecting the server to the internet sporadically announces its presence to the other servers. The other servers, in turn, dump their old routing table information and begin including the new server configuration on the internet.

Then the server with the bad interface board no longer broadcasts its presence to the other servers, who then again drop the server with the bad board from their routing information. This game can make the internet sluggish and can eventually tie up all the server's time keeping up routing information. These problems can best be discovered through point-to-point testing programs, such as NetWare Care, Thomas-Conrad's TXD, and others. Protocol analyzers like Network General's Sniffer or Novell's LANalyzer can also find these types of problems.

2. Check the cabling specifications.

Cabling specifications for the three major topologies—ARCnet, Ethernet, and Token-Ring—are described on pages 22-27.

3. Check the bridges, hubs, and terminators.

While hubs and terminators have been covered in previous sections, bridging has not. NetWare uses local and remote bridging procedures to connect servers and workstations together. Local bridging is divided into two parts: internal and external. NetWare allows up to four network interface boards and board drivers to reside in the server; this arrangement is known as internal bridging. When information comes in on one cable, NetWare can internally route the information to another cable.

External bridging takes place when a workstation runs NetWare's routing software, allowing the workstation to have up to four network interface boards and board drivers. These workstations bridge other workstations and servers together through the routing software and offload the routing services, leaving the server to perform other tasks.

While bridges are routing information in the workstation's background, you can treat bridges much the same as servers when you are troubleshooting a cabling problem. The only difference is that you have one more station in the loop; you will need to check the cable going into the workstation, the workstation's network interface board, the cable going out from the workstation to the server, and the server's network interface board. Each location is a potential point of failure. When you choose diagnostic software, be sure if you are using external bridges that the software can check through bridges (most do).

D. *The workstation ran properly before the problem occurred.*

1. The workstation displays an error message on the screen.
2. You have recently added software to the workstation.
3. You have recently added hardware to the workstation.

1. The workstation displays an error message on the screen.

Error messages you see on the screen come from four sources: BIOS, DOS, NetWare, or the current application. BIOS errors are usually configuration errors, and some workstations will perform a BIOS test every time you turn the workstation on. When you see a configuration error, run SETUP. DOS error messages occur when you first bring up the workstation, or when you are running a DOS utility and that utility cannot complete a specified task. For a list of DOS error messages, consult the appendices in the DOS manual for the error message section.

For NetWare v2.0a, v2.1x, and v3.0 error messages originating from the IPX and/or the NetWare shell or from NetBIOS drivers, see page 109 in this book for explanations and some solutions. For NetWare error messages originating at the server, consult the NetWare System Messages manual for explanations and possible solutions.

Error messages can also be application-related. Application error messages appear when an application cannot perform a particular task. The error message you see describes a problem with the application itself or with the network connection. Even though the application may be a network version, the application often thinks it is requesting DOS to perform a task (see page 51), but the NetWare shell has sent the request to the server instead. If the server is down or the cabling is not working properly, the application will attach an error message to the unperformed task. This message is usually DOS-related, since most applications expect DOS to handle the application's requests. What you see on the screen—for example, an "Error Reading Disk" message or an "Error Writing to Disk" message—can actually indicate a cable/network interface board-related problem or a downed server.

First, see if other workstations running this or other applications are having the same types of errors; universal problems usually point to the server or its cabling connection. This cautious look ensures the server is still operational; if more than one workstation is affected, go back to "C. More than one workstation is affected."

Next, check the error message to learn what task the workstation was trying to perform when the error occurred. Again, you have three error message references: DOS, NetWare, and the application. If you are in an application when the error occurred, check the application's error messages first for an explanation. If the error is not covered in the application manual, consult secondary sources such as the DOS or NetWare manuals (or the *DOS Technical Reference* manual). If during a file update the workstation receives a "disk read" or "disk write" error, the workstation may be having problems with the network interface board, driver software, cable, or cable connection.

The server is a constant medium; anytime an application has to go to the server to retrieve information or perform a process, the workstation/server connection must be working. When applications have any problems along this connection line, you will see error messages, or the application will "hang" during one of its operations.

2. You have recently added software to the workstation.

You may have a software conflict caused by two programs' using the same memory address. This problem normally occurs when the workstation is loading a string of programs and it suddenly stops the process, leaving you with a blank screen or a blinking cursor. Perhaps an application does not have enough memory to run properly after the network utilities and TSRs have loaded, or perhaps there is a software conflict.

In the DOS environment, software conflicts usually involve a TSR conflicting with an application or another TSR. Unload the new software (or TSR) and reboot the workstation to see if it can again run properly. Sometimes you just have to play with TSRs to see if loading them in a different order will work. Certain TSRs take over keyboard buffers, which conflict with other applications that do the same. When this occurs, you may need to first unload the TSRs through programs like MARK and RELEASE utilities before accessing the applications (see page 52).

In the NetWare environment, some TSRs conflict with the NetWare shell, so you will need to experiment, or simply cut out the TSRs and other convenient-but-not-essential programs that are causing these problems.

Sometimes, when an application or modem program redirects serial and parallel printing and you leave that application or modem program and go into a different application, the workstation gets confused, resulting in all sorts of strange glitches and errors that simply make no sense. The best thing to do is to get out of the program, log out, log back in again, and go back into the application. Other times it is best to turn off the workstation, wait about twenty seconds, and turn on the workstation again. This flushes the workstation's memory and rebuilds the workstation's DOS environment, which has been known to cure many workstation glitches. If, after rebooting, the workstation reestablishes its connection with the server, go to the same application and see if the workstation hangs again at the same point.

If a workstation persists in having glitches, run the application on another workstation with the same memory, DOS version, NetWare shell/drivers, and directory rights. If that workstation displays the same problem, try the application on a workstation with a different configuration (if you have one). Persistent glitches can indicate a problem with an application rather than the workstation. There may be a flaw in the application that you need to report to the vendor.

Some word processing and desktop publishing applications have difficulty in handling excessively large files, especially when the files contain graphic figures. So if a particular application keeps hanging, try splitting the data files in half.

3. You recently added hardware to the workstation.

You may be experiencing a hardware conflict because two pieces of hardware are using the same DMA (direct memory access), interrupt, or I/O (input/ output) addressing scheme. This problem normally occurs when you first turn on the workstation and the workstation hangs because of the conflict. However, there are exceptions, such as when an NE-1000 network interface board is using interrupt 3 and COMM port 2 is also using interrupt 3.

Check all hardware settings by consulting the report you have created on each workstation, by consulting the manuals that come with the additional hardware for their default settings, or by looking at the boards and then referencing the settings to the manuals. Be sure to record your findings on a workstation worksheet or database.

You can also ensure that the IPX driver will not conflict with other board settings in the workstation by running the Custom Configuration option in SHGEN (see page 67).

A Quick Checklist

There are many reasons for a workstation to hang; troubleshooting often consists of simply looking for the particular software/hardware combination that will get the workstation(s) back up and running. Here is a quick list of hardware and software tools to make your life a little easier when troubleshooting a DOS workstation environment. This list is followed by some planning practices that have also proven useful.

Hardware

• Time Domain Reflectors to help you look for short circuits, crimps, kinks, impedance problems, bends, and breaks.

• Power line testing tools to ensure proper voltage in the building.

• Protocol analyzers to capture, monitor, and digest frames of information on the network.

Software

• Personal computer diagnostic software to provide you with an analysis of the workstation's hardware and software configurations. This software must describe the settings of your hardware components, ROM BIOS table readings (if you are adding hard disk drives to IBM AT compatibles), and program usage of the workstation's memory, along with a MARK and RELEASE program for TSRs.

• Network interface board diagnostic software to troubleshoot the cable layout and network boards. A point-to-point software testing program may also prove helpful.

• A DOS diskette to see if the workstation can simply load and run applications in DOS. This diskette can contain a simple CONFIG.SYS file.

• A boot diskette containing the essential NetWare shell and NetBIOS files, along with simple CONFIG.SYS and AUTOEXEC.BAT files. However, you may wish to load the shell files manually.

• Other helpful tools are TECHS (Technical Encyclopedia of Computer Hardware and Software), or, for Certified NetWare Engineers, the TIDB (Technical Information DataBase) software. These databases contain an impressive amount of technical information for troubleshooting and diagnosing LAN problems.

For a notebook or database

• Create a workstation listing, showing the network interface board type and settings, monitor type, memory configuration, hard and floppy disk drive types, DOS version, NetWare version, and, when appropriate, NetBIOS information. Also note any problems you have had with that workstation. (See Appendix A for a worksheet you can use to track this data.)

• Create a cable map. Employees in testing labs normally name or number cables for access and connecting information; this practice is helpful in real life as well. It is also important to keep a cable map showing the location of cables and workstations. Remember, you are dealing with two types of networks: the physical location of your people and their workstations, and the logical location of your people and their workstations (based on which server they log in to).

• Create a user listing, showing the directories each user has rights in and the groups each user belongs to. Create this listing by creating a directory called LISTINGS, then go into SYSCON and give the group EVERYONE write rights (RWOCDSM) to the directory as a trustee assignment. Then go into the system login script and create a temporary directory path in the system login script—for example, MAP Q:=SYS:LISTINGS <Enter>.

• Have all the users on your network go into the Q directory (Q:<Enter>) and type WHOAMI /A > LIST.user's initials <Enter>. For example, a user with the initials EAL would type WHOAMI /A > LIST.EAL <Enter>. The greater-than (>) sign saves the group, security equivalences, and effective rights information to the LIST file. Once everyone has followed this procedure, put a couple of stars in front of the MAP command in the system login script (this nullifies the command). Then when you need to gather some information later on, you can take off the stars and reuse the MAP command. You can then print out the LIST files for your notebook through the NPRINT command or any word processor.

• Create a database containing the applications you are using and the problems you have experienced, along with your solutions. Since certain problems tend to repeat themselves, you will have for future reference a running database of possible solutions. You must practice this method each day, however, or you will never do it. During the troubleshooting procedure, take quick notes of the problem and solution, then leave fifteen minutes at the end of the day to transfer that information to the database. It takes effort, but this list will become invaluable.

• Have on hand the phone numbers of earlier supervisors, software and hardware vendors, network designers, and consultants you use. Also, attend user groups in your area; they can be an invaluable source of problem-solving information.

You won't be able to implement these procedures right away. But organize the information dealing with one aspect of troubleshooting—for example, workstation information—before going on to another project. Plan on spending a half hour a day on paper or database updating.

8 Workstation Error Messages

Some error messages received by the workstation can come from IPX or from the NetWare shell. Here is a list of error messages you can receive from the NetWare shell (for v2.0a) or from IPX and the NetWare shell (for v2.1x and v3.0). These messages apply to the workstation environment.

Listed in alphabetical order, the entries indicate which error messages you will see with which version of the NetWare shell, as well as the page number of this handbook where you can find the message.

Shell Messages

A File Server could not be found. (v2.0a, v2 .1x, and v3.0, page 110)

Batteries are low. Server will go down in one minute. (v2.0a, page 111)

(CTRL-ENTER to clear) (v2.0a, v2.1x, and v3.0, page 111)

Commercial power has been restored to server. (v2.0a, page 112)

File Server has no free connection slots. (v2.1x and v3.0, page 112)

Invalid Parameter. Use "I" option to query shell type. (v2.0a, v2.1x, and v3.0, page 112)

IPX has not been loaded. Please load and then run the shell. (v2.1x and v3.0, page 113)

IPX/SPX already loaded. (v2.1x and v3.0, page 113)

Net Driver Crash: <driver error message> (v2.0a and v2.1x, page 113)

NetWare Workstation Shell has already been loaded. (v2.0a, v2.1x, and v3.0, page 114)

Network Error: <error> during <operation>. File = <drive>:<filename> (v2.0a, v2.1x, and v3.0, page 115)

Network Error on Server <servername>:<error> (v2.0a and v2.1x, page 120)
Network Spooler Error: (probably out of space on SYS: volume) (v2.0a, v2.1x, and v3.0, page 124)
Not running on top of DOS version 2.x (v2.0a, v2.1x, and v3.0, page 124)
Not running on top of DOS version 3.x (v2.0a, v2.1x, and v3.0, page 124)
Not running on top of DOS version 4.x (v2.1x and v3.0, page 125)
PIPE not found in transient portion of COMMAND.COM (v2.0a, v2.1x, and v3.0, page 125)
Program Aborted (v2.0a, v2.1x, and v3.0, page 125)
Shell Error: No active File Server attachments (v2.0a, v2.1x, and v3.0, page 125)
The Network is inactive or you are not connected properly. (v2.0a, v2.1x, and v3.0, page 126)
Too many devices defined in DOS (over approx 32). Device Table Overflow (v2.0a, v2.1x, and v3.0, page 126)
Warning: Byte value greater than 255 was truncated (v2.1x and v3.0, page 126)
Warning: disk write error in file <filename> (v2.0a and v2.1x, page 126)
You are not connected to any file servers. The shell will try to connect to a file server whenever the current default drive is changed to an invalid drive. (v2.1x and v3.0, page 127)
You are on auxiliary power. Server will go down in xx minutes. (v2.0a, page 128)

A File Server could not be found.

(v2.0a, v2.1x, and v3.0)

Explanation. You have loaded IPX and the NetWare shell (in v2.0a, just the shell); the shell broadcasts for a server, but cannot find one before it times out and stops broadcasting. The workstation might have a poor cable connection or a bad cable segment. Or perhaps the hardware settings on your network interface board do not match the configuration you selected when generating the LAN driver in SHGEN or GENSH. In this case, the shell cannot communicate properly with your network board; it therefore concludes that there are no servers out there with which to connect.

In the case of a single-server network, either your server cannot communicate over the cable or the server is down. If the server cannot properly communicate with the bridge driver and cable, workstations will again time out as they try to establish a connection to that server (Server servername could not be found).

Solution. If other workstations can log in to the server, the problem is probably not server-based. If other workstations cannot log in to any servers and the servers are connected through internal bridging (not using a backbone method), the problem lies in the connection between the server and those workstations physically attached to that server. But start with basics: see if the server you wish to log in to is still running. If all workstations except those on a particular cable segment can log in, the problem lies in that cabling segment. If only one workstation is receiving the error message, the problem could be with the cabling, or the shell driver is not communicating properly with the network interface board. Trace backwards until you isolate the problem.

When you generate the shell, you link a hardware-specific LAN driver into the IPX services. Make sure the IPX.COM file or (for v2.0a) ANETx.COM file is properly configured to the hardware settings on the workstation network interface board. Check the cabling to make sure you have a firm connection between the cable and the board. If those components are functioning properly, try a new shell and driver. Next, try replacing the network interface board, then the cable to the active or passive hub, terminator, or bridge.

Batteries are low. Server will go down in one minute.
(v2.0a)

Explanation. A power outage has disrupted the server's normal power, and the server's UPS is running low on battery power. Unless normal power is restored within one minute, the server will shut down. You will see this message on all workstations connected to the server. (In later versions of the shell, this message is moved out of the shell and into the UPS monitoring software.)

Solution. This is a warning message; all workstations will have their connection cleared when the server downs itself. When the server clears the workstation's connections, users will lose their data unless the applications they are running save the data files to a back up file. Log out all workstations immediately when you see this message; reboot the server when you once again have normal AC power.

A poor power supply marked with brown-outs and power spikes can cause you no end of cabling, workstation, and server problems. Make sure you have a reliable power supply and a good UPS that can handle the disk subsystems that your server supports. Otherwise, you will be chasing phantoms and gremlins around the network every time a brown-out occurs. A good UPS will also protect your disk drives from premature crashing due to brown-outs.

(CTRL-ENTER to clear)
(v2.0a, v2.1x, v3.0)

Explanation. This message appears at the bottom right-hand corner of the workstation monitor when you receive a message from another person through the SEND command, from the supervisor through the BROADCAST command, or from NetWare itself through the BROADCAST command.

Solution. Press the <Ctrl> and <Enter> keys simultaneously; the message will disappear. If another message is saved in the sending buffer, you will see that message after you press the <Ctrl> and <Enter> keys. To prevent your workstation from receiving further messages, type CASTOFF <Enter> at the network prompt. Some applications may be performing database manipulations or linking processes that should not be disturbed by SEND messages, so run the CASTOFF utility before entering such applications and the CASTON utility when the users leave them.

Commercial power has been restored to server.

(v2.0a)

Explanation. Normal AC power has been restored, and the server is now running from that power supply. You will see this status report to all users only if the server has not yet downed itself from running out of battery power. Otherwise, you will have lost workstation connections to the server.

Solution. You need do nothing but get back to work.

File Server has no free connection slots.

(v2.1, v3.0)

Explanation. The connection table listing all the attached workstations is full. Servers running NetWare 286 can handle up to 100 simultaneous connections; servers running NetWare 386 can have up to 250 attached connections. When these connections are all in use, you will not be allowed to establish a connection with this server.

Workstations can also see this message even though you go into FCONSOLE and see there are connections free. You can see this message if you lack service processes in NetWare v2.1x, if your cabling system exceeds recommended cabling distances, or if you are having communication errors, such as problems sending and receiving packets to and from the server.

Solution. Until a workstation terminates its connection, you will not be able to attach to that server. If a person simply shuts off a workstation instead of logging out, you must wait about fifteen minutes for the server's Watch Dog process to query the workstation, which will respond with an "I'm still alive" packet if it is able. After fifteen minutes of unsuccessful Watch Dog queries, the server terminates the connection and frees up a slot in the connection table. Then, as that connection becomes available, you will be able to attach to the designated server.

For supervisors running NetWare v2.1x, if you go into FCONSOLE and discover there are plenty of connections free but you are still getting this error message, select the Statistics option from the "Available Options" window, then the Summary option. If you have less than four file server processes, that might be your problem (this depends upon how busy the server is). You might also want to make sure you have kept the cabling system within recommended specifications, which will also take care of communication errors, such as problems with sending and receiving packets to and from the server.

Invalid Parameter. Use "I" option to query shell type.

(v2.0a, v2.1x, v3.0)

Explanation. Either you typed in the IPX or NETx commands with extra characters after the command, or your AUTOEXEC.BAT file has extra characters after the IPX or NETx or ANETx commands.

Solution. Be sure there are no extra parameters in the syntax when you type the NetWare shell name to load the shell. If you want to see which IPX or shell version you are running, follow the shell name with the "I" parameter. For example, if IPX and NET3 are on your A: drive, type A:IPX I <Enter> at the network prompt.

You will see something like:

```
Novell IPX/SPX V2.15
(C) Copyright 1985, 1988 Novell Inc.  All Rights Reserved

LAN Option: NetWare Ethernet NE1000 V2.31EC (881024)
Hardware Configuration: IRQ = 3, I/O Base = 300h, no DMA or ROM
```

This method also works for the NetWare shell.

If you prefer, use the NVER utility to see the IPX and NetWare shell version (if you have v2.1x or v3.0).

IPX has not been loaded. Please load and then run the shell.
(v2.1x and v3.0)

Explanation. You are trying to load the NetWare shell (NETx.COM) without first loading IPX.

Solution. Load IPX first, then load the NetWare shell. If you are booting from an AUTOEXEC.BAT file, be sure the IPX command is listed before the NETx command in that file. The minimum commands you need in an AUTOEXEC.BAT file to load the shell and establish a login connection for NetWare v2.1x are:

```
IPX
NET3                (if you are running DOS v3.x)
F:                  (or the next drive after the LASTDRIVE parameter you designated in
                    the CONFIG.SYS file)
LOGIN servername/username
^Z
```

IPX/SPX already loaded.
(v2.1x and v3.0)

Explanation. You will see this message if you have already loaded IPX (which loads SPX at the same time) and then try to reload IPX again. You cannot load IPX on a workstation more than once during a single work session.

Solution. Once you have loaded IPX, simply load the NetWare shell (NETx.COM) and log in to your designated server. To load a different IPX.COM file, you must reboot your workstation. A program called Marknet and Relnet from Kim Kokkonen works like MARK and RELEASE utilities, except that it works on the NetWare shell. Run Marknet before loading IPX or the NetWare shell; you can then drop the IPX and Netx.COM TSRs by running Relnet without resorting to <Ctrl-Alt-Del>.

Net Driver Crash: <driver error message>
(v2.0a, v2.1x, and v3.0)

Explanation. When you generate a NetWare shell through GENSH or SHGEN, you link a hardware-specific LAN driver into the IPX services. GENSH or SHGEN, therefore, links a slightly different IPX to the LAN board in either the IPX.COM file (for v2.1x) or the ANETx.COM file (for v2.0a). You see this error when that LAN driver or NetWare shell encounters a critical problem, producing an

ABEND (ABnormal END) condition. The ABEND halts communication with the network to prevent further problems to the system. You receive this error message only if you have a hardware problem with the network interface board or cabling, or if you have workstation memory problems.

Solution. Examine the driver error message for some indication of the cause of the problem. Each LAN driver gives different error messages, which vary with each network interface board. Since there are over 17 different brands of boards (and over 115 types of boards), listing them all would be arduous. But as an example, the NE/2 Ethernet board produces the following driver error messages after the "Net Driver Crash:" message:

```
NE/2 is Hung
NE/2 Failed Reset
```

If you are curious about the error messages specific to your network interface board, perform a string or character dump on your IPX.COM file. You can do this with a String program that simply dumps any character string of a specified length to a file. Since IPX is modified to accommodate the board settings and board type, you will see a string of characters, similar to the NE/2 messages, that do not match any of the error message fragments explained in this section. These are the error messages you will see in the <driver error message> section of the error message.

Try to reboot your workstation. If the problem reoccurs, check to see if your IPX file is properly configured to match the physical settings on your network interface board; make sure as well that you chose the appropriate LAN driver option to link to the board in SHGEN or GENSH. You will have to deal with enough idiosyncracies in network interface boards without the added complications of mismatched LAN drivers or configuration settings.

If rebooting the workstation produces the same error message, make a new boot diskette, or use the spare boot diskette containing the correct version of IPX and NETx (or ANETx) and load those files. If the problem persists, replace the network interface board, remembering to match the configuration settings to the settings on the board you just removed. If the problem persists, remove the board and try it in a different workstation, along with the old boot diskette. If the board functions properly, check the cabling at the problem workstation site by replacing a cable segment (when possible) and trying the cable at another workstation; if the cabling works, you may have a hardware problem with the workstation and the network interface board type or the workstation's memory.

NetWare Workstation Shell has already been loaded.
(v2.0a, v2.1x, and v3.0)

Explanation. You have already loaded the NetWare shell (NETx.COM file), and you are trying to reload the shell. The shell will not allow itself to be loaded more than once on a workstation.

Solution. Once you load the NetWare shell, log in to a designated server. To load a different NETx.COM file, you must reboot your workstation. However, a program called Marknet and Relnet from Kim Kokkonen works like MARK and RELEASE utilities, except on the NetWare shell. Run Marknet before loading IPX or the NetWare shell; you can then drop the IPX and NETx.COM TSRs by running Relnet without resorting to <Ctrl-Alt-Del>.

Network Error: <error> during <operation>. File = <drive>: <filename> Abort, Retry? or Abort, Retry, Fail? (v2.0a, v2.1x, and v3.0)

Explanation. You are performing an operation in a NetWare utility that requires the workstation shell to send its requests to the file server (as opposed to an operation performed locally). The request is trying to perform a function call or use a DOS interrupt, but that operation cannot be performed. Instead of sending back a reply to the request, the server sends an error code sequence with which the shell constructs the above message. The <drive>:<filename> aspect of the message tells you which file on which drive is causing the error. If the "PUBLIC:" drive is specified, the bad file is located on a search drive.

Solution. Try pressing the "R" key to see if the retry will work. For the most part, if a retry works, it simply means that your server is busy, or that a bad cable or network interface board is causing interference on the network. Use the information in the <error> and <operation> part of the message to help you chase down the causes. This information may be enough to help you fix the problem, which can be anything from a failing network interface board, cable, or bridge to faulty software (which can lead to problems with the disk drive). Most likely you will have to abort or reboot the workstation to escape your present difficulty.

Below are the <error> and <operation> portions of this error message. When the workstation or server cannot perform a particular request or task, NetWare halts the process and displays the error it receives for the operation that NetWare is trying to perform. An error message, then, tries to describe what the workstation and server were doing when a particular task could not be completed.

Keep in mind that applications do not necessarily put these specific NetWare messages on your screen, for they most likely have incorporated their own explanations for the <operation> messages. For example, if you are in WordPerfect and your communication with the server is interrupted, you will receive a "Disk error 88: error writing to disk. Retry 0, Cancel 1" message.

<error>:

The following messages could appear in the <error> portion of the message.

Bad Directory Handle. This message usually means that the application is mishandling its directory resources and is passing an invalid directory handle to the <operation> part of the message; the application probably has a bug in it. This message can also indicate an internal error problem, such as a memory error.

File Detached. An application that usually locks, uses, and unlocks a file is trying to use the file again without going through the same locking and unlocking procedure. A likely cause of the error message is a file-locking problem with the application. Sometimes the application simply becomes confused; exiting and reentering the program may fix the problem. Sporadic but consistent error messages on a single workstation can indicate a memory chip with a faulty connection.

File in Use. Another process or application is already using the file specified in the <filename> parameter. That process or application must release the file before you can enter it.

File Server Went Down. This message appears when the server goes down during the specified operation that generated this error message.

Illegal Completion Code. This internal consistency check error message means that a utility (or application) was performing an operation and received an invalid completion code. You should rarely get this error message, for it indicates that you may have corrupted NetWare files, or that you have intermixed different versions of the NetWare operating system, shells, and utilities. In this case, you may need to reinstall the NetWare operating system and utilities, or update the workstation shell (a good place to start).

Invalid File Handle. This message usually means that the application is mishandling file resources and passed an invalid file handle to the <operation> part of the message; the application probably has a bug in it. The message can also indicate an internal error problem, such as a memory error.

IO Attempted to Physically Locked Area. Your current application tried to read or write to a part of a file that is locked with a physical record or file lock. Someone else is in that physical area of the file. That person must release the file before you can enter it.

IO Error in Directory Area. The application or utility you are running received an error message while trying to read or write to the directory entry. It usually means that the server is experiencing a hardware failure at the disk drive, the disk controller, or the disk cables. Start your troubleshooting there.

IO Error Network Disk. The application or utility you are running received an error message while trying to read or write to the network drive. This message usually indicates that the server is having a hardware failure at the disk drive, the disk controller, or the associated cables. Start your troubleshooting there.

No Read Privilege. You do not have Read rights in the directory containing the file you wish to access, or, for NetWare v3.0, no Read privileges to the file itself. For you to be able to read the contents of the file, your effective rights in that directory or file must include the Read right. For NetWare versions before 3.0, this usually means Read, Open, and Search rights.

No Write Privilege or File Read Only. This is similar to the "No read privilege" message; you are trying to write to the file that appears in the <filename> portion of the message, but you have no Write rights in that directory, or the file itself has been flagged to only be read (for NetWare v2.0a and v2.1x—Read/Only, for NetWare v3.0—Read). To write to the file, you must flag the file Read-Write or grant Write privileges (for NetWare v3.0), and you must have Write effective rights in this directory. For NetWare versions before 3.0, this usually means Write, Create, Delete, Open, and Search rights.

To see what rights you do have, type RIGHTS <Enter> in that directory. If you are using a NetWare version prior to v3.0, you can also type FLAG filename <Enter> to see how the file has been flagged. For NetWare v3.0, type RIGHTS filename <Enter> to see your rights to that particular file.

Out of Directory Handles. The server has run out of directory handles. Go into INSTALL or NETGEN and allocate more directory handles (directory handles are self allocated with NetWare 386). You may also ask the users on your network to delete unnecessary files and directories, and get rid of any extra drive mappings they have in their login scripts (which is a good general house-keeping procedure).

Out of Disk Space. The directory named in the File – <drive>:<filename> portion of this message is out of space. When you see this message, first back up the system and have everyone delete any files they have not accessed for however many months you specify, such as the last six months, or three months. Then, if someone needs to access an archived file, restore that file only.

For NetWare v2.1x and v3.0 users, NDIR shows you when files were last accessed. For example, suppose you are using NetWare v2.1x and today's date is August 1, 1990, and you want to make a list of all files on the volume that have not been accessed since August 1, 1989. Go to the volume root and type NDIR * FILES ONLY ACCESSED BEFORE AUG 1 1989 SUB >DATES <Enter>. To use NDIR's shorthand, you can type NDIR * FO AC BEF AUG 1 1989 SUB >DATES <Enter>. NDIR will save the information to the DATES file; you can then print out the DATES file and methodically get rid of all files listed. (Be sure you have enough disk space for the file you are about to create; it may be quite large.)

Another option at this point is to add another disk drive.

Out of Dynamic Work Space. Your NetWare operating system has run out of dynamic memory work space, as measured in Memory Pool 1 in NetWare v2.1x. NetWare failed its own internal consistency check, which could mean you are having a hardware memory problem, the operating system became confused, or the operating system has become corrupt. First, down the server and reinstall the operating system. If the problem persists, have your server's memory checked first, or rerun INSTALL (for NetWare v2.0a and v3.0) or NETGEN (for NetWare v2.1x).

For v2.1x supervisors, go into FCONSOLE, choose the Statistics option and then the Summary option, and watch the Dynamic Memory 1 entry. If the Maximum Used and Peak Used entries match closely, have the users on your network delete as many unnecessary drive mappings as possible. A simple way to do this is to set up a MENU system that CDs (Changes Directories) to the applications and personal directories that people need to use.

Check the "Number of File Service Processes" entry; make sure you have at least three processes for thirty users or more. (Depending on your number of users, you can have two processes if you are using applications that are not I/O-intensive—for example, word processing, spreadsheets, and E-mail activities).

For NetWare v3.0 supervisors, run the MONITOR utility at the server console to see the number of server processes. Since NetWare 386 can allocate this resource for itself, you need not worry if the server processes are no more than 1.

Out of File Handles. The server is out of file handles. Go into INSTALL or NETGEN and allocate more file handles. As a general housekeeping activity, you may also ask the users on your network to delete unnecessary files and directories, and get rid of any extra drive mappings they have in their login scripts. NetWare 386 automatically allocates extra file handles as they are needed.

<operation>:

The operation messages appearing in the <operation> part of the message are the DOS function calls that the application was trying to perform when the error occurred. As an application asks for a request, it executes an Int 21h command to awaken DOS to perform a function. The NetWare shell intercepts the request going to the Int 21h command and sends that request to the network when necessary. What you are seeing is a list of NetWare Core Protocol references and their accompanying DOS function calls. Consult the *DOS Technical Reference* manual for the DOS function call explanations.

CHANGE FILE MODE. The Change File Mode (CHMOD) call corresponds to the DOS Function Call 43h.

CHANGE THE CURRENT DIRECTORY. The Change the Current Directory (CHDIR) call corresponds to the DOS Function Call 3Bh.

CLOSE. The Close call corresponds to the DOS Function Call 10h.

CLOSE A FILE. This call, which closes a file handle, corresponds to the DOS Function Call 3Eh.

CREATE. This call, which creates a file, corresponds to the DOS Function Call 16h.

CREATE A FILE. This Create A File Handle call corresponds to the DOS Function Call 3Ch.

CREATE A SUBDIRECTORY. The Create a Subdirectory (MKDIR) call corresponds to the DOS Function Call 39h.

CREATE NEW FILE. This request, corresponding to the DOS Function Call 5Bh, is used to create a new file.

CREATE TEMP FILE. This call, corresponding to the DOS Function Call 5Ah, creates a unique file.

CURRENT DIRECTORY. The Get Current Directory call corresponds to the DOS Function Call 47h.

DELETE. This request, corresponding to the DOS Function Call 13h, deletes a file.

DELETE A FILE. This request, corresponding to the DOS Function Call 41h, deletes a file from a specified directory.

FIND FIRST MATCHING FILE. The Find the First Matching File (FIND FIRST) call corresponds to the DOS Function Call 4Eh.

FIND NEXT MATCHING FILE. The Find the Next Matching File (FIND NEXT) call corresponds to the DOS Function Call 4Fh.

GET CURRENT DIRECTORY. This request corresponds to the DOS Function Call 47h.

GET SET A FILE DATE AND TIME. The application or utility uses this request to Get and/or Set a file's date and time. The call corresponds to the DOS Function Call 57h.

IO CONTROL FOR DEVICES. The I/O Control for Devices (IOCTL) call corresponds to the DOS Function Call 44h.

MOVE FILE POINTER. The Move File Read Write Pointer (LSEEK) call corresponds to the DOS Function Call 42h.

OPEN. This call, corresponding to the DOS Function Call 0Fh, opens a file.

OPEN A FILE. The request uses this call, corresponding to the DOS Function Call 3Dh, to open a file handle.

READ FROM A FILE. The request uses this call, corresponding to the DOS Function Call 3Fh, to read from a file or device.

REMOVE A SUBDIRECTORY. The Remove a Subdirectory (RMDIR) call corresponds to the DOS Function Call 3Ah.

RENAME A FILE. The request uses this call, corresponding to the DOS Function Call 56h, to rename a file.

SEARCH FIRST. This request corresponds to the DOS Function Call 11h and searches for the first matching file name in the current directory.

SEARCH NEXT. This request corresponds to the DOS Function Call 12h and searches for the next matching file name in the current directory.

SET ATTRIBUTES. The Network Environment Function 228, Set File Attributes call, corresponds to the NetWare Function Call 228 (E4h).

UPDATE FILE SIZE. The Network Environment Function 229, Update File Size (FCB) call, corresponds to the NetWare Function Call 229 (E5h).

WRITE TO A FILE. This request, corresponding to the DOS Function Call 40h, writes to a file or device.

Network Error on Server <servername>:<error> Abort or Retry?
(v2.0a, v2.1, and v3.0)

Explanation. This message appears when the server in the <servername> portion of the message returns the error in the <error> portion of the message while communicating with the workstation. This type of message results from cabling problems—for example, improper bus termination (make sure your terminator Ohm match your cable Ohm), cable distance exceeding the recommended length on a cable segment, or broken or bad cables and/or connectors.

This message may also indicate that a bad board or cable is causing interference so that other workstations cannot communicate efficiently with the server. This message also appears when the server goes down because of power failures or backups. Pressing "A" for "Abort" usually brings you to a LOGIN prompt, as the "Abort" sequence rebroadcasts IPX to attach a connection to any server on the network. If you have more than one server on your network, you may need to specify the servername in your login procedure (LOGIN servername/ username).

Solution. Depending on the amount of interference you are experiencing, pressing the "R" key will not usually work. If the problem is with cabling, start narrowing down the options. If it entails all workstations, start at the server (see if it is running) and work back through your bridging and cabling schemes. If only one workstation has the problem, start with that workstation's network interface and cable that connects the workstation to the network. If several workstations display this error message, start with their most common element.

<error>:

Here is an explanation of the statements you might see in the <error> portion of the message.

Attempted Access To Illegal or Down Server. You are trying to communicate with a downed server. Simple problems to check for are correct server spelling (an unlikely cause of the error), a downed server, or a bad cable segment.

Bad Local Network Address. The address scheme for NetWare's IPX includes network, node, and socket information in the packet. Each packet sent to the server from a workstation contains those three address portions in order for the request to reach its proper server destination (node) and to be serviced by the proper process in the server (socket). The network portion of the address determines the physical LAN cable to which the workstation is attached. You see this message when a driver/network interface board, a bad cable, or a bad bridge connection corrupts the network address.

First, find out if other workstations are experiencing the same events. If other workstations are receiving the same message, begin at the server and work back. If the problem is a single workstation, try a new shell and driver and make sure the network interface board is jumpered correctly, matching the interrupt selection you chose in SHGEN. (For NetWare v2.0a, make sure the board is set to the default setting.)

Next, try replacing the network interface board, then the cable to the active or passive hub, terminator, or bridge. In this case, you're working up to the server until you solve the problem.

For NetWare 386, go to the server console and bring up the monitor screen (LOAD MONITOR <Enter> at the command prompt). At the "Available Options" window in MONITOR, select the LAN Information option. The "LAN Driver Information" window will list the drivers that you have loaded. Choose the driver that pertains to the workstations and press <Enter>. Under the General Statistics, see if the Total Packets Sent/Received entry is incrementing. This may take some time, so try logging in again and see if the numbers increment.

If there is no activity on the LAN board, either replace the board or cabling segment to the server. If you replace the board, make sure the I/O and interrupt settings match how the board is jumpered; otherwise you won't be able to load the LAN driver. Then get back into the MONITOR utility and see if the Total Packets Sent/Received entry increments as you try to log in. Work back down the cabling until you can log in a workstation.

The above procedure somewhat applies to NetWare v2.1x as well. Go into FCONSOLE, choose the Statistics option, then the LAN I/O Statistics option. If the server shows Reexecuted Requests, Duplicate Replies Sent, and Positive Acknowledges Sent entries are consistently in the hundreds, you are having problems with cabling, a network interface board, or faulty drivers somewhere on the network. To pinpoint the problem, use a point-to-point diagnostic utility, such as NetWare Care.

Connection No Longer Valid. This is the message you will probably see most often; it means your workstation no longer has a valid connection to the server. With NetWare v2.0a and v2.1x, the server can have 100 connections; with NetWare 386, that number is 250. The server keeps track of its connections in the connection table. If you simply turn off a workstation without logging out, you sever the connection but still occupy a connection slot in the connection table.

The server handles this problem by keeping track of the last time it heard from a workstation. If it has heard nothing from the workstation in five minutes, the server begins sending an "Are you there?" message once every minute. When your workstation has been unable to communicate with the server for 15 minutes, the server will invalidate the connection. This loss of connection can mean that you have some bad cable or that your route to the server, or the server itself, has gone down.

Could Not Route to File Server. The 12-byte node address that is part of the request packet contains an invalid server destination. Perhaps the server you usually log in to was once a valid destination, but has since been downed. The message can also mean that the bridge's routers have become corrupted and can no longer show a valid route to your server.

First make sure that the server is still running. If you must go through a bridge to get to the server, make sure the bridge is running. If the problem persists, attach a workstation directly to the server and try logging in.

For NetWare 386, go to the server console and bring up the monitor screen (LOAD MONITOR <Enter> at the command prompt). At the "Available Options" window in MONITOR, select the LAN Information option. The "LAN Driver Information" window will list the drivers that you have loaded. Choose the driver that pertains to the workstations and press <Enter>. Under the General Statistics, see if the Total Packets Sent/Received entry is incrementing.

If there is no activity on the LAN board, either replace the board or cabling segment to the server. If you replace the board, make sure the I/O and interrupt settings match how the board is jumpered; otherwise you won't be able to load the LAN driver. Then get back into the MONITOR utility and see if the Total Packets Sent/Received entry increments as you try to log in.If the workstation can log in, reconnect the bridge to the server and check your cabling connections between the servers or bridge. Do the same procedure with MONITOR to ensure that packets are being sent and received. Work your way back to the workstation if necessary.

It's not likely that a single workstation will get this error. But if one does, try a new shell and driver and make sure the network interface board is jumpered correctly, matching the interrupt selection you chose in SHGEN. Next, try replacing the network interface board, then the cable to the active or passive hub, terminator, or bridge.

Error Locating Router. The shell cannot find a route to the server. Most likely the server or bridge has gone down. The message can also indicate a bad cable segment or poor cable connection. When you reboot, type SLIST to see if the server is listed; that will give you an idea if the server or the connection between the bridge/ server is in question.

Error Reading (Receiving) from Network. The workstation shell is having problems receiving packets from the network. This error message usually results from a hardware problem, so start your search by looking for broken cables, bad connections, or a faulty network interface board. If you are performing an initial network installation, make sure you have the bus properly terminated. This error message can also mean that the server or bridge went down, or that the network is very busy, so first see if the error affects more than one workstation.

Error Writing (Sending) to Network. When you see this error, first look at the workstation; the message tells you that hardware problems are causing formatting and sending errors. It can also mean the workstation LAN driver/board is having problems, or that you have broken or bad cables and cable connections or bus termination.

Reply Invalid Header. The server sent the workstation a reply packet with an invalid IPX packet header. Either the packet was corrupted coming to the workstation, or the memory in the workstation has become corrupted. Try turning off the workstation and then restarting it. Check cabling connections next. If several workstations are receiving the error message, the problem may be with a common cable, or that the server's LAN driver has become corrupted. In the latter case, down the server and reinstall the server operating system (for NetWare 386, you need only reinstall the driver).

Reply Invalid Sequence Number. The server sent the workstation a reply packet that has an invalid packet sequence number. Either the packet was corrupted coming to the workstation, or the memory in the workstation has become corrupted. Try turning off the workstation and then restarting it. Check cabling connections next. If several workstations are receiving the error message, the problem may be with a common cable, or that the server's LAN driver has become corrupted. In the latter case, down the server and reinstall the server operating system (for NetWare 386, you need only reinstall the driver).

Reply Invalid Slot. The server sent the workstation a reply packet with a packet header containing an invalid slot number. Either the packet was corrupted coming to the workstation, or the memory in the workstation has become corrupted. Try turning off the workstation and then restarting it. Check cabling connections next. If several workstations are receiving the error message, the problem may be with a common cable, or that the server's LAN driver has become corrupted. In the latter case, down the server and reinstall the server operating system (for NetWare 386, you need only reinstall the driver).

Reply Packet Lengths Don't Match. The server has sent a reply packet whose actual length does not match its expected length. This, too, is a failed internal consistency check, sometimes caused by corrupted workstation memory. Try turning off the workstation and then restarting it. Check cabling connections next. If several workstations are receiving the error message, the problem may be with a common cable, or perhaps the server's LAN driver has become corrupted. In the latter case, down the server and reinstall the server operating system (for NetWare 386, you need only reinstall the driver).

Unknown Communications Error Code. When the file server sent a reply packet, the ECB (Event Control Block) completion code has become corrupted by the time it reached the workstation shell, and the corrupted packet doesn't match a known error. Such packet corruption is often caused by interference or bad cabling.

Check your cabling connections and anything (such as bad termination or ground or incorrect Ohm terminators for the cabling you are using) that can cause interference to cabling. There may also be a problem with the driver/network interface board, or with flaky workstation memory. Try turning off your workstation and then restarting it, thus reinstalling the LAN driver. You could also have one of the network problems mentioned earlier—problems with terminators, cables, routing through bridges, or the server.

Network Spooler Error: (probably out of space on SYS: volume).
(v2.0a, v2.1x, and v3.0)

Explanation. The network spooler can no longer operate, usually because the spooler ran out of print job storage space on the SYS: volume.

Solution. Either delete or move files from volume SYS: to other volumes to allow the network spooler to work. If you have only one volume, back everything up and delete the files that no one has accessed for the last three or six months. You may also consider adding a new disk drive and moving all users to the newly created volume, leaving only applications and utilities stored on the SYS: volume.

Not running on top of DOS version 2.x.
(v2.0a, v2.1x, and v3.0)

Explanation. Your DOS version does not match the NET2.COM or ANET2.COM (NetWare shell) file you are using. You may have simply installed the wrong shell file from GENSH or SHGEN for your DOS type.

Solution. Make sure you are running the correct version of DOS with the correct NetWare shell file. It is much easier to manage network data if you purchase the same DOS version for everyone on the network rather than having to keep track of many DOS versions.

Not running on top of DOS version 3.x.
(v2.0a, v2.1x, and v3.0)

Explanation. Your DOS version does not match the NET3.COM or ANET3.COM (NetWare shell) file you are using. You may have simply installed the wrong shell file from GENSH or SHGEN for your DOS type.

Solution. Make sure you are running the correct version of DOS with the correct NetWare shell file. It is much easier to manage network data if you purchase the same DOS version for everyone on the network rather than having to keep track of many DOS versions.

Not running on top of DOS version 4.x.
(v2.1x and v3.0)

Explanation. Your DOS version does not match the NET4.COM or ANET4.COM (NetWare shell) file you are using. You may have simply installed the wrong shell file from GENSH or SHGEN for your DOS type.

Solution. Make sure you are running the correct version of DOS with the correct NetWare shell file. It is much easier to manage network data if you purchase the same DOS version for everyone on the network rather than having to keep track of many DOS versions.

PIPE not found in transient portion of COMMAND.COM.
(v2.0a, v2.1x, and v3.0)

Explanation. The NetWare shell cannot locate the file name DOS uses for DOS PIPE functions. The problem usually stems from a corrupt COMMAND.COM or shell. The shell changes this file name for the DOS PIPE function to work properly with the server.

Solution. Recopy the COMMAND.COM file onto the workstation's boot diskette (be sure to copy the correct DOS version). If the workstation reboots but still receives the error message, try replacing the NetWare shell. With the workstations using the COMMAND.COM file on a network search drive (you can set up the COMSPEC command in the system login script), you might want to replace that COMMAND.COM file as well.

Program Aborted
(v2.0a, v2.1x, and v3.0)

You chose the "Abort" option from an error message displaying the "Abort, Retry, Fail?" or "Abort, Retry?" choices. The "Abort" option usually returns you to DOS, displaying the above message as it does.

Shell Error: No active File Server attachments.
(v2.0a, v2.1x, and v3.0)

Explanation. The workstation was logged in or attached to a server/bridge, but that server/bridge has gone down.

Solution. First make sure the file server is running; then make sure your bridge connection is still functioning. If only one workstation is experiencing this error, start with its cable/hub connections and work back to the shell. However, this error message usually means that you once had a connection, but something has disrupted that connection.

The Network is inactive or you are not connected properly.

(v2.0a, v2.1x, and v3.0)

Explanation. This error message appears only if the workstation shell attaches and begins to initialize, but the shell loses its connections to the server. A bad or faulty cable/network interface board can cause this problem.

Solution. Make sure the cable connections are secure; this error usually occurs because of a poor cable connection, faulty terminator, or faulty network interface board. So start your troubleshooting with network interface board settings and cable connections.

Too many devices defined in DOS (over approximately 32)...Device Table Overflow.

(v2.0a, v2.1x, and v3.0)

Explanation. You filled DOS's device table before NetWare inserted its device name. Filling the device table with approximately 32 entries before the shell loads will abort the NetWare shell.

Solution. Remove some device drivers from that workstation's CONFIG.SYS file and reboot the workstation shell.

Warning: Byte value greater than 255 was truncated.

(v2.1x, v3.0)

Explanation. You will see this message only if you accidentally put in a number greater than 255 in the SHELL.CFG file. NetWare brings the number back to 255 (the maximum value permitted). When the workstation initially boots up and loads IPX and the NetWare shell, you will see which parameter is not correct in the SHELL.CFG file.

Solution. Go into the SHELL.CFG file and change the option within the proper values. (See page 77 for details on when to use the SHELL.CFG file.)

Warning: disk write error in file <filename>.

(v2.0a, v2.1x)

Explanation. This command is usually relegated to the server console. It appears when NetWare performs a read-after-write verification when writing to the hard disk, but that verification fails and NetWare could not HotFix the block(s). Go to the server console; you will see a part of the error message there: "Write Error: dir = sss file = FILENAME.EXT vol = VOLUMENAME."

NetWare verifies what is written to disk by immediately reading back what was written to disk, thus verifying a correct write. With Hot Fix installed, NetWare will automatically redirect the bad block, rewriting the data to another part of the disk. This error message means that the network disk you are writing to has gone bad and Hot Fix is not functioning properly. Other possible sources of difficulty are the server's Disk Coprocessor Board (DCB), disk controller, or disk drive.

Solution. If the user who receives this message is in an application, have that user save the file under a different name; for example, if the filename is WARE.LST, have the user save the contents of the file with a name like WARE2.LST and rename the corrupted file to something like FILEIS.BAD. Leave the bad file in place; if you erase it, another file will try to write to the bad block and will have the same problems. Since this is a write error, try copying the file to another file name, such as COPY FILEIS.BAD WARE.LST. See how much of the data remains uncorrupted.

For v2.1x supervisors, go into FCONSOLE and select the Statistics option. Choose the Disk Statistics option from the "File Server Statistics" window, then select the physical disk that is having the problem. If you do not know which physical disk is servicing which volume, choose the Volume Information option from the "File Server Statistics" window and look at the "Primary Disk Number" entry. This entry tells you the physical disk drive number of the drive used for this particular volume. When you know the physical disk number, you can then choose the physical disk number for the Disk Statistics option.

Once you choose the physical disk, check the Hot Fix status line, which tells you if Hot Fix is enabled, disabled, or not available. If you once had Hot Fix, but it is now disabled, it could mean that the disk is going bad and Hot Fix has disabled itself. You can check this by looking at the "Hot Fix Table Size" and "Hot Fix Remaining" entries; if the numbers are about the same, the disk is going bad. Try to back up and get ready to replace the drive.

You can also try running VREPAIR, which may or may not fix the problem at hand. For those of you running NetWare v2.15 with NetWare for Macintosh value-added processes (VAPs), running VREPAIR won't fix the Macintosh file structures if there are problems.

For v3.0 supervisors, go into the Monitor utility at the server console (Load MONITOR <Enter>). Choose the Disk Information option from the "Available Topics" window, then choose the System Disk Drives option. You'll see how the disk drives are split into volumes as well as the Hot Fix status. You'll also see the Redirection Blocks and Redirected Blocks entries. If the Redirected Blocks are on the rise, the disk may be going bad. Try to back up and get ready to replace the drive.

You are not connected to any file servers. The shell will try to connect to a file server whenever the current default drive is changed to an invalid drive.

(v2.1x and v3.0)

Explanation. The NetWare shell lost all of its server connection(s) and cannot find any servers on the network to which to connect.

Solution. When you see this message and choose one of the network drive letters, NetWare will try to attach the workstation to another server without the user having to perform a <Ctrl-Alt-Del>. If NetWare is unsuccessful, you will again see the same message. If the attempt proves successful, you will see the LOGIN prompt, just as you do when you log out.

At the prompt, type SLIST to see if your server is on the network. If the server is present, log in. If the shell cannot connect you to another server, the workstation has lost its means of communicating with the network. This loss of communication points to a problem with the network interface board and/or cabling.

If other workstations cannot log in, start with the server and/or bridge and work down to isolate the problem. If the problem involves only a single workstation, first try rebooting; then make sure the network interface board is securely fastened and that you are using the correct shell and driver for the board you are running. Then reboot. Next, check the cable and its connections.

You are on auxiliary power. Server will go down in nn minutes.
(v2.0a)

Explanation. This error message relates to the other two UPS-generated messages for shell version 2.0a. You see this message when your normal power has been interrupted and the server is now running off the backup battery. When the server has only one minute of power remaining, the NetWare shell will generate the "Batteries are low. Server will go down in one minute" message. You will see the above message when you are running SFT or TTS software and you have an intelligent power supply that is initiated when battery power gets low. The message will appear on all workstations connected to the server.

Solution. The server will run on its battery backup until it has one minute of backup power left. You will then receive the "Batteries are low. Server will go down in one minute" message. Have all your people log out, for after the one minute, the server will down itself until normal power is restored. But if normal power is restored, you will not see the one-minute message.

NetBIOS Error Messages

NetBIOS does not need the NetWare shell (NETx.COM) running in order to run on the network. However, there are three error messages specific to Novell's implementation of NetBIOS. You may not find these exact error messages if you are using another vendor's NetBIOS, but you will probably see something similar. These errors are all ABEND (ABnormal END) error messages. In the case of NetBIOS, ABENDs are fatal errors that stop NetBIOS's processing before anything else goes wrong. (For a brief explanation of NetBIOS, see page 91).

Active NCB Re-passed to NetBIOS

Explanation. When an application submits a request for services to NetBIOS, the application must fill out a NetBIOS Control Block, or an NCB. Inside the NCB is all the information NetBIOS needs to handle the request. The above ABEND error message is saying, in effect, "I have an active NCB, but you've given me another NCB that is pointing to the same area." This most likely means that the application tried to use that control block again before NetBIOS was through with it. NetBIOS therefore performed an ABEND before causing any damage to data.

Solution. For some reason, NetBIOS is submitting an NCB to an area where another NCB is still processing, and the application did not check to see if that resource was freed up. This is usually an application problem rather than a NetBIOS problem. When you see this error message, write down the circumstances under which you experienced the error; then call the vendor of the application and explain what you have seen.

Free IPX Block Failed

Explanation. NetBIOS is trying to free up an Event Control Block (an "ECB" initiates a request process in IPX—think of it as IPX's equivalent to a NetBIOS NCB) and failed in the attempt. This mishandling of the ECB resource confuses NetBIOS, and NetWare halts processing after displaying this error message.

Solution. NetBIOS, IPX, or the LAN driver is mishandling available resources—in this case, the ECB. When you see this error message, check first to make sure you are running the current NETBIOS.EXE file that comes with the SHGEN utility diskette(s) (with NetWare v2.1x and above, NetBIOS is no longer generated as it was with the GENSH utility).

If you are running v2.0a, be sure you use the NETBIOS.EXE file that you generate with the ANETx.COM file through the GENSH utility. Make sure the LAN driver you are using is certified. If you get this error message, talk to the application vendor, who, in turn, should talk to Novell; they both need to find out why IPX, NetBIOS, and/or LAN drivers are mishandling the ECB resources.

Get IPX Block Failed

Explanation. NetBIOS is trying to obtain an Event Control Block (an "ECB" initiates a request process in IPX—think of it as IPX's equivalent to a NetBIOS NCB) and failed in the attempt. As NetBIOS tries to allocate an ECB, the pointer to the ECB is out of a memory range where all ECBs are known to be. Somewhere in IPX, the LAN Driver, or NetBIOS, this pointer has been set to an invalid value. This mishandling of the ECB resource confuses NetBIOS and it halts processing after displaying this error.

Solution. NetBIOS, IPX, or the LAN driver is mishandling the available resources—in this case, the ECB. When you see this error, first make sure you are running the current NETBIOS.EXE file that comes with the SHGEN utility diskette(s) (with NetWare v2.1x and above, NetBIOS is no longer generated as it was with the GENSH utility). If you are running v2.0a, use the NETBIOS.EXE file that you generate with the ANETx.COM file through the GENSH utility. Make sure the LAN driver you are using is certified. If you get this error message, talk to the application vendor, who, in turn, should talk to Novell; they both need to find out why IPX, NetBIOS, and/or LAN drivers are mishandling the ECB resources.

Numeric List of Return Codes

Below is a list of the IBM NetBIOS return codes. These error messages, because they are part of the standard NetBIOS protocol specification, are generic to every NetBIOS implementation but may be handled differently by every application. In this respect, you may never see the hex values of NetBIOS return codes, but there is a good chance that the error description will be similar.

Hex Value	Error Description
00	Command complete or command has no immediate errors
01	Invalid buffer length
03	Invalid command
05	Command timed out
06	Message incomplete
08	Invalid local session number
09	No resource available
0A	Session closed
0B	Command canceled
0D	Duplicate name in local name table
0E	Name table full
0F	Command completed (name has active sessions and is now deregistered)
11	Local Session table full
12	Session open rejected
13	Invalid name number
14	No answer (cannot find the name called)
15	Invalid name
16	Name in use on remote node
17	Named deleted
18	Session ended abnormally
19	Name conflict detected
21	Interface busy
22	Too many commands outstanding
23	Invalid number in NCB_LANA_NUM field
24	Command completes while cancel is occurring
26	Command not valid to cancel
40	Adapter malfunction
50 to F6	Adapter malfunction
FF	Command pending status

Section 2

OS/2 and NetWare

9 The OS/2 Environment: A Primer for Beginners

This book is about NetWare, not DOS or OS/2 or Macintosh. So why a section devoted entirely to Operating System/2, rather than NetWare? The answer is simple. This book is intended for the system administrator or curious NetWare user who either has, or will soon have, a heterogeneous Novell network on his or her hands. That network could include DOS, OS/2, and/or Macintosh workstations.

In the old days, it was necessary for a NetWare network administrator to have a good understanding of the DOS environment to be an effective resource to the network users. However, with the latest and greatest versions of NetWare, support for Macintosh and OS/2 has been added. The system administrator must now be prepared to install, maintain, and troubleshoot a variety of workstation environments, including OS/2.

OS/2 is a newcomer to the PC marketplace; therefore, many of the hundreds of thousands of NetWare system administrators, and the millions of users, have had no experience with OS/2 or only cursory exposure. It is for that majority that this primer is included.

For the serious OS/2 guru-to-be, a variety of excellent books teach in more detail the principles presented here. But if you are a NetWare user who does not want (or need) that level of detail, this brief introduction provides a synopsis of the issues most important to you. This section should tell you just about everything you need to know about maintaining an OS/2 workstation on a Novell network.

Historical Overview

The rise of DOS, courtesy of IBM, Microsoft, and wunderkind Bill Gates, is now legendary. DOS has been the industry-standard operating system for Intel-based personal computers since the early 1980s.

The limitations of DOS throughout its almost decade-old existence are also legendary. An inadequate file-naming convention, the inefficient FAT file system, a cryptic command-line interface, and the inability to run more than one program at a time are among the pet peeves of DOS users and industry pundits alike.

Several products have attempted to overcome some of the inherent problems with DOS. Among them are DESQview, Microsoft Windows, various file name extender utilities, and a plethora of "graphically pleasing" command shells. Each of these products attempts in its own way to overcome one or more of the inadequacies of DOS. Microsoft itself released Windows, one of the most commercially successful of the "DOS Extender Programs."

Although these packages differ in their approach and value, they have a common thread: they all run under DOS. None of them is really a departure. Rather, each is simply an extension, albeit a niftier or more user-friendly one.

Birth of a New Operating System

In August of 1985, Microsoft and IBM signed a joint development agreement to create a new operating system for the personal computer. They called it "Operating System/2" (or OS/2). IBM shipped OS/2 Standard Edition version 1.0 in December of 1987. IBM followed in July of 1988 with Extended Edition version 1.0, which contained a more robust set of workstation management tools, including Communication Manager and Database Manager.

The most significant difference between DOS and the new operating system was that OS/2 did true multitasking. As an operating system concept unfamiliar to the DOS environment, multitasking in OS/2 deserves a brief discussion here. The rest of this chapter will address other pertinent multitasking operating system concepts which will aid you in understanding OS/2.

Multitasking Operating System Concepts

DOS is a single-tasking operating system. This makes it a relatively simple creature to understand and work with. First of all, each program which runs under DOS controls the entire machine. Programs can take over every byte of memory, change interrupt vector tables, reprogram chips, and directly access video RAM, and can perpetrate an endless number of indignities to which the computer patiently submits. Indeed, it has become typical in the DOS environment to access any number of these programming "hooks" to get better performance out of the machine.

In the DOS world, there is no harm in this total control as long as the program puts everything back in place when it leaves. There are no other active programs to be harmed. (Terminate-and-stay-resident [TSR] programs are a single exception to this rule.)

In a true multitasking operating system, certain conditions affect the way in which the operating system must be designed. The first of these conditions is the existence of multiple processes in the system. Each instance of a program in execution is termed a "process" (hence the term "multiprocessing").

Among the requirements of a multitasking operating system are:

• The operating system must time-slice fairly between processes.
• The operating system must allocate resources fairly between processes.
• The operating system must protect the machine's resources from processes.
• The operating system must protect processes from other processes.

The "protection" and "resource allocation" roles are central to the design of a multitasking operating system. Typically, the core of such an operating system is referred to as a "kernel," while user interfaces to it are often referred to as "shells."

Running Rings around the Machine

The nature of a multitasking operating system makes security an important issue. OS/2 was designed with several protective rings (or privilege levels), the innermost ring designated Ring 0, and the outermost designated Ring 3. Those processes running in Ring 0 are trusted, and are allowed certain privileges in order to accomplish their work. Ring 0 processes include installable and base device drivers, as well as the kernel itself, and are referred to as "Kernel Mode."

Applications have very limited privileges, and therefore run in Ring 3. If an application misbehaves (for example, if it attempts to directly access workstation memory), the kernel will terminate the process so as to protect other processes or the rest of the system.

Sessions and Screens Groups

OS/2 allows multiprocessing on several levels. The most obvious to the new user is the existence of *sessions*, or *virtual screens*. There is only one "physical" or "foreground" screen at any given time, that screen being the one visible on the monitor. Each of the virtual screens can be brought to the foreground by the user. (In the early days, these were referred to as "screen groups," but the term seems to have given way to "sessions"; in either case, we are talking about virtual screens.) This means that OS/2 can remember several different activities and allow the user to return to any of those activities at a moment's notice.

In OS/2, there is always an initial session to greet the user. In version 1.0, this initial session was the Program Selector, a text-based shell of sorts, which allowed a user to see all sessions, and either switch to one of them, kill a session, or initiate a new session. Under OS/2 1.1, there is a Presentation Manager (PM) equivalent, called Task Manager.

The most common screen group is the OS/2 Command Prompt. This session can be created over and over, with multiple occurrences existing at the same time within the machine. Each of these command prompts works in much the same way as the old arcane "C>" prompt from DOS. However, by default the prompt now appears as "[C]", and the user is no longer tied to a single prompt, but may have many

OS/2 command prompts in multiple sessions. Each call to create a new OS/2 command prompt creates a new session or virtual screen. From an OS/2 command prompt, any OS/2 program may be executed. The big difference from DOS, of course, is that the program may be left running while the user moves on to something else.

By pressing "<Alt-Esc>", the user may leave the current screen and move through all the virtual screens, eventually returning to the starting point. "<Ctrl-Esc>" sends the user quickly back to the Task Manager (or Program Selector in 1.0). After the user leaves a screen, the actions which were taking place before the move continue, even though the screen is not visible. For example, a programmer might have an editor in one session and a compiler in another. The programmer can move to the session where the compiler is, begin compiling, and immediately return to the editor to initiate the next change. The compiler will continue uninterrupted (albeit much slower) while the programmer continues to edit the program. To terminate a session, the user may type "Exit" from the OS/2 command line. This removes the session as one of the "virtual screens" available on the workstation and returns the user to the original Presentation Manager screen.

The OS/2 Command Prompt has a little brother that tags along. (Some consider him a pal, and others a nuisance.) He is the DOS Compatibility Box (also referred to as the DOS Box, the Compatibility Box, the DOS 3X Box, or the 3X Box). The DOS Box is essentially good-old-though-not-quite-as-reliable DOS 3.3 running as a virtual screen under OS/2.

The original intent of the DOS Box was to maintain a certain amount of backwards compatibility, allowing users to run existing DOS applications under a screen group in OS/2. Several problems have plagued this approach:

(1) Applications in the DOS box stop working when the DOS Box is not the active screen group.
(2) This little DOS is not quite the reliable version that real DOS is. Not all DOS applications will run here, especially those using many dirty programming hooks.
(3) There is only one DOS box, so you cannot plan on running all your DOS programs as a way to take advantage of OS/2.

In addition to running multiple programs in multiple screen groups or sessions, you can initiate programs which own no virtual screen at all. You can do this by using the "run" command in the CONFIG.SYS file, or the "detach" command from an OS/2 Command Prompt. A program initiated in this way will lurk in the background, using CPU cycles like any other process, but it cannot be accessed by switching between sessions. It may, however, appear in the foreground, via a pop-up window, and temporarily take over the current session.

Threads of Execution

Besides the running of programs under OS/2, there is another level of multitasking that deserves mention. In typical multitasking operating systems on minis and mainframes, the primary goal is to service many clients at the same time.

The illusion to each of the users logged in at various terminals is that the machine is his or her own. In reality, each user's program has become a process to the operating system, which quickly time-slices between the processes. To the operating system, the advantage is that it can use its time more efficiently. While one user's process blocks for I/O, the kernel can give the CPU to another process waiting for service.

In OS/2 there is still just one user, even though true multitasking is available. Partially for this reason, OS/2 approaches multitasking at an even finer level than that of multiple screen groups. Each program is itself made up of individual and autonomous *threads*. The OS/2 kernel keeps track of the threads and time-slices between them. Each program that begins running starts life out as a single thread. Through various calls to the kernel, a program can spawn threads which will run independently and accomplish pre-defined tasks.

The advantage to an OS/2 user is that programs written to utilize threads effectively can dramatically increase performance, even with the increased overhead that OS/2 carries with it. For example, a word processing program under OS/2 can spin off a thread to handle print jobs whenever they are requested by a user, while the main thread continues to service the user. All of the time-slicing is maintained by the kernel, and the user never has to wait for the printer before continuing his or her work. Likewise, any I/O-intensive operations can be placed into separate threads, to be done on the side by the operating system, while the user continues other actions uninterrupted.

Protected Mode and Real Mode

The Intel 80286 was the first CPU in a personal computer to offer what is called "protected mode." Supported by the chip, this mode allows hardware enforcement of certain rules, such as the protection mechanisms mentioned previously. In "real mode," an application has free reign over the machine, with little or no protection enforced. DOS does not utilize the protected mode of the 80286 and 80386 chips, and hence always runs in real mode. The DOS Box also runs in real mode (although OS/2, unlike DOS, restricts its access to most of the machine).

Device Drivers

Device drivers are nothing new to personal computers. Every controller in the machine needs some sort of software interface to allow the operating system to access it. Under DOS, most of the device drivers are either in ROM BIOS or in routines loaded into memory at boot time (for instance, from IBMBIO.COM).

What is new in OS/2 is that the ROM BIOS is not used. The reason is simple: virtually all BIOS routines in today's PCs were written in violation of many protected-mode rules. Most of these routines would not run to completion without being either trapped by the CPU or stopped by the operating system.

For this reason, under OS/2 all controllers and devices are handled through either base or installable device drivers. The only difference between these is that base device drivers are included in a list made known to the kernel at boot time, and they are automatically loaded by the operating system. Standard and essential drivers (keyboard, monitor, printer, and so on) are typically included as base drivers. Installable drivers are those placed in the CONFIG.SYS file with the command "device=".

Regardless of the method for loading, the effect is the same. Device drivers may run in Ring 0 and manipulate various pieces of hardware. Most of the NetWare Requester system operates as device drivers. As you will see in later chapters, installing the Requester consists primarily of moving these drivers to the hard disk and installing them via the CONFIG.SYS file.

What Have OEMs Got to Do with It?

There were always two flavors of DOS: Microsoft's MS-DOS and IBM's PC-DOS. Despite subtle quirks between these two, they were essentially the same operating system, with PC-DOS for true-blue PCs, and MS-DOS as the "vanilla" operating system for all PC-compatibles. With OS/2, there is no longer the vanilla operating system which runs on all PC-compatible hardware.

Even though many machines are dubbed "PC-compatible," there are actually small hardware differences between most PCs and the IBM PC. In the DOS world, this offers few problems, since each machine also ships with its own ROM BIOS. Since DOS relies on these BIOS calls, and each machine comes with those customized calls on-board in ROM, there are few problems.

As we discussed earlier, OS/2 cannot rely on a machine's BIOS. As a result, it also cannot run transparently on any machine other then a true IBM or a 100% compatible clone. Consequently, the old two-flavor approach has changed somewhat. There are still the two main players, IBM and Microsoft, but the rules have changed a little. Microsoft does not ship its own competitive product (like MS-DOS). Instead it works directly with hardware manufacturers in the form of Software Developer Kits (SDKs) and Binary Adaptation Kits (BAKs).

As a hardware manufacturer readies a machine, it must create the OS/2 device drivers needed to handle its own quirks. It will then take the BAK from Microsoft and make its own release of OS/2, complete with its own customized drivers. The company then becomes a reseller (or OEM) of OS/2.

There is no guarantee that IBM OS/2 will run out of the box on anything but an IBM PC or PS/2. However, practical experience demonstrates that IBM's version of OS/2 1.1 will run on a Compaq without problems.

OS/2 Version 1.1

While the initial release of OS/2 took a beating in the press, it was also accepted throughout the industry that the first version was primarily a developer's release of sorts, and that better things would be along in later releases.

Two major problems were solved with the release of OS/2 version 1.1 in November of 1988. First of all, most of the critical problems went away; OS/2 was becoming a realistic environment in which to function. Second, a **real** graphical interface was unveiled, replacing the minimal Program Selector. This new interface was dubbed "Presentation Manager" (PM).

To a certain degree, the initial release of PM was simply a much better-looking version of the Program Selector. It was still the first and default screen group; all the same functionality was still there. To some, it was just Microsoft Windows for OS/2. Certainly its look and feel were reminiscent of Windows. But it was much more. Part of its significance was that it was not just an extension for those who wanted to go buy it, like Windows is for DOS. PM was actually *the* user interface for OS/2. Period. It was standard equipment, and this was certainly a departure. OS/2 applications can write to the PM interface, just as they can under Windows.

Another feature brought to us by Presentation Manager is the Windowed Command Prompt. This feature allows us to run OS/2 command-line operations in multiple windows on the same screen.

Since the release of OS/2 version 1.1, IBM has issued updates. The various versions since the first release can each be identified by a unique time stamp which appears at boot time. Figure 1 gives an example of the time stamp as it appears at boot time. The initial release was time-stamped 88300, which indicates the 300th day of 1988. Since then there have been updates in the form of Corrective Service Diskettes. As OS/2 continues to solidify, these updates are inevitable. To run the NetWare Requester 1.1 you must use the 89039 version or later. Table 1 lists the versions of IBM OS/2 from its initial release to the time of this writing.

OS/2 Version 1.2

In October of 1989, IBM released OS/2 version 1.2. At the time of this writing, Microsoft is still working with OEMs on individual releases of OS/2 1.2. While version 1.2 does not represent a radical improvement over version 1.1, there are significant differences.

The most immediately noticeable change is that the look of Presentation Manager (PM) has changed. The Desktop Manager and main group windows now include icons, and the overall look and feel of PM are more Mac-like. Less noticeable, but much more important, is the file system. Under previous versions, users were still tied to the old file allocation table (FAT) system which DOS used. Some problems with the FAT system are short names, limited attributes, and slow performance. The new file system is designed to be installable—hence the name Installable File System (IFS). This different approach means that the portion of the kernel which handles the file system is actually installed as a series of drivers at boot time.

The High Performance File System (HPFS) is shipped with OS/2 1.2 as one IFS you can install, but you could use any other third-party IFS instead. The file system you use can actually vary, depending upon the file system which you load. The options available are (1) the FAT system, (2) HPFS, and (3) any third-party IFS.

Among the features available in the HPFS are long file names (more than eight letters per name, and more than a single extension), and extended attributes (which are similar to extended attributes in the Macintosh file system). In addition, the performance of the HPFS is far superior to the old FAT system.

In keeping with its policy of providing leading-edge OS/2 support, Novell has already shipped Requester support for OS/2 version 1.2.

Future Versions of OS/2

IBM has announced that a future release of OS/2, written specifically for 80386 machines, will take advantage of the 32-bit bus of the 80386. When IBM releases OS/2 version 2.0, Novell will certainly follow with appropriate OS/2 support for the environment.

Figure 1

```
IBM Operating System/2 Version 1.10
(C) Copyright IBM Corp. 1981, 1988. All rights reserved
(C) Copyright Microsoft Corp. 1981, 1988.

89039
```

Table 1

Here is a list of the IBM OS/2 releases from the first release to the time of this writing:

Standard Edition	Extended Edition	Release Date	Form of release
88300	E8300	30 Oct 88	Product Release
89039	E9039	08 Feb 89	Corrective Services Disks
89158	E9158	07 Jun 89	Corrective Services Disks
89256	E9256	14 Sep 89	Corrective Services Disks

10 OS/2 Workstation Theory of Operations

Many NetWare users are familiar with the way the DOS shell allows a DOS workstation to hook into a Novell network. Since the NetWare Requester for OS/2 is still relatively new technology, this chapter offers an overview of how the Requester works, how it interacts with OS/2, what its parts are, and how those parts fit together.

The World According to DOS

Because DOS enforces no protection mechanisms, the DOS shell is free to steal interrupts and act as a front end, filtering commands before DOS sees them. Because of the nature of OS/2, this approach will no longer work.

The Requester's Approach

Because it is a multitasking operating system, OS/2 protects the workstation hardware from misguided processes, as well as processes from each other. Because of this protective nature, an approach like the DOS shell will simply not work. No one is allowed to steal interrupts and be a front end to the system under OS/2. Instead, special programs called device drivers are allowed a certain number of privileges, including the opportunity to *request* the chance to be a back end to the system. Device drivers may sign up with the OS/2 kernel to look at interrupts which the system does not know how to handle. These device drivers may also perform privileged operations otherwise forbidden to ordinary applications.

This approach is the exact opposite of the DOS approach. Under OS/2 the device drivers make requests and hence become a back end, while under DOS they steal interrupts and act as a front end. It is this requesting nature of the OS/2 approach that leads to the name **NetWare Requester**.

Device Drivers

The Requester system is actually composed of two types of programs: device drivers and daemons. Device drivers are programs which have the file name extension **.SYS**, and run in the privileged Ring 0 of the kernel. As the name implies, device drivers are most commonly used to service various devices. In general, a device driver registers with the OS/2 kernel and requests to be the handler of a particular interrupt line. For example, the OS/2 keyboard driver (KBD01.SYS) registers at boot time as the handler for both Interrupt 9 (keyboard hardware interrupt) and Interrupt 16 (keyboard software interrupt). Any interrupts triggered through these interrupt vectors cause the keyboard driver to begin executing an appropriate interrupt handling routine.

Apart from handling interrupts, device drivers may also exist simply to perform actions at Ring 0, without actually being tied to specific interrupt lines. The flexibility of device drivers under OS/2 allows the NetWare Requester to hook into the OS/2 kernel in a variety of ways, making network connectivity a reality for OS/2 workstations.

There are actually two basic types of OS/2 device drivers: base drivers and installable drivers. Base drivers are those standard drivers that must be in place for the system to run. The keyboard, clock, and disk drivers are examples of base drivers. They are loaded automatically by the kernel at boot time. Installable drivers are all other drivers which are not automatically loaded. These drivers must be included in the CONFIG.SYS file with the command "device =". All of the drivers which make up the NetWare Requester for OS/2 are installable, and must be explicitly loaded via the CONFIG.SYS file.

Even though device drivers run in privileged mode, they are limited in what they can do and how they can interact with the kernel. For example, a device driver cannot pop up a window under OS/2 or accept keyboard input like an ordinary application could. Some of the functions of the Requester demand this sort of access. For example, when an error message needs to be displayed due to some condition in the driver, there must be some mechanism to allow a message window to appear. This is where the daemons come in.

Daemons

Daemons are simply executable programs which are detached at boot time. They are tightly paired with device drivers, and you will often see two files installed in CONFIG.SYS to effect a single action. In these cases, one of these files is usually the device driver, while the other is the daemon. An example is SPX, which is implemented as a device driver (SPX.SYS) and a daemon (SPDAEMON.EXE).

Since the daemon is a normal process (with the same privileges as any other application program), it can access everything—for example, screen and keyboard I/O—that is available to other programs. Because the daemon is intended to work closely with the device driver, hooks are built in which allow the two to communicate at run time. This provides the duality of Requester implementation: the device driver, which runs at Ring 0 and has low-level privileges; and the daemon, which runs at Ring 3 and has high-level privileges.

The Parts

Now that you understand the basic way in which the Requester accomplishes its interaction with the OS/2 kernel, it is time to introduce the parts. There are essentially four layers in the Requester: the LAN card driver, the link support layer, the IPX protocol stack, and a higher layer composed of four distinct parts: the Requester, the SPX protocol stack, the Named Pipes protocol, and the NetBIOS emulator. Each of these seven pieces is diagrammed in Figure 2 and described in the sections which follow.

LAN Card Driver

At the foundation of any network workstation is a network interface board, or card. This is the hardware that physically connects the workstation to the wire, and hence to the network. The very first layer of workstation software is a device driver specifically designed to interface with and control this board. This is the LAN card driver. The NetWare Requester v1.1 provides a choice of 14 such drivers, with the appropriate choice dictated (naturally) by the actual card installed in the machine. The LAN card driver registers with the OS/2 kernel to service the interrupts generated by the LAN card. Its job is fairly simple and straightforward: Take packets from the card and give them to the link support layer (LSL), and take packets from the LSL and give them to the card. This is its sole purpose for existence.

Link Support Layer

The next part of the picture is the link support layer (LSL). This layer is intended to buffer device drivers from protocol stacks. In the case of the current Requester, that protocol stack is IPX/SPX, but others are possible. The LSL is actually capable of supporting multiple protocol stacks simultaneously, even where the protocol stacks are different. For example, when there is a TCP/IP protocol stack available for OS/2, it will be possible for an application to write directly to TCP/IP, which would interface with the LSL and achieve seamless interaction with a UNIX workstation at the packet level. Because of the multitasking nature of OS/2, it would conceivably be possible to have different processes on the same machine sending different packets through different protocol stacks, all going through the same LSL, all on the same machine.

IPX Protocol Stack

While we refer to the IPX/SPX protocol stack, they are actually two distinct layers, implemented in different drivers and daemons. As under DOS, IPX provides non-guaranteed delivery of packets and forms the foundation for all communication on the workstation. The OS/2 implementation is written to comply with the Open Data-link Interface (ODI) standard, and so it will interface transparently with the LSL. All other protocols, as well as the Requester itself, are built on IPX. Direct access to IPX is available through a set of twelve APIs.

SPX

SPX is the portion of the IPX/SPX protocol stack which guarantees sequenced delivery of packets. Since SPX is built upon IPX, it utilizes IPX sockets. However, while under DOS SPX communication was made using IPX sockets, under OS/2 the user must always request sockets from SPX, which administers the sockets to the user programs and makes its own internal requests of IPX for more resources. Because of its guaranteed delivery, SPX provides the basis upon which Named Pipes is built. Direct access is available to SPX through a set of sixteen APIs.

Named Pipes

Named Pipes is a relatively new protocol, made popular as a form of local interprocess communication (IPC) on OS/2 workstations. Novell's implementation of the Requester includes Named Pipes support, which works transparently across a Novell network.

The basic concept behind Named Pipes is that a process may create a pipe (and then additional instances, or virtual occurrences of that pipe) and give it a name. The process which creates the pipe is referred to as a server. The pipe name is actually part of the file system space. Once the instances of the pipe are available, other processes (known as clients) may open communication with the pipe server simply by opening the pipe name as a file. When the client writes to the file, the server may read from its end (as if it were a file), and communication is established. Likewise, when the server writes to the file, the client may read from its end.

Various options that are available to the creator of the pipe affect the nature of the pipe and hence the modes in which it may be accessed. For example, a Named Pipe may be created as inbound (client to server only), outbound (server to client only), or duplex (both directions). It may be in byte stream mode or message mode, and it may have many instances or just one.

Each time a client opens a Named Pipe, an SPX connection is established behind the scenes. The Requester system performs reads and writes by sending and receiving SPX packets. In this way the communication is still SPX/IPX, but the interface presented to the user is much more usable from both a conceptual as well as a programming perspective.

When a workstation loads the Named Pipes driver and daemon, it automatically has access as a client to any Named Pipe on the network. It must indicate a workstation name in the CONFIG.SYS file at the time the daemon is detached in order to be able to operate as a Named Pipe server.

NetBIOS Emulator

The NetBIOS emulator is the last of the protocols available as part of the Requester product. It is functionally equivalent to the DOS version of the same protocol. It follows the IBM NetBIOS standard, providing another form of guaranteed delivery (in addition to SPX). NetBIOS for OS/2 is also built upon IPX. Direct access is available to NetBIOS through programming function calls.

The Requester

The last piece to this puzzle is the Requester itself. It is the link which allows an OS/2 machine to become a Novell NetWare workstation. As explained above, it makes requests of the OS/2 kernel to be given a chance to do certain things that the kernel cannot handle (like file I/O on a network drive). It also sits on top of IPX, allowing it to send appropriate packets to a file server when network services are required. Requester services are provided to applications through an exhaustive set of function calls. Available areas include Bindery Services, Connection Services, Directory Services, File Services, File Server Environment, Message Services, Print Services, Queue Management Services, Synchronization Services, and Transaction Tracking Services.

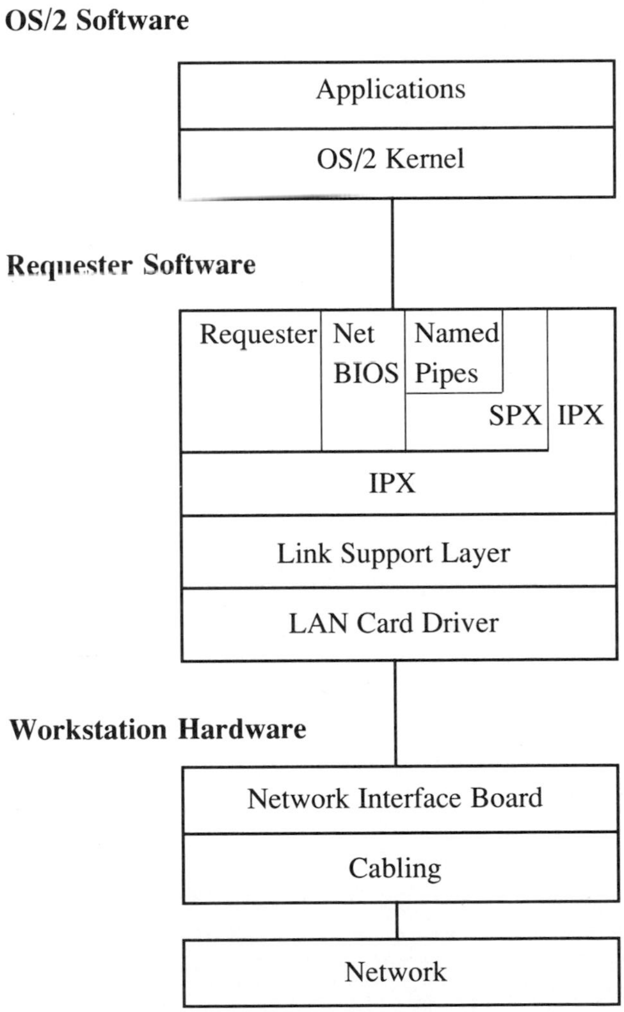

OS/2 Software

Requester Software

Workstation Hardware

Figure 2: Architecture of the NetWare Requester.

11 OS/2 Workstation Hardware

Despite the differences between OS/2 and DOS, the two operating systems share one strong similarity: They both run on Intel-based personal computers. Granted, OS/2 runs only on the more powerful 80286 or 80386 platforms, but the basic hardware requirements are the same. An earlier chapter presented an overview of workstation hardware in the DOS arena; virtually all of what was written there applies equally to OS/2. The intent of this chapter is to clarify those hardware issues which specifically affect OS/2 workstations.

The Workstation

OS/2 was intended to run on Intel-based personal computers. While DOS will run on anything from an 8088 to an 80486, an OS/2 workstation must be either an 80286, 80386, or 80486 machine. The protected mode available on these chips, their fast speeds and wide buses, and their ability to address large amounts of memory make them suitable to support a multitasking operating system like OS/2.

Machines suitable for use as OS/2 workstations include all Micro Channel Architecture (MCA) machines, including the PS/2 line from IBM; all IBM-compatible Industry Standard Architecture (ISA or AT) machines, including Compaqs and other compatibles; and Extended Industry Standard Architecture (EISA) machines, including new machines recently announced by Compaq, Hewlett-Packard, and other manufacturers.

If you are using an IBM-compatible as a workstation, you should probably use the version of OS/2 released by that computer manufacturer. Although Novell does not officially certify personal computers for use as OS/2 workstations, you will most likely have no trouble as long as you use the OEM version designed for your particular workstation. Not all personal computer manufacturers are adapting OS/2 to their machines. Contact your PC manufacturer for detailed information.

In addition to the CPU platforms required for OS/2, a variety of workstation peripherals is involved in using OS/2 in a network environment. These include memory, disk drives, monitors, pointing devices, network boards, and cabling.

Random Access Memory (RAM)

One of the notable negatives typically associated with OS/2 is its seemingly insatiable thirst for RAM. Unlike DOS, which fits snugly into a few hundred kilobytes, OS/2 begins by gobbling several megabytes of RAM just for an appetizer. You should have at least 4MB of RAM on your OS/2 workstation, and preferably several megabytes more. (Large OS/2 database applications such as Microsoft SQL Server may require 8MB or more.)

Several problems can occur when an OS/2 workstation has an inadequate amount of RAM installed. The first is a condition called "thrashing." To understand thrashing, you must first understand the virtual memory system which OS/2 uses.

Regardless of how much memory is installed, if memory on an OS/2 workstation is ever entirely allocated, the Memory Manager begins swapping portions of memory to its hard disk. This allows several programs to each access a large virtual memory, even though the physical memory might be relatively small. For example, you could load ten programs, each utilizing a full megabyte of RAM, even though your machine may have only 4MB of memory installed. When conflicts occur in RAM, portions are swapped out to disk, then brought back when needed.

In most situations, this swapping of RAM to disk represents relatively little overhead. However, as RAM access increases or RAM availability decreases (through too little RAM installed), the number of disk accesses increases dramatically. Spending a large percentage of system time swapping memory to disk is known as "thrashing." Needless to say, when the operating system is spending the bulk of its time doing disk access for virtual memory, system performance suffers severely. A powerful OS/2 machine with too little memory installed can spend several minutes doing a simple DIR.

The second problem is less obvious to the user, but far more pernicious. It is simply that unpredictable problems arise when there is not enough RAM installed on an OS/2 workstation. In the kernel, as well as in many drivers, some portions of code can never afford to be swapped to disk. These portions of memory are marked internally as non-swappable, and must always reside in RAM. When too little RAM is installed in a workstation, these non-swappable portions of code can completely gobble up the available RAM, resulting in unpredictable behavior on the part of the machine (commonly manifested in mysterious workstation hangs or an inability to boot).

When dealing with RAM on an OS/2 workstation, a single rule applies: If you can afford it, err on the high side when installing memory in your OS/2 machine.

Disk Drives

Many DOS workstations have no hard disk, but are either diskless or one-floppy systems. However, neither is a viable alternative for an OS/2 workstation. The next section should help you understand why these are not options, and what disk drive configurations are appropriate for an OS/2 workstation.

Why Not a One-Floppy System?

OS/2 occupies around 10MB of disk storage—far more than can fit on a single floppy disk. Chapter 13 will describe how it is possible to set up your OS/2 workstation to boot from a floppy. But even in this case, the floppy disk will contain only the minimum software necessary to boot the system. The bulk of the operating system must still reside on a hard disk.

Why Not a Diskless System?

Some systems under DOS come without disk drives (hard or floppy) in the workstation. These systems do not rely on local disks from which to boot, but rather utilize boot ROMs on the network interface boards. Some network cards come with boot ROMs, which can be used to boot the machine at power-up time, gathering the appropriate software for the machine from the network file server. However, these boot ROMs are not written in such a way as to allow OS/2 to boot—they work only under DOS. The diskless workstation, therefore, is simply not an option under OS/2, until manufacturers begin shipping OS/2 boot ROMs.

Hard Drives

An OS/2 workstation must be equipped with a hard disk. The size, speed, and brand of hard disk you put in the workstation is largely up to you, but 20MB is recommended as an absolute minimum, with 40MB preferred. As long as there is a hard disk in the machine, it is also practical to place on it frequently used tools, rather than having to constantly access the network file server for personal tools and files.

Floppy Drives

An OS/2 workstation must be equipped with at least one floppy disk drive. The standard for these machines is either 5 1/4" floppies with 1.2 MB capacity, or 3 1/2" floppies with 1.4 MB capacity. All OS/2 application and operating system software which you will need for these machines will come in these formats.

Be aware that, although you can write to a low-density floppy from a high-density drive, you may have problems. This is because the track on a high-density drive is so much narrower than that on a low-density drive. Once you have written to a low-density disk from a high-density drive, you may find that a low-density drive does not have an adequately refined head to read the narrow track. To be safe, you should begin migrating your workstation environments to use high-density drives as a standard.

In deciding between 5 1/4" and 3 1/2" drives, keep in mind that IBM uses 3 1/2" disks as a standard, and ships most of their software on this medium. The PS/2 line comes standard with 3 1/2" drives, while 5 1/4" drives are available only as add-ons. If your budget allows, it may be advantageous to have at least one machine with both sizes of high-density floppy drives, just to cover your bases.

Monitors

Although OS/2 has no required monitor option, some recommendations are in order. For example, if your OS/2 workstation is using a monochrome text monitor, you cannot run Presentation Manager. You can turn off Presentation Manager in the CONFIG.SYS file, as described in Chapter 13. You must decide how much money it is worth to be greeted with nifty graphics and a mouse interface.

Keep in mind that users of OS/2 workstations will insist that they must have a graphics monitor so that they can run Presentation Manager. All graphics monitor options are usable in an OS/2 workstation, with EGA/VGA being preferred. A monochrome graphics monitor, standard with some PS/2 models, functions effectively, but color is certainly more appealing. CGA monitors are supported, but their screen appearance is not as pleasing as that of a higher-resolution monitor. Besides, you may make enemies of your network users if you force them to look at poor graphics all day. The choice is yours.

Pointing Devices

The entire OS/2 system, including Presentation Manager (PM), can be accessed without a mouse or other pointing device. However, the tedious nature of using a windowed user interface without a mouse makes a pointing device almost standard equipment on an OS/2 workstation.

Since OS/2 supports the same wide range of devices as user interfaces under DOS, the choice of mouse is largely up to you. None of the issues involved in your choice is unique to OS/2, so a discussion is beyond the scope of this section.

Network Interface Cards and Cabling

The topologies supported by the OS/2 Requester are a subset of those supported by DOS. For a detailed discussion of the issues involved in installing and maintaining the network interface cards, or issues involving cabling, refer to the discussion in Chapter 1. For the most comprehensive discussion of the boards themselves, refer to the documentation which Novell provides for each of the boards it supports.

Table 2 outlines the network interface cards available for OS/2 workstations. Of particular interest is the NE/2-32 card, which was not supported in the initial release of the Requester v1.1, but which was supported in later releases, including v1.2. All other cards have been supported by the Requester since the initial release.

Table 2

Here is a comprehensive list of the network interface cards supported by the OS/2 Requester versions 1.1 and 1.2:

ARCnet

AT	MCA
Novell RX-Net	Novell RX-Net/2
SMC PC110	SMC PS110

Ethernet

AT	MCA
3Com EtherLink Series 501	3Com EtherLink/MC Series 523
3Com EtherLink Series 503	Novell Ethernet NE/2
3Com EtherLink Series 505	Novell Ethernet NE/2-32
Novell Ethernet NE1000	Novell Ethernet NE2000

PCN/2

AT	MCA
IBM PC Network Adapter II	IBM PC Network Adapter II/A

Token Ring

AT	MCA
IBM Token-Ring PC Adapter	IBM Token-Ring MCA Adapter

12 OS/2 Requester Software

This chapter discusses the software you will need from Novell in order to set up your OS/2 workstation environment. Chapter 13, on the workstation environment, will cover software installation (both OS/2 and the Requester) as well as other OS/2 environment issues.

Each section below describes a separate piece of the software package and explains how it fits into the whole. Since Chapter 10 has already covered the OS/2 workstation theory of operations, each piece should be somewhat familiar to you. This chapter should help you connect the software pieces of the Requester product with the logical pieces of the Requester design.

The Product

Novell's Requester for OS/2 includes protocol drivers, network card drivers, utilities, the LSL, and the Requester itself. Each of these pieces is discussed separately below. With version 1.1, all of the files mentioned in the sections below, with the exception of utilities, are shipped on the disk labeled SYSTEM. Table 3 lists the files on the SYSTEM disk. Because of some additional features of version 1.2, the contents of the main Requester disk have changed. DOS Box support is provided by DOSBOX.EXE, and file I/O support is provided by NWIFS.IFS. Two subdirectories are also included: DOSNP and SQL. DOSNP contains the DOS Named Pipes file, and SQL contains files necessary to run Microsoft's SQL Server. The name of the disk has also changed to REQUESTER. Table 4 lists the contents of the REQUESTER disk.

The NetWare Requester

Although the product is referred to as "the NetWare Requester," in actuality the Requester consists of two pieces: NWREQ.SYS and NWDAEMON.EXE. NWREQ.SYS hooks into the OS/2 kernel at load time as an installable device driver, while NWDAEMON.EXE exists as a daemon, or background process, within the system.

The Link Support Layer

A key piece of the workstation software is the LSL, which acts as an interface between network board drivers and one or more protocol stacks. The LSL consists of a single piece, LSL.SYS, which is implemented as an installable device driver.

Ddaemon

The sole purpose of the Driver Daemon (or Ddaemon) is to allow network card drivers to display error messages on the screen when they encounter exceptions which they cannot handle. Ddaemon is implemented in a single file called DDAEMON.EXE.

Protocols

The NetWare Requester supports a variety of communication protocols: IPX, SPX, NetBIOS, and Named Pipes. Each of these has been described in detail in previous chapters. The sections which follow outline and describe briefly the files which make up each of these protocols.

IPX

IPX forms the foundation of the IPX/SPX protocol stack, upon which all other protocols in the Requester are built. It is implemented in a single installable device driver, IPX.SYS, which must be loaded for the Requester to function.

SPX

SPX provides the guaranteed sequenced packet delivery in the IPX/SPX protocol stack. SPX, the base upon which Novell's remote Named Pipes support is built, must be loaded to enable the use of Named Pipes. It is implemented in two files: SPX.SYS and SPDAEMON. SPX.SYS is an installable device driver which loads at boot time, while SPDAEMON.EXE is a background process within the system.

NetBIOS

Like SPX, the NetBIOS emulator is another form of guaranteed sequenced packet delivery. It also runs on top of IPX, and is implemented in two analogous files: NETBIOS.SYS and NBDAEMON.EXE.

Named Pipes

As described in Chapter 10, Named Pipes is a protocol at a much higher level. Novell's implementation follows the IBM/Microsoft standard outlined for local Named Pipes in an OS/2 workstation. Named Pipes functionality is provided by two files: NMPIPE.SYS and NPDAEMON.EXE. NMPIPE.SYS is an installable device driver, while NPDAEMON.EXE is a background process within the system. Since Named Pipes is built upon SPX, SPX must be loaded in order for Named Pipes to function across the network.

As mentioned previously, DOS Named Pipes support is available on the 1.2 REQUESTER diskette in a separate subdirectory called DOSNP. Within that directory, the file DOSNP.EXE is the DOS program necessary for running a Named Pipes client from a DOS workstation.

Network Interface Board Drivers

For each of the network boards listed in the previous chapter, the Requester product includes an installable device driver which allows the workstation to communicate with the installed network board. Table 5 contains a list of the network interface board device drivers, together with the topologies they support. A device driver for the board must be installed in the machine.

A variety of options is available via the NET.CFG file for some of these device drivers, which are selectable at load time. These options, and troubleshooting issues associated with loading these drivers, are explained in Chapters 13 and 14, which discuss the workstation environment and the NET.CFG file.

Utilities

As should be obvious, the DOS NetWare utilities will not run in the OS/2 environment. Although their file systems are compatible, DOS and OS/2 are different enough that programs written for one environment will not run in the other. However, Novell has provided a set of NetWare utilities written to run under OS/2. While Novell has tried to keep these utilities consistent with their DOS counterparts, there are naturally some differences between the OS/2 and DOS utilities.

There are 44 utilities included with the OS/2 1.1 Requester. The 1.2 Requester utilities are different only in the area of printing. The 1.2 release includes all of the 1.1 utilities except PSTAT, but adds four print utilities: PCONSOLE, PRINTCON, PRINTDEF, and PSC. All of these utilities are OS/2 programs, intended to run from the OS/2 command prompt. Tables 6 (command-line utilities) and 7 (menu utilities) list the OS/2 NetWare utilities common to both 1.1 and 1.2 releases of the Requester.

In version 1.1, the utilities were shipped on two disks labeled PUBLIC1 and PUBLIC2. A list of the files on PUBLIC1 and PUBLIC2 is included in Tables 8 and 9. With the additional utilities included in the 1.2 release of the Requester the number of utility disks rose to three, and the names changed to OS2UTIL-1, OS2UTIL-2, and OS2UTIL-3. A list of the files on the 1.2 utility diskettes is included in Tables 10, 11, and 12.

Note that many DOS NetWare utilities are not available in the OS/2 Requester. In most cases, the utility is missing simply because there is no purpose for it under OS/2. For example, there is no shell in OS/2, hence no SHGEN.

Several differences between DOS and OS/2 are worth mentioning. Each of the affected utilities is listed below with a brief description of how it is different from DOS.

PURGE and **SALVAGE**. When OS/2 is running on a NetWare v2.15 file server, PURGE and SALVAGE both operate as command-line utilities, and function the same as under DOS. However, when OS/2 is running on a 386 file server, PURGE goes away completely, and SALVAGE becomes a menu utility, performing the functions of both utilities. In other words, to purge files on a 386 file server, you must use SALVAGE.

SYSCON and **Login Scripts**. While SYSCON itself is no different in OS/2, login scripts are different. Since login scripts can be accessed only through SYSCON, we will discuss them here.

You must remember two things about login scripts under OS/2. The first is that they are not compatible with DOS login scripts. This means that if you create a login script in SYSCON with a DOS workstation, your OS/2 workstation will not see it. You must create the login script with SYSCON on an OS/2 workstation for OS/2 workstations to see it.

The second point is that login script search mappings are not implemented under OS/2, and will be ignored by an OS/2 workstation when it reads the login script. Fortunately, there is a relatively painless way around this: use the OS/2 PATH environment variable to implement the search mappings. Here's how.

The first step is to use SYSCON to map the drives that you wish to eventually use as search drives. As an example, here is a walkthrough of the process of mapping K: to your work area on the file server. Figure 3 shows how to do this within the login script.

Under OS/2, L: is the default map to the file server volume containing utilities (such as LOGIN), so there is no need to specifically map L: in the login script. After you log in to the file server, K: and L: will be mapped to network drives. At this point, the drive mappings do not yet function as search drives. That is the next step.

Now use the OS/2 system search path to provide the equivalent of search mappings, using the two network drives that we have mapped. There are actually five different ways to affect the PATH environment variable on an OS/2 workstation. The most obvious way is by using AUTOEXEC.BAT, as you would under DOS. Unfortunately, this is the only *wrong* way to do it. Changing the PATH variable in AUTOEXEC.BAT affects only the PATH variable associated with the DOS Box and has no affect whatsoever on the OS/2 Command Prompts. Using AUTOEXEC.BAT is therefore not an option.

The other four methods are equivalent in their effect, but slightly different in their implementation. They are CONFIG.SYS, STARTUP.CMD, OS2INIT.CMD, and Command Line. Like the DOS equivalent, an OS/2 CONFIG.SYS is read by the system at boot time, and it contains information which allows you to customize your environment, most typically by loading various drivers. Under OS/2, its functionality has been expanded to the point that it can deal with functions which are almost exclusively the domain of AUTOEXEC.BAT in the DOS world. When OS/2 is installed on a workstation, the PATH variable is set in CONFIG.SYS as a default. This makes it a logical place to implement your fix.

Since OS/2 will look at this variable each time it tries to execute a file, by placing your network drives into this PATH variable, you will have effectively implemented search mappings under OS/2. Figure 4 shows the PATH variable as set within the CONFIG.SYS. Notice that L: has been expanded to L:\OS2. This is because by default L: maps to the DOS utilities, while the OS/2 utilities are in a subdirectory called OS2. By placing L:\OS2 into the search path, you correctly set the search path to look at the OS/2 utilities.

You should also note that if one or more of the network drives in your path becomes invalid, OS/2, unlike DOS, will not complain. This allows you the flexibility to use this method without having to endure warnings about invalid directories each time OS/2 sees the bad network drives.

We mentioned STARTUP.CMD and OS2INIT.CMD earlier, but failed to explain them. Under OS/2, a file with the .CMD extension is a batch file. The new extension distinguishes OS/2 batch files from the .BAT DOS batch files, which must coexist on the same disk. STARTUP.CMD is in many ways OS/2's equivalent of AUTOEXEC.BAT. The instructions contained in STARTUP.CMD are executed in a Presentation Manager window when the workstation boots. OS2INIT.CMD functions similarly, except that it is run each time an OS/2 session begins (so long as the PROTSHELL command in CONFIG.SYS includes the /K option). Its effect is therefore felt only by the OS/2 session, and not by the Presentation Manager.

Because of the order in which these three batch files run, the effects of one may nullify the effects of another. For example, even if CONFIG.SYS sets the PATH, STARTUP.CMD may set a PATH and completely override the original. Likewise, if OS2INIT.CMD sets an environment PATH, it will supersede any PATH previously set in either CONFIG.SYS or STARTUP.CMD.

The remaining option is the OS/2 Command Prompt. As in DOS, you are free at any time to type in the SET PATH command from the Command Prompt in order to change the PATH variable. While this provides the most flexi-bility, it is also certainly the most tedious.

CAPTURE and **NPRINT**. Under DOS, these print utilities can access a small database, maintained by PRINTCON, which contains various print job definitions. By using the "j=" parameter, these utilities can designate which print job should indicate default settings for a particular call to CAPTURE or NPRINT. Since PRINTCON does not exist under OS/2 v1.1, neither does the database, nor does the option of specifying a print job as a command-line parameter.

One other feature which affects CAPTURE and NPRINT is the No Tabs option (/NT). Using this option with CAPTURE or NPRINT causes them to operate in byte-stream mode, a mode otherwise impossible to use under OS/2.

File Server Requirements

Although file server requirements for running the Requester are not a part of the Requester software, it is appropriate to discuss them here as part of this discussion of Novell software. The Requester needs NetWare v2.15 or above to run.

These file server requirements apply only to those Requester functions, such as attaching or logging in, which directly interact with a file server. A variety of functions available with the Requester require no file server at all. Examples are SPX and Named Pipes communication protocols, which can run peer-to-peer without a file server. However, where there is a need to interact with a file server (as there is in most cases), the restrictions on file server versions will apply.

Table 3
Contents of SYSTEM disk

3C501.SYS	NPCALLS.DLL
3C503.SYS	NPDAEMON.EXE
3C505.SYS	NWAFP.DLL
3C523.SYS	NWCALLS.DLL
DDAEMON.EXE	NWCONFIG.DLL
INSTALL.EXE	NWDAEMON.EXE
INSTALL.HLP	NWREQ.SYS
IPX.SYS	NWSPOOL.EXE
IPXCALLS.DLL	PCN2.SYS
LSL.SYS	RXNET.SYS
NBDAEMON.EXE	RXNET2.SYS
NE1000.SYS	SPDAEMON.EXE
NE2.SYS	SPX.SYS
NE2000.SYS	SPXCALLS.DLL
NET.MSG	SYS$ERR.DAT
NETAPI.DLL	SYS$HELP.DAT
NETBIOS.SYS	SYS$MSG.DAT
NETH.MSG	TOKEN.SYS
NETOEM.DLL	TOKENEE.SYS
NMPIPE.SYS	

Table 4
Contents of REQUESTER disk

READ.ME	IPX.SYS
3C501.SYS	IPXCALLS.DLL
3C503.SYS	LSL.SYS
3C505.SYS	NBDAEMON.EXE
3C523.SYS	NE1000.SYS
DDAEMON.EXE	NE2.SYS
DOSBOX.EXE	NE2-32.SYS
INSTALL.EXE	NE2000.SYS
INSTALL.HLP	NET.MSG

NETAPI.DLL	PCN2.SYS
NETBIOS.SYS	RXNET.SYS
NETH.MSG	RXNET2.SYS
NMPIPE.SYS	SPDAEMON.EXE
NPCALLS.DLL	SPX.SYS
NPDAEMON.EXE	SPXCALLS.DLL
NWAFP.DLL	SYS$ERR.DAT
NWCALLS.DLL	SYS$HELP.DAT
NWCONFIG.DLL	SYS$MSG.DAT
NWDAEMON.EXE	TOKEN.SYS
NWIFS.IFS	TOKENEE.SYS
NWREQ.SYS	DOSNP <DIR>
NWSPOOL.EXE	SQL <DIR>

Table 5
Network Interface Board Drivers

Here is a list of network interface board device drivers included with the NetWare Requester, together with the boards that each driver supports.

Topology	Device Driver	Boards Supported
ARCnet	RXNET.SYS	Novell RX-Net (AT)
	RXNET2.SYS	Novell RX-Net/2 (MCA)
Ethernet	NE2.SYS	Novell Ethernet NE/2 (MCA)
	NE2-32.SYS	Novell Ethernet NE/2-32 (32-bit MCA)
	NE1000.SYS	Novell Ethernet NE1000 (AT)
	NE2000.SYS	Novell Ethernet NE2000 (AT)
	3C501.SYS	3Com EtherLink Series 501 (AT)
	3C503.SYS	3Com EtherLink Series 503 (AT)
	3C505.SYS	3Com EtherLink Series 505 (AT)
	3C523.SYS	3Com EtherLink Series 523 (MCA)
PC Network/2	PCN2.SYS	IBM PC Network Adapter II (AT) IBM PC Network Adapter II/A (MCA)
Token Ring	TOKEN.SYS	IBM Token-Ring PC Adapter (AT) IBM Token-Ring PC Adapter (MCA)
	TOKENEE.SYS	IBM Token-Ring PC Adapter (AT) IBM Token-Ring PC Adapter (MCA)

Table 6
Command Line Utilities

Here is a list of command-line utilities included with the NetWare Requester 1.1.
Asterisks indicate utilities which have changed from their DOS counterparts.

ALLOW	NPRINT*
ATOTAL	PAUDIT
ATTACH	PURGE*
CAPTURE*	REMOVE
CASTOFF	REVOKE
CASTON	RENDIR
CHKDIR	RIGHTS
CHKVOL	SECURITY
ENDCAP	SEND
FLAG	SETPASS
FLAGDIR	SETTTS
GRANT	SLIST
LISTDIR	SMODE
LOGIN	SYSTIME
LOGOUT	TLIST
MAP	USERLIST
NCOPY	VERSION
NDIR	WHOAMI

Table 7
Menu Utilities

Here is a list of menu utilities included with the NetWare Requester 1.1. Asterisks
indicate utilities which have changed from their DOS counterparts.

DSPACE
FILER
MAKEUSER
SALVAGE*
SYSCON*
USERDEF
VOLINFO

Table 8
Contents of PUBLIC1 disk

ALLOW.EXE	LOGIN.EXE
ATOTAL.EXE	LOGOUT.EXE
ATTACH.EXE	MAKEUSER.EXE
CAPTURE.EXE	MAKEUSER.HLP
CASTOFF.EXE	MAP.EXE
CASTON.EXE	NCOPY.EXE
CHKDIR.EXE	NDIR.EXE
CHKVOL.EXE	NPRINT.EXE
DSPACE.EXE	PAUDIT.EXE
DSPACE.HLP	PSTAT.EXE
ENDCAP.EXE	PURGE.EXE
FILER.EXE	SERVINS2.BAT
FLAGDIR.EXE	SERVINS2.CMD
GRANT.EXE	SERVINST.BAT
LISTDIR.EXE	SERVINST.CMD

Table 9
Contents of PUBLIC2 disk

REMOVE.EXE	SYS$ERR.DAT
RENDIR.EXE	SYS$HELP.DAT
REVOKE.EXE	SYS$MSG.DAT
RIGHTS.EXE	SYSCON.EXE
SALVAGE.EXE	SYSCON.HLP
SALVAGE.HLP	SYSTIME.EXE
SECURITY.EXE	TLIST.EXE
SEND.EXE	USERDEF.EXE
SERVINS3.BAT	USERDEF.HLP
SERVINS3.CMD	USERLIST.EXE
SETPASS.EXE	VERSION.EXE
SETTTS.EXE	VOLINFO.EXE
SLIST.EXE	VOLINFO.HLP
SMODE.EXE	WHOAMI.EXE

Table 10
Contents of OS2UTIL-1 disk

ALLOW.EXE	LISTDIR.EXE
ATOTAL.EXE	LOGIN.EXE
ATTACH.EXE	LOGOUT.EXE
CAPTURE.EXE	MAKEUSER.EXE
CASTOFF.EXE	MAKEUSER.HLP
CASTON.EXE	MAP.EXE
CHKDIR.EXE	NCOPY.EXE
CHKVOL.EXE	NDIR.EXE
DSPACE.EXE	NPRINT.EXE
DSPACE.HLP	PAUDIT.EXE
ENDCAP.EXE	PCONSOLE.EXE
FILER.EXE	SERVINS2.BAT
FILER.HLP	SERVINS2.CMD
FLAG.EXE	SERVINST.BAT
FLAGDIR.EXE	SERVINST.CMD
GRANT.EXE	

Table 11
Contents of OS2UTIL-2 disk

PCONSOLE.HLP	SECURITY.EXE
PRINTCON.EXE	SEND.EXE
PRINTCON.HLP	SETPASS.EXE
PRINTDEF.EXE	SETTTS.EXE
PRINTDEF.HLP	SLIST.EXE
PSC.EXE	SMODE.EXE
PURGE.EXE	SYS$ERR.DAT
REMOVE.EXE	SYS$HELP.DAT
RENDIR.EXE	SYS$MSG.DAT
REVOKE.EXE	SYSCON.EXE
RIGHTS.EXE	SYSCON.HLP
SALVAGE.EXE	SYSTIME.EXE
SALVAGE.HLP	TLIST.EXE

Table 12
Contents of OS2UTIL-3 disk

SERVINS3.BAT	VERSION.EXE
SERVINS3.CMD	VOLINFO.EXE
USERDEF.EXE	VOLINFO.HLP
USERDEF.HLP	WHOAMI.EXE
USERLIST.EXE	

Figure 3
Login script line to do simple mapping.

```
map K := fserver/user:chuck
```

Figure 4
Lines from CONFIG.SYS to set path to include L: and K:.

```
SET PATH=C:\OS2;C:\OS2\SYSTEM;C:\OS2\INSTALL;C:\;L:\OS2;K:\
```

13 Setting Up the OS/2 Workstation Environment

We've already talked about the actual Requester software—what it is and how it works—but in order to maintain a Novell network with OS/2 workstations, you must understand all the issues involved in setting up an OS/2 workstation environment. This chapter discusses the essentials of setting up and maintaining an OS/2 workstation on a Novell network.

Installing OS/2

You must first install the operating system on the workstation. You may find yourself having to install OS/2 under a variety of circumstances, from upgrading a DOS machine to OS/2 to setting up a new machine right out of the box. Although installing OS/2 is not a Novell issue, your NetWare users will still expect you to understand each workstation environment on the network, including OS/2. Therefore, some helpful hints are in order. The sections which follow discuss four installation scenarios which you may encounter.

Upgrade from DOS

As you begin to move portions of your network toward OS/2, upgrading from DOS to OS/2 may become a common experience. The OS/2 installation program will present upgrading from DOS as one of the installation options; in that case, simply select it when it is presented. For OS/2 1.1, you do not run the risk of losing any files, since the file system is identical to that under DOS. However, version 1.2 offers you the chance to install the High Performance File System (HPFS), which is non-DOS compatible. We'll discuss this in greater detail a little later. Keep in mind also that you may preserve the ability to boot your machine under DOS, even after you have installed OS/2. We'll also talk about that later.

OS/2 as First OS

Installing OS/2 in a brand-new machine will probably be the next largest percentage of your OS/2 installations, as the network grows to include new OS/2 workstations. This option is also presented to you during the OS/2 installation program. One consequence of this option is that the hard disk must be formatted during this step, and formatting is a time-consuming process. As long as you are either installing version 1.1 or using 1.2 without the HPFS, you can boot the machine with a DOS diskette and format the disk under DOS. Having done this, simply skip the format option during installation. However, if you wish to use HPFS, let the installation program take you by the hand and walk you through it. As with the upgrade-from-DOS option, you may still have the option of booting with DOS, as discussed later.

Upgrade from OS/2

Since IBM and Novell have discontinued support for OS/2 1.0, the upgrade path from OS/2 1.0 to 1.1 is already a historical side note. However, there may still be OS/2 1.0 machines out there to contend with. In any event, you may already be faced with upgrading from version 1.1 to 1.2 (and eventually to 2.0). Since version 1.1 used the DOS FAT file system, the HPFS issues are the same ones you will face when performing an upgrade from DOS. The actual upgrade should provide no problems, although installing the new Requester could create some difficulties. These problems, together with solutions, are discussed later in this chapter, in the section on installing the Requester.

Corrective Services

Even if you have the most recent version of OS/2 on your workstation, you may still be faced with an upgrade situation. IBM has issued several maintenance releases of OS/2 1.1 and a couple for OS/2 1.2 since their original shipments. These maintenance releases have been in the form of Corrective Services Diskettes. These upgrades simply replace the kernel and other important files (device drivers, libraries, and so on). Since these free updates correct known problems with OS/2, you should greet them eagerly and quickly install them on your OS/2 workstations. If you are sitting on an original version of OS/2 1.2, get your update as quickly as possible.

Using OS/2 without Losing DOS

The faint of heart need not make the leap of faith to OS/2 without a parachute. There are several options for using OS/2 without losing access to your comfortable DOS environment. Indeed, in some network environments, there will be software (E-mail or games, for example) which is not OS/2 compatible and which cannot run from an OS/2 workstation.

Dual-Boot Software

Originally, OS/2 1.0 came with a dual-boot option. The idea behind dual-boot is that when you boot your machine, a simple menu comes up asking whether you want DOS or OS/2. You select the one you want, and then proceed with your work. In some systems, if you don't make a selection after a predefined period of time, the system defaults to OS/2.

Originally, with version 1.1, the powers that be took the dual boot out of OS/2, despite the cries of new OS/2 users. Since then, dual boot has reapperared in OS/2 with version 1.2, so now the choice is easy.

DOS on a Floppy

Essentially, this is the poor man's dual boot. You simply create a DOS boot diskette, complete with the DOS network software (IPX and NET3), and keep it handy. When you need to work in DOS, or play a game, or read your E-mail, simply put the disk into the drive and reboot. This approach is cheaper than buying dual-boot software; it also saves you from having to see the menu each time you boot, or *having* to make a selection just to boot, in those programs not providing a default OS/2 boot after a timeout.

OS/2 on a Floppy

In a macabre twist of the DOS-on-a-floppy method, the reverse approach is possible. Although the choice is certainly not recommended, you can allow your machine to remain a DOS workstation and place OS/2 on a floppy disk. To use this method, you will need the OS/2 kernel and loader programs (the hidden files OS2KRNL and OS2LDR) on a floppy disk, together with the CONFIG.SYS and STARTUP.CMD.

Since there is not enough room on a floppy disk for all of the software which OS/2 requires, you must have your hard disk set up like a normal OS/2 installation. However, the hard disk must have the DOS system files IBMBIO.COM and IBMDOS.COM, and its own copies of CONFIG.SYS and AUTOEXEC.BAT, containing DOS-specific commands. When creating the OS/2 boot floppy, you must use CONFIG.SYS to set default directories to the hard disk so that the operating system will never get confused if you remove the original OS/2 boot diskette.

Using the DOS Box on a Network (with Version 1.1)

This is not a good option for a fake DOS workstation environment. For one thing, simple commands, such as LOGIN and ATTACH, will not function in the DOS box because they need to interact with the DOS shell. Since the DOS shell must steal interrupts to get its job done, and since OS/2 does not allow applications to perform such objectionable tasks as stealing interrupts, this approach simply does not work—the DOS shell cannot be loaded in the DOS box. Hence, normal workstation actions like those mentioned above will not work from the compatibility box.

However, on the bright side, you can still access the network from the DOS compatibility box. As long as you don't try anything complicated, but simply use the network drives you've already mapped under OS/2, you can move around your network drives and even run DOS programs from the network. This method works because all file I/O is handled by OS/2, and access to network drives is passed to the Requester, as described in Chapter 10. This approach can provide a partial solution when you have a real need to access DOS programs on the network, but you must work from an OS/2 workstation. However, the DOS box is not (I repeat, not) a reasonable place to do the bulk of your work on an OS/2 workstation.

Using the DOS Box on a Network (with Version 1.2)

DOS Box reality changed somewhat with the release of the 1.2 Requester. For one thing, enhanced DOS Box network support is now available. A sort of pseudo-DOS shell is loaded within the DOS Box; this shell allows the Requester to handle the various network calls made in the DOS Box. Under this system, you should be able to log in, log out, map drives, and perform most other network operations from the DOS Box. This approach should give you greater convenience when you are working in the DOS Box, but it is not a viable alternative to working from the OS/2 interface. A powerful OS/2 workstation with most work being done in the DOS Compatibility Box is really just an overpriced DOS workstation.

New Features—New Installation Problems

As I mentioned earlier, several new features appear in OS/2 1.2, and these features are accompanied by a couple of installation challenges. One pleasing feature is the return of dual boot. Having a choice in the matter is comforting, even if you never use that choice.

The second feature is a bit more challenging—the High Performance File System (HPFS). This system is a variation of the normal FAT system under DOS. The first two versions of OS/2 also used FAT, but with version 1.2 HPFS was made available. The challenge is not in the installation itself, but rather in the fact that HPFS becomes a non-DOS partition, and thus requires that the hard disk be properly configured. The menu provides no way to set up a non-primary disk partition as an HPFS; rather, it provides only for setting up the boot partition—and that partition must be at least 10MB. However, you may use the OS/2 FDISKPM utility to manipulate the hard disk after installation. In this way, you can control the nature of the other partitions on the disk.

Installing the Requester

Once OS/2 is installed and running in the workstation and all network hardware is in place, it's time to install the Requester. The INSTALL program is on the SYSTEM disk in version 1.1 and on the REQUESTER disk in version 1.2. INSTALL is fairly simple and straightforward—even easier than doing a SHGEN under DOS.

One small glitch in INSTALL should be noted here, just because it is potentially annoying. The first two windows of INSTALL ask you for the "Source Disk" (where the INSTALL program is), and the "Destination Disk" (the hard disk on which the Requester will be installed). The defaults for these disks are "A" for Source, and "C" for Destination. These windows appear with the cursor under the default drive letter. If you wish to change one of these, simply typing a different letter will not overwrite the default. You must either press "<Del>" or move the cursor to the right of the letter, backspace to remove it, then type the desired letter.

As you work through the installation program, it prompts you for directories into which to put the various parts of the Requester. The INSTALL program looks at the Requester files in four categories: DLLs, background tasks, message files, and device drivers. Each is discussed below.

Some commonalities exist between these installation areas. For example, each offers "C:\" as an option. Considering how quickly the root directory becomes cluttered in OS/2, this is almost certainly the worst option in every case. However, "C:\NETWARE," also offered in each one, is a reasonable option. It will place every Requester file into the same directory on the hard disk. But keeping all these files together requires changing some lines in the CONFIG.SYS file to reflect the presence of the Requester files in that directory. (See the CONFIG.SYS discussion later in this chapter.) Other options, such as "C:\OS2" and "C:\OS2\SYSTEM," reflect common subdirectories which OS/2 should already recognize and look for. Selecting these subdirectories allows you the option not to modify CONFIG.SYS, while removing the benefit of having all of the Requester files grouped together.

DLLs

DLLs are the dynamic link libraries, consisting of files with the extension .DLL. The available directories are:

        C:\NETWARE
        C:\
        C:\OS2\DLL

Background Tasks

These are the various daemons run from the CONFIG.SYS file. The daemons are all of the files on the disk with the extension .EXE (except IN-STALL.EXE). The available directories are:

        C:\NETWARE
        C:\OS2
        C:\OS2\SYSTEM
        C:\

Message Files

These files, which contain message strings used by pieces of the Requester, consist of files with the extension .MSG. The available directories are:

        C:\NETWARE
        C:\
        C:\OS2\SYSTEM

Device Drivers

These are all of the installable device drivers, consisting of all files in the directory with the extension .SYS. The available directories are:

    C:\NETWARE
    C:\OS2
    C:\OS2\SYSTEM
    C:\

Installing the Requester from a Network Drive

INSTALL will most commonly be run from a floppy drive, as appropriately indicated by the default Source Drive offered in the first installation menu. However, running INSTALL from a floppy is not the only option available. If you are already running some form of the Requester, you can upgrade by installing the Requester from a network drive. Obviously, if you are installing the Requester for the first time on an OS/2 workstation, this option is not available, since you need the Requester to access the network in the first place.

In order to install from a network drive, first create on the file server a directory called SYSTEM into which to copy the files from the original SYSTEM (version 1.1) or REQUESTER (version 1.2) floppy from the Requester installation diskettes. As mentioned above, you must already be logged in to the file server from the workstation to use this method.

From the workstation, map a drive to the SYSTEM subdirectory, such that the root of the network drive is the SYSTEM directory. The installation program always assumes that it is operating from the root of the letter you gave it in the Source Drive menu. If you map to the root, then change directories to SYSTEM, INSTALL will not find the files. Once the mapping is complete, the installation will run to completion with the same results as installing from floppies.

Troubleshooting Requester Installation

If you are installing the Requester for the first time, there should be no glitches. However, problems may arise if you run the Requester installation program from within OS/2 while a previous version of the Requester is running.

In order to install the Requester, the installation program must kill the Requester daemons which exist in the system. If for some reason a daemon cannot be killed and the installation fails, don't panic. Some inconsistencies in the way in which daemons are killed can lead to this situation. If this problem occurs, there are two good solutions.

Load without the Old Requester

You can avoid the problem of killing stubborn daemons by simply running the installation program without the Requester loaded. Do this either by removing references to the Requester from the CONFIG.SYS, or by REMing it out and then rebooting the workstation. The system will come up *without* the Requester loaded; hence there will be no daemons to kill and therefore no conflicts.

Install under DOS

Another solution is to reboot your workstation with DOS (see above), and simply copy the Requester files manually into the correct subdirectories. In either case, the essence of the solution is to avoid the potential conflict with stubborn daemons.

Using CONFIG.PST

Running INSTALL creates a file called CONFIG.PST in the root directory of your hard disk. This file, which contains all of the statements necessary to execute daemons and install the device drivers for the Requester, should become part of your CONFIG.SYS file. Either use your favorite editor to cut and paste this file into your CONFIG.SYS, or type the following at the command prompt:

```
COPY CONFIG.SYS + CONFIG.PST CONFIG.SYS
```

Once the contents of CONFIG.PST are in the CONFIG.SYS file, remove the REM statements from the correct lines in the file. The following section explains how to correctly un-REM lines from the CONFIG.PST.

Setting Up the CONFIG.SYS

Once the CONFIG.SYS file has the CONFIG.PST file pasted into it, you must remove REMs in an intelligent manner. To help you understand this process, a brief explanation of each of the sections in CONFIG.PST follows. First, however, here is a brief explanation concerning the commands in the CONFIG.PST file.

Each line in CONFIG.PST falls into one of three categories:

device=
run
comment

The *device=* statement instructs the kernel to load the installable device driver whose name follows. The *run* statement instructs the kernel to detach, as a daemon, the program whose name follows. This process is logically equivalent to running the DETACH command from the command line. Technically, any statement which begins with REM is a *comment*, and is ignored by the operating system when it examines CONFIG.SYS. While REM is useful for keeping commands from being seen by the system, a number of lines in CONFIG.PST are simply comments for the sake of clarification. We will look at all of these more carefully as we examine the parts of the CONFIG.PST file.

The following is an overview of each group of statements in CONFIG.PST. Since each of these pieces has been explained in previous chapters, we will not delve into what they are, but simply how they should be placed within the CONFIG.SYS file. Where subdirectories are indicated in CONFIG.PST, they reflect the directories selected during the installation process. In each of the cases below, the destination directory chosen during installation was C:\NETWARE.

NetWare Spooler

The NetWare Spooler is set up to run by default. There is no REM statement before the command to run the spooler daemon. The lines from CONFIG.PST are:

```
rem start NetWare Spooler
run=C:\NETWARE\nwspool.exe
```

You may disable the NetWare Spooler by placing "REM" before the run command as follows:

```
rem start NetWare Spooler
rem run=C:\NETWARE\nwspool.exe
```

LSL

The LSL is also installed by default, since the command to load the device driver is not REMed out. Likewise, the ddaemon is set to detach at boot time. The lines are:

```
device=C:\NETWARE\lsl.sys
run=C:\NETWARE\ddaemon.exe
```

These lines must remain exactly as is, or the Requester will not function.

NIC Drivers

There are thirteen lines for installing network board drivers. All of these lines are set with the REM as a default. You should select the driver which supports the board installed in the workstation by removing the REM from in front of the line. The lines below indicate the drivers in the CONFIG.PST, on a workstation with a Novell Ethernet NE2000 board installed:

```
rem device=C:\NETWARE\pcn2.sys
rem device=C:\NETWARE\rxnet.sys
rem device=C:\NETWARE\rxnet2.sys
rem device=C:\NETWARE\ne2.sys
rem device=C:\NETWARE\ne2-32.sys
rem device=C:\NETWARE\ne1000.sys
device=C:\NETWARE\ne2000.sys
rem device=C:\NETWARE\token.sys
rem device=C:\NETWARE\tokenee.sys
rem device=C:\NETWARE\3c501.sys
rem device=C:\NETWARE\3c503.sys
rem device=C:\NETWARE\3c505.sys
rem device=C:\NETWARE\3c523.sys
```

There should usually be only one network card driver loaded in this section of the CONFIG.PST. If you remove the "REM" from more than one driver, only the first driver will be recognized by default. By using NET.CFG, as described in the next chapter, you may remove the "REM" from more than one and specify which network card driver the Requester should work with.

IPX

IPX loads as a single device driver, and has no REM by default. The line is:

```
device=C:\NETWARE\ipx.sys
```

This line must be exactly as found in the CONFIG.PST file, or the Requester will not function.

SPX

Since SPX is an optional protocol, its lines are preceded by REMs as a default. The first line installs the device driver, and the second detaches its daemon. Remove the REMs from both lines to install SPX. SPX is required to run applications which use either SPX or Named Pipes. The lines are:

```
rem device=C:\NETWARE\spx.sys
rem run=C:\NETWARE\spdaemon.exe
```

Named Pipes

Installing Named Pipes is probably the trickiest of all. (In fact, the CONFIG.PST file comes with six lines of comments to explain three lines of commands.) The first line loads the Named Pipes device driver. The last two lines are different ways of detaching the Named Pipes daemon. Since the daemon is an executable program, it can be passed a command-line parameter. This parameter is indicated by COMPUTERNAME in the CONFIG.PST file. If you wish your workstation to be a Named Pipes server (and client), you should give a string in the place of COMPUTERNAME and remove the REM from the third line. The string you give will uniquely identify your workstation as a Named Pipe server, and will be part of the string used by a Named Pipe client to open a named pipe on your machine.

If you want your workstation to act simply as a Named Pipe client, remove the REM from the second line, giving no command-line parameter. (Refer to Chapter 10 for a discussion of Named Pipes servers and clients.) SPX must have been previously loaded in order to use Named Pipes. The following lines are the defaults from CONFIG.PST:

```
rem device=C:\NETWARE\nmpipe.sys
rem run=C:\NETWARE\npdaemon.exe
rem run=C:\NETWARE\npdaemon.exe   COMPUTERNAME
```

The following lines show Named Pipes loaded as a Named Pipe server called NPSERVER:

```
device=C:\NETWARE\nmpipe.sys
rem run=C:\NETWARE\npdaemon.exe
run=C:\NETWARE\npdaemon.exe   NPSERVER
```

The following lines show Named Pipes loaded only as a client:

```
device=C:\NETWARE\nmpipe.sys
run=C:\NETWARE\npdaemon.exe
rem run=C:\NETWARE\npdaemon.exe   COMPUTERNAME
```

NetWare Requester

The NetWare Requester device driver and daemon are loaded here. The lines are:

```
device=C:\NETWARE\nwreq.sys
run=C:\NETWARE\nwdaemon.exe
```

These lines must remain exactly as they appear in the CONFIG.PST file, or the Requester will not function.

NetBIOS

The NetBIOS protocol does not depend upon any other protocols except IPX. Remove the REMs from the last part of the CONFIG.PST file to run programs which use NetBIOS. The lines in CONFIG.PST are:

```
rem device=C:\NETWARE\netbios.sys
rem run=C:\NETWARE\nbdaemon.exe
```

The order in which these groups of statements appear in the CONFIG.SYS is important because it preserves certain important dependencies. For example, the LSL must be loaded before a network card driver can load. The network card driver must be loaded before IPX can successfully load. IPX is the foundation for every protocol, so it naturally comes before the others. The Named Pipes protocol is built on SPX, so it comes after. You must preserve the order in which these statements appear in CONFIG.PST when you cut and paste them into CONFIG.SYS. The most obvious approach is to leave these statements alone, except for removing the appropriate REM statements.

Default Directories

During the installation of the NetWare Requester, you were asked to select directories in which to place the various Requester files. That discussion mentioned default search paths which OS/2 uses, and changes needed to CONFIG.SYS if the C:\NETWARE directory were chosen. In order to help you understand these default paths, we will discuss here what those paths are, what portions of the Requester are affected by them, and how to update them in the CONFIG.SYS file.

There are two OS/2 environment paths which you should be concerned about: DPATH and LIBPATH.

DPATH

This is the search path used by OS/2 to find data files. Whenever a program attempts to access a data file, OS/2 looks through this path for the file. It will use the first occurrence of the file name it finds along the path. The default DPATH command in CONFIG.SYS is the same as PATH. The Message files are the part of the Requester which will be affected by this search path. If you installed the Messages into the C:\NETWARE directory, you should change DPATH as indicated below:

```
SET DPATH=C:\OS2;C:\OS2\SYSTEM;C:\OS2\INSTALL;C:\;C:\NETWARE
```

LIBPATH

This is the search path which OS/2 uses to locate libraries. All the OS/2 Dynamic Link Libraries (DLLs) are in the directory C:\OS2\DLL, so the default LIBPATH contains only this directory. If you installed the Requester DLLs into this directory, no change to CONFIG.SYS is needed. If you installed the Requester DLLs into C:\NETWARE, then you should add this directory to LIBPATH. The CONFIG.SYS entry would then be:

```
LIBPATH=C:\OS2\DLL;C:\NETWARE
```

Notice that the command to set the LIBPATH does not include the word "SET." This is not a typo, and the command must appear as indicated or OS/2 will not even boot.

You should note that in either of the cases discussed, you must add C:\NETWARE to these paths if you installed the Requester there. If you used other directory options during installation, you won't need to actually change either of these.

Other Environment Issues

We have talked about CONFIG.SYS, an important tool in configuring the environment on an OS/2 workstation. This file also exists in the DOS world, and should be somewhat familiar to you already. Three other OS/2 system files help tailor your environment: AUTOEXEC.BAT, STARTUP.CMD, and OS2INIT.CMD. These three files are discussed in the following sections. A fourth file, NET.CFG, allows you to reconfigure the Requester, and is discussed in the following chapter.

Setting Up AUTOEXEC.BAT

The AUTOEXEC.BAT file is familiar to most users of DOS. It is a batch file which executes as soon as DOS loads. On an OS/2 workstation it has a very specific purpose, one perfectly analogous to its function under DOS. AUTOEXEC.BAT executes in the DOS compatibility box the very first time the DOS box is entered after the workstation boots. As far as networks are concerned, this file has very little practical value, but you should at least understand it as part of the workstation environment. To the extent that you can access network drives from the DOS box, some DOS environment variables (like PATH) could be affected.

Setting Up STARTUP.CMD

Under OS/2, any file ending with the extension .CMD is a batch file. The .CMD extension (CoMmanD) differentiates OS/2 batch files from DOS batch files on the same hard disk. STARTUP.CMD is to OS/2 what AUTOEXEC.BAT is to DOS. As soon as the OS/2 workstation boots, OS/2 executes STARTUP.CMD in a windowed command prompt. It will be typical for you to place the LOGIN command in this batch file to prompt the user to log in as soon as the system boots. Once having logged in, the user is already logged in from every screen group in the machine, including the DOS box. Any actions which you wish to take place every time the machine boots (but not every time a new screen group is created) should go into STARTUP.CMD. If you wish the windowed command prompt to go away after having done its duty, include the command "EXIT" as the last command in the file. This will close the window and return you to the Presentation Manager screen.

Setting Up OS2INIT.CMD

OS2INIT.CMD is another in a series of useful "do-this-once" batch files available in OS/2. This one executes each time a screen group is created, so long as the PROTSHELL command in CONFIG.SYS includes the /K option. The actions taken under OS2INIT.CMD pertain only to the session under which the batch file was executed, and go away with the session when it is closed.

Installing Utilities

If you are a system administrator maintaining a Novell network with both DOS and OS/2 workstations, you will have to deal with the differences between DOS and OS/2 utilities for NetWare, both of which will probably be installed on the same file server. As a default, the DOS utilities are always stored on a file server in SYS:LOGIN, SYS:PUBLIC, and SYS:SYSTEM. Since the names of DOS and OS/2 utilities are the same, you cannot put the OS/2 utilities in the standard places in these volumes. To get around this conflict, you should create OS/2 directories in SYS:LOGIN and SYS:PUBLIC.

The NetWare Requester provides a utility installation program, SERVINST.CMD, which places the OS/2 utilities into the OS/2 directories in these two places. (SERVINST can be run from either OS/2 or DOS.) Before running SERVINST.CMD, you should map drive L to SYS:LOGIN/OS2, and drive P to SYS:PUBLIC/OS2. SERVINST is located on the PUBLIC1 diskette in version 1.1 and on the OS2UTIL-1 diskette in version 1.2. It will take you through loading the utilities from both diskettes into the appropriate directories on the file server. In particular, SERVINST places ATTACH, LOGIN, MAP, and SLIST in SYS:LOGIN/OS2, while placing all other utilities into SYS:PUBLIC/OS2. Figure 5 shows the steps you would take to do this from the OS/2 Command Prompt.

The OS/2 utilities must be installed on the very first file server to which an OS/2 workstation attaches. (This is the default attachment which occurs when your workstation boots up.) Without the OS/2 NetWare utilities available in the L: drive of the OS/2 workstation, that workstation cannot log in to a file server. If you always know which file server will be the first that the OS/2 workstation will attach to, install the OS/2 NetWare utilities on that file server. (You can only guarantee attachment to a single file server if there is only one file server on the same wire with your workstation. It will attach first to that file server whether it is the only file server on the net, or even if that file server then bridges to an internetwork.)

When there is more than one file server on the same wire with your workstation, you can never be sure which file server the OS/2 workstation will see first. In this case, either install the OS/2 utilities on every file server to which you might attach, or place the key OS/2 NetWare utilities, such as ATTACH, LOGIN, MAP, and SLIST, on the workstation hard disk in a directory that will be seen by the workstation's search path. This will allow you to work around the inconvenience which would occur each time the OS/2 workstation found itself attached to a file server without the OS/2 NetWare utilities.

Figure 5
Steps to install OS/2 utilities on a file server.

```
C:> A:
A:> MAP L:=FSERVER/SYS:LOGIN/OS2
A:> MAP P:=FSERVER/SYS:PUBLIC/OS2
A:> SERVINST
```

14 Reconfiguring the Requester with NET.CFG

NET.CFG is a configuration file, provided by the Requester, which allows you to tailor the NetWare Requester to your particular workstation environment. NET.CFG is examined by the Requester as soon as it loads, and it allows you to reconfigure various parts of the Requester.

To use the configuration options, create NET.CFG as a text file in the root directory of your hard disk. You can include any of the commands available under each heading. Where no explicit command is given (or where no NET.CFG is present) the Requester uses default values.

There are a couple of tricks in setting up NET.CFG that you should keep in mind. There are a variety of functional categories available within NET.CFG, and each category is indicated to the Requester by the presence of a header, occurring at the very beginning of a line, with no leading blanks or tabs. Specific commands under this header follow immediately after, and must have at least one leading blank or tab. The commands within NET.CFG are not case-sensitive.

There are seven major categories in which you can reconfigure the Requester: Link Support, Protocol Stack IPX, Protocol Stack SPX, NetWare Requester, Link Driver, NetWare NetBIOS, and NetWare Spooler. The following sections discuss each of these categories.

Link Support

This option allows you to reconfigure the number of buffers used in the Link Support Layer (LSL) as well as the size of those buffers. The syntax is:

```
Link Support
     Buffers count [buffer size]
```

You can use any values you wish when setting the number and size of buffers, so long as the total space occupied by all buffers (*count* times *buffer size*) is less than or equal to 64KB. While *count* must be given, *buffer size* is optional. If *buffer size* is ignored, the default buffer size of 1,130 bytes is used with the new count. When no Link Support option is indicated in NET.CFG, the default is 20 buffers of 1,130 bytes each (or 22KB).

Examples of Link Support configurations are:

```
Link Support
        Buffers 30 2000
```

This configuration would yield 60,000 bytes of buffer space (30 buffers at 2,000 bytes each).

```
Link Support
        Buffers 30
```

This configuration would yield 33,900 bytes of buffer space (30 buffers at a default size of 1,130 bytes each).

Protocol Stack IPX

Three options are available to reconfigure the IPX protocol stack: Sockets, Router Mem, and Bind. These are described below.

Sockets

This option sets the number of sockets which IPX can have open on the OS/2 workstation. The syntax is:

```
Protocol Stack IPX
        Sockets count
```

The default number of sockets available is 64, which is also the maximum. This means that the actual available number of IPX sockets can only be lowered, not raised.

Router Mem

The Requester includes a small local router. This router concerns itself only with issues pertinent to the local workstation. For example, if an application performs a Get Local Target operation, the router within the Requester will attempt to find the shortest path. However, it will not function for other workstations the way NetWare routers and bridges do.

This option affects the size of the router memory pool. The router memory pool is the amount of memory used for local router tables. It is influenced by the number of cards in the workstation. The syntax is:

```
Protocol Stack IPX
        Router Mem size
```

The default size is 450 bytes, which is also the minimum. For a typical OS/2 workstation (even one with more than one card), this value should not have to change. In an unusual situation with a bus extender and many LAN cards, this value may have to be increased.

Bind

This last option available for the IPX protocol stack is used when there is more than one board installed in the workstation. Using the Bind option allows you to indicate which board is the primary board. It does this by creating a logical link between the IPX protocol stack and the LAN card driver indicated. In the future, when other protocol stacks are available, a user will be able to bind different protocol stacks to different drivers using this option. If you don't use this option, the default is whichever driver was loaded first in the CONFIG.SYS file. The syntax is:

```
Protocol Stack IPX
        Bind name
```

The parameter name should be replaced with the name of one of the thirteen supported board drivers. The parameter names are listed in Table 13, together with the boards to which they refer.

Summary

The following is an example of how you might alter all of the available IPX protocol stack options in a NET.CFG file:

```
Protocol Stack IPX
        Sockets 32
        Router Mem 600
        Bind NE2000
```

Protocol Stack SPX

There are six configurable options for the SPX protocol stack: Sockets, Sessions, Abort Timeout, Verify Timeout, Listen Timeout, and Retry Count. These are described in the sections which follow.

Sockets

This option allows you to set the number of SPX sockets available on the OS/2 workstation. The syntax is:

```
Protocol Stack SPX
        Sockets count
```

The default number of SPX sockets is 16, with a minimum value of 8, and a maximum of 64. Remember that since SPX sits on IPX, every time you open an SPX socket, an IPX socket is also used. These two socket values should therefore be the same.

Sessions

This option allows you to alter the number of SPX connections your work-station can support at any given time. The syntax is:

```
Protocol Stack SPX
        Sessions count
```

The default number of connections is 16, with a minimum number of 8, and a maximum of 256.

Abort Timeout

This option affects the number of milliseconds SPX waits without response from a connection before terminating the connection. The syntax is:

```
Protocol Stack SPX
        SPX Abort timeout = number
```

The default timeout number is 30,000 milliseconds (30 seconds), with a minimum value of 10 milliseconds. You can set this value as large as you wish.

Verify Timeout

This option allows you to adjust the time that SPX will wait before sending a packet to the other side of the connection to see if the other partner is still there. The syntax is:

```
Protocol Stack SPX
        SPX Verify Timeout = number
```

The default value for timeout verification is 3,000 milliseconds (3 seconds), with the minimum being 10 milliseconds. Again the value may be as large as you want.

Listen Timeout

When SPX doesn't hear from the other side of a connection for a certain amount of time, it will send a packet demanding acknowledgment. This next option allows you to adjust the time which passes before SPX sends such a packet. The syntax is:

```
Protocol Stack SPX
        SPX Listen Timeout = number
```

The default value for a listen timeout is 6,000 milliseconds (6 seconds), with the minimum again being 10 milliseconds. This number may be as large as you wish.

Retry Count

When an SPX packet is not acknowledged by the other side of the connection, SPX will send another copy of the same packet. This last option allows you to change the default number of times SPX will try and send a packet before giving up. The syntax is:

```
Protocol Stack SPX
        SPX Retry Count = number
```

The default number of retries is 20, with a minimum number of 1 and a maximum of 255. Keep in mind that the value you configure here represents the default value presented to the actual SPX session. Any program writing to SPX may change this value on the fly, for the purpose of that session only, using the SPX function calls.

Summary

The following is an example of how you might alter the SPX protocol stack options in NET.CFG:

```
Protocol Stack SPX
        Sockets 32
        Sessions 32
        SPX Abort Timeout = 20000
        SPX Verify Timeout = 2000
        SPX Listen Timeout = 3000
        SPX Retry Count = 40
```

NetWare Requester

Three options allow you to configure the Requester itself: Cache Buffers, Sessions, and Request Retries.

Cache Buffers

This option affects the number of buffers which the Requester uses for local caching of open file data. The syntax is:

```
NetWare Requester
        Cache Buffers count
```

While the number of buffers can be altered, the size of these buffers is fixed. The actual size of the buffers is determined by the maximum packet size of the card installed in the machine. The number of buffers can vary, so long as the total memory used is within 64KB. For example, if the topology you were using had a maximum packet size of 4KB (such as Token-Ring), you could change *count* to as much as 16. If the maximum packet size of the card is smaller, *count* could be larger. The default number of cache buffers is 8.

Sessions

This option determines the maximum number of file server connections available at one time. The syntax is:

```
NetWare Requester
        Sessions count
```

The default number of file server connections is 8 (the minimum number allowed), and the maximum is 20.

Request Retries

This last option lets you determine the number of times the workstation will resend a packet following a communication error. If your network is prone to losing packets, increasing this value may help; however, other network functions will then experience a performance degradation. The syntax is:

```
NetWare Requester
        Request Retries count
```

The default number of retries is 20, with a minimum of 5 allowed. You may set this number as high as you want.

Summary

The following is an example of how you might reconfigure some of the Requester options using the NET.CFG:

```
NetWare Requester
        Cache Buffers 10
        Sessions 16
        Request Retries 10
```

Link Driver

The Link Driver options are different from the other NET.CFG options in that the header itself takes a parameter. The syntax is:

```
Link Driver name
```

In this header, *name* is the name of a network interface board, as indicated in Table 13. Any options listed beneath this header pertain to the board indicated in the header. You may also include this header more than once for different boards in your machine, but there must be a separate header each time, and the options below each header will pertain only to that network interface board. Keep in mind that even if you have more than one of the same type of board (for example, two NE2000 boards) in your machine, you will use the Link Driver header once for each board in the machine, even if each occurrence of the line looks exactly like the previous one. The Requester will look at each board in the machine as it sees each Link Driver header.

For each Link Driver header, there are six different options available which affect the way the device drivers interact with the network interface boards. These options are DMA, Int, Mem, Port, PS/2 Slot, and Envelope Type. Most of these options allow the driver to know what settings have been on made on the board itself. While most of these options are not necessary on a PS/2, where intelligent boards are able to communicate their settings to the rest of the system, the first four options (DMA, Int, Mem, and Port) will be typically used with AT-bus machines where the boards do not have the same ability to communicate. They will also be used on PS/2 machines when multiple boards of the same type are present, allowing the Requester to distinguish between like boards based upon board settings. PS/2 Slot will be used exclusively with PS/2 machines (not surprisingly). Envelope Type is independent of hardware platform.

DMA

If you have a network interface board that supports two DMA channels, this option is your method of informing the Requester of which DMA channel to use in place of the defaults. You may reconfigure one or both channels in the same statement. The syntax of this option is:

```
Link Driver name
        DMA [#1|#2] channel
```
or
```
Link Driver name
        DMA #1 channel
        DMA #2 channel
```

When you reconfigure only channel #1, you need not include the number, since it is assumed as a default. The statements:

```
Link Driver name
        DMA #1 4
```
and
```
Link Driver name
        DMA 4
```

have exactly the same effect. In either case, DMA channel 4 will be used by the network interface board device driver in place of DMA channel 1. If you configure both DMA channels, you must indicate both #1 and #2. Below is an example of changing both DMA channels in the same statement.

```
Link Driver name
        DMA #1 4
        DMA #2 3
```

Int

This option works much like the DMA option. It allows you to tell the Requester which IRQ lines the network interface board will be using instead of the defaults. The syntax is as follows:

```
Link Driver name
        Int [#1|#2] IRQ
```

or

```
Link Driver name
        Int #1 IRQ
        Int #2 IRQ
```

When you reconfigure only IRQ #1, you need not include the number since it is assumed as a default. The statements:

```
Link Driver name
        Int #1 3
```

and

```
Link Driver name
        Int 3
```

have exactly the same effect. In either case, IRQ 3 will be used by the network interface board device driver in place of the default for IRQ line 1. If you configure both IRQ lines, you must indicate both #1 and #2. Below is an example of changing both IRQ lines in the same statement.

```
Link Driver name
        Int #1 3
        Int #2 2
```

Mem

If you have configured your network interface board for a memory range other than the default, this option allows you to inform the Requester, so the board device driver can correctly interface with the board. The syntax is:

```
Link Driver name
        Mem [#1 | #2] starting_address size
```

The *starting_address* should be the physical address in memory, in hexadecimal notation. The size is the number of paragraphs which make up the memory area. For example, if the memory range of the board is from C000 to C400, *starting_address* will be C000, and size will be 400. The following gives an example using these values:

```
Link Driver name
        Mem C000 400
```

If your LAN board has shared memory (either RAM or ROM) and you wish to configure one or both, you can do so by indicating either #1 or #2, depending on the way in which your board treats shared memory. The LAN board documentation is your only source to know whether #1 or #2 means RAM or ROM for the particular board. Where a board has only one (either RAM or ROM) but not both, there is no need to indicate a number (#1 or #2).

Port

Where there are a number of I/O ports available on your network board, this option allows you to tell the Requester what the appropriate range of ports is. The syntax is:

```
Link Driver name
        Port [#1 | #2] starting_port count
```

If you have a board with multiple ports available (#1 and #2), the same rules apply as for Int and DMA in using these to change one or two default values. The *starting_point* is the hexadecimal value of the starting I/O port. The *count* indicates the number of I/O ports in the range. In the following example, the first I/O port available on the board is 0400, and there are 32 I/O ports available.

```
Link Driver name
        Port #2 0400 32
```

PS/2 Slot

This option comes into play only when you have more than one network interface board of the same type in a PS/2 machine. For example, if you install two NE/2 boards in a PS/2 workstation, use this option to tell the Requester where the two boards are. The actual lines from NET.CFG would look like this:

```
Link Driver NE2
        PS/2 Slot 4
Link Driver NE2
        PS/2 Slot 1
```

The board which first appears in the NET.CFG file will be the primary board recognized by the Requester. Keep in mind that the PS/2 machine will still search the slots and find all of the boards installed even without this option. Without this option the Requester would determine the primary board on its own.

Send Retries

This option allows you to instruct the network board driver how many times to resend a packet following an error. Do not confuse this with other retry values previously mentioned for the Requester or SPX. This value concerns only the particular device driver associated with a LAN board. The syntax is:

```
Link Driver name
        Send Retries count
```

The default value is established by the individual device drivers. For example, if you want to set the device driver retry count to 16, place the following in the NET.CFG:

```
Link Driver name
        Send Retries 16
```

Envelope Type

Some network interface boards support multiple media types. This option allows you to specify the media type to be used with the board. Table 14 lists the possible media types supported by this option. The syntax is:

```
Link Driver name
        Envelope Type name
```

The media type, indicated by name, must be given exactly as listed in Table 14 to be recognized. An example of this option implemented in NET.CFG is:

```
Link Driver NE2000
        Envelope Type ETHERNET_II
```

Summary

The following gives an example of using all of the Link Driver options in a single NET.CFG. It assumes a single board is installed in the machine.

```
Link Driver NE2000
        DMA #1 4
        DMA #2 3
        Int #1 3
        Int #2 2
        Mem C000 400
        Port #2 0400 32
        Send Retries 16
        Envelope Type ETHERNET_II
```

NetWare NetBIOS

Just as IPX and SPX have configurable options, NetBIOS has analogous options. The eleven configuration options available for NetBIOS are Sessions, Commands, Send Buffers, Retry Count, Retry Delay, NetBIOS Internet, Broadcast Count, Broadcast Delay, Abort Timeout, Verify Timeout, and Listen Timeout. Descriptions of each of these options follow.

Sessions

This option allows you to set the number of NetBIOS sessions allowed at one time. The syntax is:

```
NetWare NetBIOS
        Sessions count
```

The default number of sessions is 32, with the minimum allowed being 4 and the maximum being 128.

Commands and Send Buffers

These two options are somewhat interrelated, and so will be discussed together. Commands allows you to change the number of NCBs which may be posted at any given time; Send Buffers allows you to change the number of ECBs posted at any given time. The syntax is:

```
NetWare NetBIOS
        Send Buffers = number
        Commands = number
```

Each posting of an NCB in NetBIOS will always result in the posting of an ECB. For this reason NetBIOS will take the larger of the two values and use it for both. In other words, if you set Send Buffers to 20 and Commands to 18, NetBIOS will set each of them internally to 20. The default number of both Commands and Send Buffers is 12, with a minimum of 4 and a maximum of 128.

Retry Count

This option indicates the number of times NetBIOS should resend a request to establish a connection. The syntax is:

```
NctWare NetBIOS
        Retry Count = number
```

The default Retry Count is 20, with no limit on either minimum or maximum.

Retry Delay

Since NetBIOS provides guaranteed delivery, it will resend packets when there is a problem. This option allows you to determine the amount of time between packet resends. The syntax is:

```
NetWare NetBIOS
        Retry Delay = number
```

The actual number of times NetBIOS will resend a packet is determined by the value that is used by IPX. It will either use the IPX default, or the new number given through the IPX options described earlier in this section. The time given as *number* must be specified in milliseconds. The default Retry Delay is 500 milliseconds (1/2 second), with the minimum delay being 1 millisecond and the maximum being 65,535 milliseconds (65.5 seconds).

NetBIOS Internet

When NetBIOS does broadcasts, it has the option of broadcasting either to the internet or to the local network. With Internet ON (the default), help will be sought from bridges and routers to allow broadcast packets to move across the internet. With Internet OFF, no such help is solicited. This option allows you to toggle between the two. The syntax is:

```
NetWare NetBIOS
     NetBIOS Internet ON|OFF
```

Broadcast Count

This option allows you to determine the number of times NetBIOS will resend a packet when doing a broadcast. NetBIOS broadcasts occur when doing a name claim (generated by adding a name) or name query (generated by establishing a connection), or when sending a broadcast datagram. The syntax is:

```
NetWare NetBIOS
     Broadcast Count number
```

The default Broadcast Count is 4 when the Internet option is ON and 2 when it is OFF. There is no limit to either the minimum or maximum value you can set.

Broadcast Delay

This option allows you to determine the amount of time NetBIOS will wait before resending a broadcast packet. The syntax is:

```
NetWare NetBIOS
     Broadcast Delay number
```

The default Broadcast Delay is 2000 milliseconds when the Internet option is ON and 1000 milliseconds when Internet is OFF. There is no limit to the minimum and maximum.

Abort Timeout

This option allows you to change the amount of time NetBIOS will wait without response from the other side before it terminates a session. The syntax is:

```
NetWare NetBIOS
     Abort Timeout = number
```

The time value indicated by *number* must be in milliseconds. The default timeout value is 30,000 milliseconds (30 seconds), with a minimum of 1 millisecond and no limit on the maximum.

Verify Timeout

Whether or not there are packets being sent by NetBIOS applications, each side of a NetBIOS session regularly sends packets to the other to assure its partner that it is still alive. This option allows you to vary the amount of time that the NetBIOS session will wait between sending these packets to its partner. The syntax is:

```
NetWare NetBIOS
     Verify Timeout number
```

The amount of time, indicated by number, must be given in milliseconds. The default timeout value is 3,000 milliseconds (3 seconds), with the minimum being 1 millisecond and the maximum being 65,535 milliseconds (65.5 seconds).

Listen Timeout

When one side of a NetBIOS session does not receive packets from the other in a certain time period, it will send a packet requesting an acknowledgement that the partner is still alive and kicking. This option allows you to vary the amount of time that the NetBIOS session will wait without packets from the other side before sending a request for acknowledgement. The syntax is:

```
NetWare NetBIOS
        Listen Timeout = number
```

The amount of time, indicated by *number*, must be given in milliseconds. The default timeout value is 3,000 milliseconds (3 seconds), with a minimum of 1 millisecond and a maximum of 65,535 milliseconds (65.5 seconds).

Summary

The following example illustrates the NetBIOS options being used together in a NET.CFG file.

```
NetWare NetBIOS
        Sessions 128
        Send Buffers = 50
        Retry Delay = 30000
        Abort Timeout = 60000
        Verify Timeout = 5000
        Listen Timeout = 5000
```

Reconfiguring the Spooler

For sending print jobs to a network printer, NetWare allows you to specify options that affect the way your job is printed. Through the NET.CFG file, you can set up defaults that will affect any job sent from the OS/2 workstation to a network printer. As with the other NET.CFG options, there must be a header included. In this case it is:

```
NetWare Spooler
```

This header is followed by any number of the options and parameters described below. Remember that since these options are configured at load time, they will remain the defaults during the entire time you are logged in to the network. You will want to seriously consider, for example, whether you really want two copies of every document you print during your day. Only those options which will be real defaults for you should be configured here. The sections which follow outline the available options, together with a brief description of each.

Four of the options below do nothing but set the default, and are therefore completely redundant, since the default will be set without them. They are Keep, Tabs, Banner, and Form Feed.

Form

Where the network printer supports multiple forms, this allows you to determine which form to print on. The syntax is:

```
NetWare Spooler
        Form number
```

Replace *number* with the form number on the network printer. The default value is 0.

Copies

This option allows you to determine the number of copies to print each time a job is printed at the network printer. The syntax is:

```
NetWare Spooler
        Copies number
```

You should indicate the number of copies to print as a default by replacing number with the number of copies. Not surprisingly, the default is 1.

Keep

This option allows you to always continue printing, even when a capture is interrupted. The syntax is:

```
NetWare Spooler
        Keep
```

There is no parameter to give here, and the default is Keep enabled.

No Keep

This option allows you to disable the default Keep enabled indicated in the previous option. The syntax is:

```
NetWare Spooler
        No Keep
```

Size

This option allows you to set the default tab size used by the printer, or in other words, the number of spaces to use when replacing tabs. The syntax is:

```
NetWare Spooler
        Size number
```

You should replace *number* with the number of spaces per tab. The default number is 8.

Tabs

With Tabs enabled, the Spooler will replace tabs with spaces, as determined by either the default or the amount designated in the Size option. This option allows you to enable this replacing of tabs with spaces. The default is No Tabs. The syntax is:

```
NetWare Spooler
        Tabs
```

No Tabs

This default option is the opposite of Tabs, turning off the translation of tabs into spaces by the Spooler.

```
NetWare Spooler
        No Tabs
```

File and Name

Jobs printed by the Spooler appear by default with a banner as the leading page of the printout. Among other information, this banner contains two fields called **File** and **Name**, which typically contain the name of the file being printed and the name of the user doing the printing. These two options allow you to determine exactly what strings will appear in these fields in the banner. The syntax is:

```
NetWare Spooler
        File string
        Name string
```

As an example of where these fields might come in handy, let's assume that you are user John Smith, with a file called BIND001.C (containing a bindery access program). By default, the banner will contain JSMITH as the user name, and BIND001.C as the file name. However, you can change to banner to something that will be more meaningful to you after you have saved the printout of the code for future reference. You could place the following lines in NET.CFG:

```
NetWare Spooler
        File Bindery
        Name John Smith
```

With a more friendly banner in your permanent source code record, it should be easier in the future to quickly see what a printout contains.

Banner

This option allows you to inform the Spooler to print a banner. The default is Banner enabled.

```
NetWare Spooler
        Banner
```

No Banner

This option is the opposite of Banner, allowing you to suppress the printing of a banner by the Spooler. As with Banner, no parameter is expected. The default is Banner enabled. The syntax is:

```
NetWare Spooler
        No Banner
```

FF or Form Feed

When jobs are printed on a network printer, there is a default form feed which follows the job. This option allows you to enable the Form Feed option. The default is Form Feed enabled. The syntax is:

```
NetWare Spooler
        FF
```

or

```
NetWare Spooler
        Form Feed
```

No Form Feed

This option is the opposite of FF or Form Feed. It allows you to turn off the default form feed after jobs. The syntax is:

```
NetWare Spooler
        No Form Feed
```

MaxSetup and MaxReset

Most printers require strings of information to be sent before and after print jobs to help it perform its task of printing. The strings sent to prepare a printer are referred to as setup strings, while the those which follow the print job restore the printer to its prior state and are referred to as reset strings. Typically the length of these setup and reset strings is fairly short. With most printers, this option should not have to be manipulated. However, some printers (such as PostScript printers) may require rather lengthy setup and reset strings. These two options allow you to set the maximum length of the printer setup and reset strings. The syntax is:

```
NetWare Spooler
        MaxSetup number
        MaxReset number
```

The default *number* is 256; the maximum is limited only by memory.

Summary

The following example illustrates configuring the NetWare Spooler with several of the options:

```
NetWare Spooler
        Copies 2
        Tabs 4
        No Banner
```

Table 13
Valid Parameters

The following are all of the valid parameters available with the Bind option of reconfiguring the IPX protocol stack in NET.CFG.

PCN2	IBM PC Network Adapter II and II/A
RXNET	Novell RX-Net
RXNET2	Novell RX-Net/2
NE2	Novell Ethernct NE/2
NE2-32	Novell Ethernet NE/2-32
NE1000	Novell Ethernet NE1000
NE2000	Novell Ethernet NE2000
TOKEN	IBM Token-Ring PC Adapter
TOKENEE	IBM Token-Ring PC Adapter using Communication Manager
3C501	3Com EtherLink Series 501
3C503	3Com EtherLink Series 503
3C505	3Com EtherLink Series 505
3C523	3Com EtherLink Series 523

Table 14
Valid Media Types

The following is a list of valid media types that can be used with the NET.CFG Envelope Type option for the Link Driver Header.

VIRTUAL_LAN	This is used where no media type is necessary.
LOCALTALK	This is the Apple LocalTalk media type.
ETHERNET_II	This is Ethernet using a DEC Ethernet II envelope.
ETHERNET_802.2	This is Ethernet (802.3) using an 802.2 envelope.
IBM_TOKEN-RING	This is Token Ring media type (802.5 envelope, and 802.5 with 802.3 envelope).
ETHERNET_802.3	This is Ethernet with 802.3 envelope type.
802.4	This is token passing bus envelope, such as ARCnet.
NOVELL_PCN2	This is Novell's PC Network 2 envelope.

15 Troubleshooting Your OS/2 Workstation

In the previous six chapters in this section of the book, we have presented concepts, principles, and information concerning all aspects of setting up and maintaining an OS/2 workstation. In this chapter, we have compiled some of the most common problems across all aspects of maintaining an OS/2 workstation. Once you have understood the concepts and information presented in the previous chapters, you can refer to this chapter as a resource should certain problems arise.

Troubleshooting Hardware

Using a DIX connector on 3Com EtherLink

If you are using a DIX connector with a 3C503 card, you need to alter the line in CONFIG.SYS to reflect this. Add the statement "1=DIX" after the 3C503 line in CONFIG.SYS. The line will then look like:

```
device=c:\netware\3c503.sys 1=DIX
```

Running Communication Manager with Token-Ring

There is a natural interrupt conflict between the Token-Ring Driver and the Communication Manager. For this reason, Novell has provided a Token-Ring Driver (called TOKENEE.SYS) which avoids this conflict. In order to run Communication Manager concurrently with a Token-Ring driver, load TOKENEE.SYS instead of TOKEN.SYS in the CONFIG.SYS file. Enable the following line in CONFIG.SYS by removing the "rem" from the beginning of the line:

```
rem device=c:\netware\tokenee.sys
```

Using Source Routing

Both TOKEN.SYS and TOKENEE.SYS support source routing. If you are going to use source routing, the following conditions must first be met: All workstations on the same ring as an IBM Token-Ring Network bridge must have source routing installed; file servers and bridges must be running source routing; all servers and bridges connected through an IBM Token-Ring bridge must be using the same address.

Once these conditions are met, actually installing source routing on the workstation is a simple process. Add "1=source" to the Token-Ring installation line in the CONFIG.SYS with either TOKEN.SYS or TOKENEE.SYS:

```
device=c:\netware\token.sys 1=source
```

or

```
device=c:\netware\tokenee.sys 1=source
```

If you have more than one board installed in the workstation, you can indicate either "1=source" or "2=source" depending upon which board you wish to support source routing. Keep in mind that the primary will be card 1, while the other card will be card 2. Since you may not know which card will be the primary card, you may want to use the PS/2 Slot option in NET.CFG to identify which card will become the primary card to the Requester.

Troubleshooting the OS/2 Environment

Private and Global Options

The NetWare Requester version 1.1 supported private and global connections. By attaching privately from one session on an OS/2 workstation, the connection could not be seen by other sessions on the same machine. Only by attaching globally could other sessions share the connection. There were some very practical uses for this option under OS/2 version 1.1, but the 1.2 NetWare Requester does not support private and global options. Any attempts to perform actions privately will default back to global. In an attempt at compatibility, the OS/2 NetWare utilities still accept the /PRIVATE parameter, but simply ignore it.

NetWare OS/2 Error Codes

Occasionally a NetWare utility will fail for some mysterious reason, and will spew forth a message containing an error code. In and of itself this type of information is utterly meaningless, but if you understand what the code means, it can at least point you at the probable source of the problem. Appendix C contains a complete list of the error codes returned by the NetWare Requester for OS/2 and their meanings. While some of the descriptions are clearer than others, they might at least point you in the right direction.

Section 3

The Macintosh and NetWare

16 Macintosh Theory of Operations in a DOS Context

When it comes to Macintosh networking, one of the most critical concerns is getting Macintoshes to interoperate with PCs. To the network manager whose default environment is DOS, Macs and PCs appear to have more differences than similarities. However, many differences between the two environments are superficial.

Looking first at the functionality of the Macintosh environment, rather than emphasizing differences in the Mac's technical implementation of functions, makes it possible to draw an analogy between the networking functions of the Mac environment and those of the PC. Drawing such an analogy gives the network manager a conceptual framework of how Macs work, and how Macs and PCs can interoperate on the same LAN.

A conceptual framework of how the Macintosh works is essential to good Macintosh troubleshooting skills. While the Mac's user interface may seem simpler and more intuitive than the DOS shell, the Mac's inner workings are complex; consequently, problems can be more difficult to isolate.

To help you gain a conceptual understanding of the Macintosh, this chapter covers first the Macintosh environment, including the System, Finder, Chooser, and Control Panel. Next, the chapter discusses LocalTalk, EtherTalk, and AppleTalk, the Mac's own networking protocols. The chapter next discusses file transfers and applications that perform file conversions. Finally, this chapter discusses distributed applications in the context of Macintosh history.

The Macintosh Operating System

While some features of the Macintosh are not analogous to those of the PC in a strict technical sense, I will generalize the differences in order to emphasize functional similarities between the two environments. The Macintosh operating system (formally named "System") has dynamic memory capabilities and is an extensible OS, meaning that programs can link additional features to the Mac OS at run time.

The Macintosh OS accomplishes dynamic memory through a group of operating system routines collectively known as the Memory Manager. The Memory Manager interacts with Macintosh applications software using a comprehensive API, the actual code of which resides in the Mac's ROM. When an application requests a block of memory from the OS, the Memory Manager allocates a block of memory and passes a memory handle to the application. A memory handle is actually a pointer to a pointer that contains the actual address of allocated memory.

When the application needs access to the allocated memory, it makes a call to the handle—not the pointer—for all memory operations. The Memory Manager intercepts the application's memory call and maps that call from the handle to the pointer. This is crucial because, while the address contained in the pointer may change, the handle stays the same until the application releases it.

The low-level double indirection accomplished by the handle and the pointer make it possible for the Macintosh OS to maintain a dynamic heap of memory. This makes it possible, for example, to load and unload Desk Accessories from memory during the execution of another program. Some applications maintain dynamic buffers and caches that improve performance, but flush those objects when the space is needed for data. The Macintosh OS itself uses its dynamic memory capabilities in scores of situations for scores of different functions.

The important thing to note about the Memory Manager is that applications and the OS have, in effect, equal access to its API. Macintosh applications that use the Memory Manager to effect virtual memory are common, in spite of the fact that version 6.x of the Operating System doesn't provide for virtual memory.

In summary, the Macintosh OS can address memory in a linear fashion, and does not suffer from the 64KB memory segmentation of DOS. (DOS' segmented memory model is the source of the hated 640KB barrier.) Currently, the unmodified Mac OS can address up to 16MB of contiguous RAM. The Mac OS allocates and deallocates memory according to requests made by applications running on the machine. From a network management standpoint, then, RAM conservation is not an issue for most Macs.

The fact that the Mac OS is extensible means that you can bind external functions and code segments to the OS at run time. There are two standard types of files that you can bind to the OS at run time: Initialization routines (INITs) and Control Devices (CDEVs). INITs typically add to the Mac OS features that are transparent to the user, while CDEVs are external functions that users can call in the same manner in which they call standard OS functions.

For example, one INIT replaces the standard Macintosh "beep" with a different sound; One CDEV replaces the standard Macintosh dialog box for opening files with a more powerful dialog box.

To use INITs or CDEVs, simply place those files in the same directory as the Macintosh OS. This directory, commonly called the "System Folder," is tagged as the directory containing the startup code for the Macintosh. When the Macintosh OS executes, it first searches the system folder for files that request binding. INITs and CDEVs have special headers that identify them as objects for binding to the OS. The OS then automatically binds in those files, and proceeds to boot the Mac.

The role and process of INITs and CDEVs and how they bind to the OS at run time is a critical subject for troubleshooting the Macintosh. Since these objects load into memory before the OS is fully initialized, they do not benefit from the same safeguards as standard applications until after the OS initializes; therefore, they sometimes conflict with each other and prevent the Macintosh from sucessfully booting.

There are several things you can do to track down an offending INIT or CDEV, including removing them all from the system folder and reinstalling them one at a time until the problem reoccurs, at which time you identify the most recently installed object as the offender. However, this process is not quite as simple as it sounds, so look for more information on INITs and CDEVs in the Macintosh troubleshooting chapter.

Macintosh Finder

The Macintosh Finder, which provides the Mac's graphical interface, is probably the most visibly distinctive element of the Mac environment. It is important to note that the Mac OS and the Finder are distinct programs, much like DOS and COMMAND.COM. In fact, most people do not even realize that it is possible to substitute other Macintosh command interfaces for the Finder. In the early days of the Macintosh, Apple shipped a file called the "MiniFinder," which was a less memory-hungry command interface many users loaded in place of the Finder. Some alternative command interfaces today include Power Station (Fifth Generation Systems) and DiskTop (CE Software). Most INITs and CDEVs are provided by third-party software developers and shareware programmers.

From a troubleshooting standpoint, the important thing to remember about the Finder is that it is a separate entity from the OS. It is totally possible to have a corrupt Finder and a perfectly healthy OS (and also the other way around). Figure 1 shows icons for the System, Finder, and a couple of CDEVs.

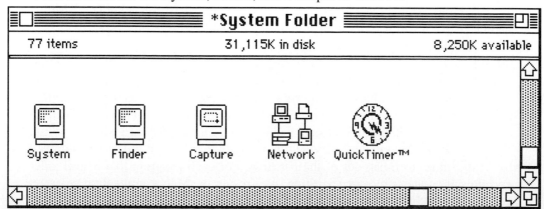

Figure 1: Example of Macintosh icons for the System, Finder, and CDEV files.

MultiFinder

MultiFinder is a program that allows the Mac to do limited multitasking. Under MultiFinder, you can load and run multiple programs concurrently. By default, the first program MultiFinder runs is the Finder. Thus, the Finder still provides the command interface; MultiFinder does not replace the Finder, as many people assume. In most cases, MultiFinder performs serial multitasking: one program stops executing and another program starts. However, MultiFinder has an API for preemptive multitasking, and some applications now can continue running in the background while MultiFinder switches the foreground application.

To run MultiFinder, you must first select the Macintosh volume containing the System. Next, choose "Set Startup" from the Special menu. The Finder will display a dialog box similar to Figure 2.

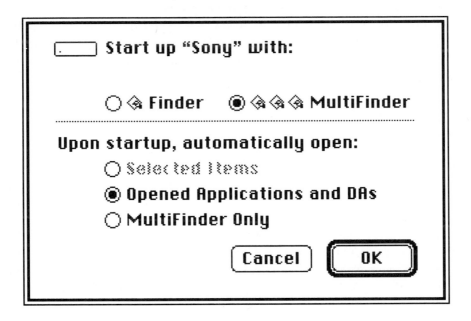

Figure 2: Startup dialog box.

If the "MultiFinder" radio box is darkened, the Mac is set to boot with Multi-Finder. You must restart the machine in order for MultiFinder to be active.

MultiFinder allows each application shared access to the system heap—the portion of RAM that holds the operating system—but otherwise does not allow shared memory. In fact, MultiFinder partially circumvents the Macintosh's dynamic memory capabilities by partioning memory each time it executes an application. For example, if MultiFinder executes Microsoft Word, it will create a partition of memory (512K is the default size) inside which Microsoft Word will run. While Word will have dynamic memory within the 512K partition, it will not be allowed by MultiFinder to break out of the partition. For each program that MultiFinder executes, it creates a memory partition. As a result, the Mac's application heap can become fragmented by MultiFinder. (See Figure 3.)

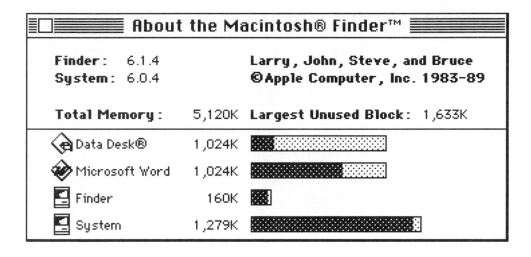

Figure 3: Example of the Macintosh Finder dialog box.

From a troubleshooting standpoint, then, memory fragmentation under MultiFinder is a key problem to look for when Macintosh applications misbehave. From a networking standpoint, however, memory fragmentation is not a concern because the Mac's client software and network drivers reside in the Mac's system memory heap, which is unaffected by MultiFinder.

Desk Accessories

Every Macintosh command interface supports Desk Accessories, special programs you can execute from the "Apple" menu—the menu that is always present in the upper left corner of the Macintosh display. Desk Accessories are analogous to DOS terminate-and-stay-resident programs, except that Desk Accessories do not stay resident. (They have no need to stay resident because of the Mac OS's dynamic memory handling.) You can execute Desk Accessories from within any well-behaved Macintosh application.

Two Desk Accessories are critical to the Mac's ability to connect to a network. These Desk Accessories are the Control Panel and the Chooser. The Control Panel allows you to change OS parameters, including the size of the Mac's built-in data cache, the date and time, the responsiveness of the mouse and keyboard, the display, and so on. The Control Panel also gives you access to each CDEV that is currently bound to the operating system.(See Figure 4.)

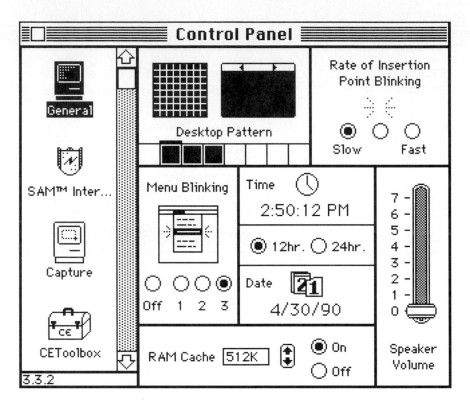

Figure 4: The Macintosh Control Panel.

One thing you use the Control Panel for is selecting a default networking shell. (More on that later.)

The Chooser is a Desk Accessory that allows you to select network devices such as printers, servers, modems, and more. Using AppleShare client software, for example, you log in to file servers using the Chooser. The Chooser also allows you to turn off AppleTalk, select different device drivers, and turn on or off the Mac's built-in print spooler.

LocalTalk and EtherTalk

Every Macintosh has a built-in network interface card that uses a physical-level protocol called LocalTalk. LocalTalk is a relatively slow protocol (230Kbps), but is reliable and inexpensive. You can connect any two Macintoshes with inexpensive twisted-pair connectors, or you can use the slightly-more-expensive LocalTalk cabling system provided by Apple, Farallon, TOPS, and others

Most PC networking vendors that support Macintoshes support LocalTalk. Both 3Com and Novell sell LocalTalk network interface boards you can use in the file server; TOPS sells LocalTalk network interface boards you can use in any PC with an AT bus.

EtherTalk is the Macintosh Ethernet shell that works with Macintosh Ethernet boards. You do not need any shell software to use LocalTalk with the Macintosh, because LocalTalk is part of the Mac OS. To use EtherTalk, you must install the Ethernet network interface board in the Mac, and install the EtherTalk software in the same directory as the Mac OS. After installation, the Mac automatically binds the Ethernet shell into its OS at run time. However, to use EtherTalk, you must explicitly select it, using the Control Panel. (See Figure 5.)

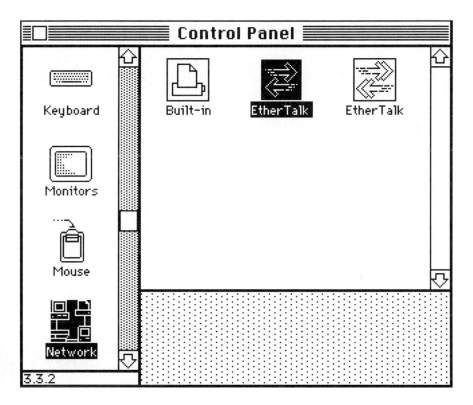

Figure 5: Selecting the network from the Macintosh control panel.

Once you select EtherTalk, the Mac OS assumes that EtherTalk is the default and selects it every time you boot. However, you can switch from EtherTalk to LocalTalk dynamically any time you wish. The Mac uses the last shell you selected as the default when it boots. If you selected Ethertalk most recently, the Mac will boot with Ethertalk; if you selected LocalTalk most recently, the Mac will boot with LocalTalk. Again, you can switch from one shell to another while running applications—you don't need to reboot.

Now that ARCnet and token-ring are available for the Mac, they work in exactly the same way as Ethernet and LocalTalk.

AppleTalk

In the DOS world, there is no entity analogous to AppleTalk. AppleTalk is the Mac's native networking protocol, built into the machine itself and into the Macintosh operating system. What makes AppleTalk different from any DOS-based networking protocol is that AppleTalk is part of every Macintosh ever built, including the very first one to roll off the assembly line. NetBIOS, which some PC users believe is the standard networking protocol for PCs, is not part of DOS per se, nor is it the dominant networking protocol for DOS-based networks. That honor belongs to Novell's IPX/SPX.

AppleTalk is not a single protocol, but rather a suite of protocols. (See Figure 6.) Starting at the bottom, so to speak, the AppleTalk Link Access Protocol (ALAP) provides a standard interface between the AppleTalk protocol suite and the underlying networking hardware (usually a network interface board). Novell's Open Data-link Interface (ODI) was modelled after ALAP, and Apple jointly developed ODI with Novell.

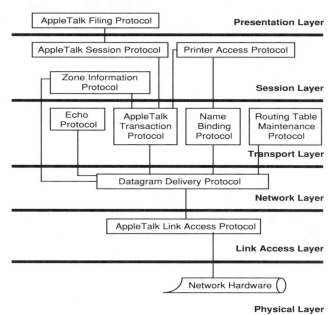

Figure 6: AppleTalk's Protocols and the OSI model.

The next level up from the ALAP is the Datagram Delivery Protocol, which defines how AppleTalk data identifies itself to other machines on the network, and how the data itself is organized within network packets. Directly above the Datagram Delivery Protocol are four distinct protocols, each performing a specific function. The Echo Protocol exists specifically so AppleTalk nodes can test other nodes to determine if they are on the network. The Echo Protocol also allows point-to-point timing tests between AppleTalk nodes. The Transaction Protocol provides guaranteed delivery of data packets; the Name Binding Protocol allows AppleTalk nodes to track the internet names and addresses of other nodes; the Routing Table Maintenance Protocol maintains routing information.

The next level up contains the Zone Information Protocol, the AppleTalk Session Protocol, and the Printer Access Protocol (PAP). AppleTalk Zones are subnetworks on a common internetwork. The AppleTalk Session Protocol provides methods by which nodes can initiate, effect, and terminate network communications. The Printer Access Protocol is a brilliant addition to AppleTalk that allows printers to be intelligent nodes on an AppleTalk Network.

Finally, the AppleTalk Filing Protocol presents network information to AppleTalk nodes by maintaining a file system the Finder can understand while retaining such information as file ownership and access rights.

The first networking product for Macintoshes was the Apple LaserWriter driver, which connected multiple Macintoshes to a single LaserWriter using AppleTalk's PAP. Today, of course, there is AppleShare, Apple's network system software. AppleShare runs on a Macintosh and (naturally) uses AppleTalk as its default networking protocol. AppleTalk client software ships with every Macintosh. All of this means that any network that includes Macs must, somehow, deal with AppleTalk.

There is more than one way to deal with AppleTalk, as three leading networking products illustrate. First, there is AppleShare, a purely AppleTalk network system. If DOS machines interoperate with Macs on an AppleShare system, they as well as the Macs use AppleTalk. In other words, every machine on an AppleTalk network does things the Apple way.

Next, there is NetWare for Macintosh, which uses IPX/SPX as its default networking protocol stack. Macintoshes, however, use the AppleTalk client software that ships as part of the Macintosh operating system. NetWare for Macintosh maps AppleTalk requests to IPX requests using what Novell calls a Service Protocol Gateway (SPG). In other words, a Macintosh requests that the file server open a file using AppleTalk. The SPG intercepts the AppleTalk message, translates it into an equivalent IPX message, and then passes the translated request to the NetWare file server. Hence, Macintoshes are able to communicate with unlike machines using AppleTalk, the native Macintosh networking environment.

The NetWare for Macintosh SPG presents some interesting troubleshooting challenges. These challenges arise mostly because there is no one-to-one correspondence between IPX/SPX functions and AppleTalk functions. Thus, a single AppleTalk instruction can pass through the NetWare for Macintosh SPG and end up as a series of several IPX instructions. Likewise, a single IPX instruction can pass through the SPG and result in several AppleTalk instructions.

Because there is no one-to-one correspondence between IPX/SPX and AppleTalk functions, the error messages a Macintosh client displays are not necessarily indicative of the real network problem.

TOPS uses a third approach. To begin with, Macs on TOPS do not use the AppleShare client software, but instead use TOPS peer software. (TOPS is a peer-to-peer network.) When two Macintoshes are interoperating on a TOPS network, they both use the AppleTalk protocol. However, when a Mac and a PC (or a Mac and a Sun workstation) interoperate over TOPS, they use TOPS' own networking protocols. This hybrid approach avoids the complexity of an SPG, while providing Macs with their native networking protocol much of the time.

There are more approaches to high-level interoperability between Macs and other computers, too. For example, Apple provides developers with a TCP/IP protocol stack that programmers can integrate with the Macintosh operating system. And several companies offer Macintosh-to-SNA and Macintosh-to-DECnet connectivity products.

File Transfers

As opposed to DOS files, which are fairly straightforward, Macintosh files have two parts: a resource fork and a data fork. A file's resource fork contains such information as which icon the Finder should display the file with, which application created the file, and more. Because of the resource fork, files can behave intelligently. For example, you can "open" a file, and the file's resource fork will make information available to the Finder that allows the Finder to execute the application that created the file and cause that application to open the file. Double-click on a PageMaker document, for example, and the Finder will execute PageMaker. PageMaker will then open the file you double-clicked on.

The problem with resource forks is that they are always binary, which means DOS doesn't understand them. Data forks contain the actual data of a file. So, in most cases, transferring a file from Mac to DOS really means transfering the data fork of that file.

One of the surest ways to transfer the data fork of a Mac file is to format that file as ASCII text. Virtually every Macintosh application provides you with an option for saving files in ASCII format. When you save a file in ASCII format, the resource fork exists, but doesn't contain any information necessary to the integrity of the file's data. DOS can ignore an ASCII file's resource fork (which DOS does) and still retain all of the file's information.

The downside of saving Mac files in ASCII format is that you lose Mac-specific formatting information such as fonts, styles, margins, and so on.

An oft-encountered problem with transfering ASCII files between PCs and Macs is the different character sets of the two machines. In addition to standard alpha-numeric characters and and punctuation symbols, both machines have different sets of extended symbols. For example, the PC has a series of line characters programmers use to build character-based user interfaces. Both machines have some typesetting characters, such as em dashes and curly quotes, but each machine uses different values to define those characters.

The result is that files containing extended ASCII characters will transfer from one machine to the other with no problems, except that the extended characters will appear differently after the transfer. For example, an em dash may appear as a box or line. The only way to prevent this type of problem from occurring is to filter out extended ASCII characters before transferring files from one machine to another. Some people like to use a discontinued programmable text editor for the Mac called QUED-M (from Paragon Concepts) to do this. Many DOS users speak highly of a programmable text editor called Brief (from Solution Systems).

With some applications, you don't need to convert a file to ASCII text in order to load it using an operating system different from the one it was created on.

These applications include PageMaker, Excel, WordPerfect, dBASE III, FoxBASE +, MacWrite II, Adobe Illustrator, and more. What each of these applications has in common with the others is that it will open and convert documents created with a different operating system (DOS, OS/2, or Mac) automatically and without losing any critical formatting information.

For example, MacWrite II contains built-in filters that allow you to open documents created on a DOS machine by applications such as WordPerfect, WordStar, Microsoft Word, and others. The applications mentioned in this and the preceding paragraph all have built-in filters that allow similar file conversion, albeit in a less flexible manner than MacWrite II, which boasts extraordinary file conversion prowess.

Some of the applications listed above, including PageMaker, Excel, Word, WordPerfect, and others, have versions running under both DOS and Mac, or both OS/2 and Mac. In each case, one version of such an application will read documents created by the other version. For example, PageMaker for OS/2 will read PageMaker for Mac documents just as easily as it will read PageMaker for OS/2 documents. In addition to built-in file conversion functions, some third party developers sell file conversion programs, including filters, for many of the more popular applications on either machine.

When using NetWare for Macintosh, you need to be especially careful when backing up or copying Macintosh files from a DOS workstation. For example, using XCOPY to copy Macintosh files will copy only the data fork, leaving the file without any formatting information. In some bizarre cases, XCOPY will copy only the resource fork of a Macintosh file.

The NetWare 386 version of NCOPY has a switch you can set to copy both forks of Macintosh files. However, unless you explicitly hit the switch from the command line when executing the NetWare 386 NCOPY, it, too, will copy only one fork of Macintosh files. Unfortunately, the NetWare 2.15 version of NCOPY doesn't feature this switch.

Some NetWare archiving products back up both forks of Macintosh files and some do not, although more and more archive vendors are offering Macintosh capability. However, if you have NetWare for Macintosh, you should be certain that the archive system you use works with Macintosh files. I suggest you try the system out by backing up Mac files and then restoring them sucessfully before relying on the archive system.

17 A Guide to Macintosh Hardware

While all Macintosh computers still in production run essentially the same operating system, there are extreme architectural differences among the different models. Before learning specific steps to setting up a Macintosh workstation, then, you must have a general knowledge of the different Macintosh machinery. So, starting from the beginning, here's a complete overview of Macintosh hardware.

The Classic Mac, Fat Mac, and Mac 512Ke

The Classic and Fat Macs are essentially the same machine: that is, the original model, a la Steven Jobs. The Classic is based on an 8MHz Motorola 68000 processor and has 128KB of soldered-to-the-motherboard RAM (the Fat Mac 512K). These machines, referred to hereafter as the "original Mac," are "clamshell" machines, meaning that their two-part case fits together like super-tight shell. You can't open the original Mac without a special Torx screwdriver and some type of tool to pry the case open without doing damage to it.

Jobs felt strongly that the user shouldn't have to open up the Mac. The good news is that the original Mac is a fairly complete package; it has LocalTalk networking hardware, a video controller, two serial ports, one mouse port, and a floppy drive controller built into the motherboard. The bad news is that the original Mac wasn't designed to be tampered with. You can't upgrade the memory on an original Mac without altering the motherboard by patching it or cutting traces. What you see is what you get, period.

Surprisingly, many original are still Macs around. You can hook up original Macs to any LocalTalk network simply by plugging a DB-9 LocalTalk connector into its printer or modem port. Although connecting isn't a problem, software is—especially the operating system. Specifically, the original Mac doesn't run the current Mac operating system, and never will, because of its outdated ROM software. Also, the original Mac's floppies format to only 340KB—not enough to hold an operating system, AppleShare or TOPS workstation software, and Desk Accessories.

You can solve the floppy capacity problem in two ways. First, you can craft a minimal operating system by using the Font/DA mover to remove all but the absolutely necessary fonts and desk accessories (certain sizes of the Geneva and Chicago fonts are reserved by the operating system and impossible to remove with the Font/DA mover). Second, you can purchase a parallel-interface hard disk drive. Apple and several other vendors formerly manufactured parallel hard drives for the Mac; these devices plug into the external floppy port on the back of every original Mac. Since these devices have been out of manufacture for several years, they're difficult to find. One good place to look is Sun Remarketing (Ogden, Utah), a firm that remanufactures old Macintosh and Lisa computers for resale.

After the introduction of the Macintosh Plus, Apple briefly offered an upgraded version of the Fat Mac called the Mac 512Ke. The 512Ke is a Fat Mac with the Mac Plus ROM software and a 740KB double-sided internal floppy drive instead of the original single-sided internal floppy. Many owners of Fat Macs purchased the upgrade from Apple dealers; others purchased a factory version of the 512Ke. A quick way to tell if an original Mac is in fact a Mac 512Ke is to insert a blank floppy in the drive and then attempt a double-sided format of the floppy. A Mac 512Ke will perform the double-sided format, while the Classic and Fat Macs won't.

The Mac 512Ke is an easier machine to network than its predecessors because it has a double-sided internal floppy drive and can run the current Mac system software.

The Mac Plus

The Mac Plus may yet be the most successful Macintosh model on the market in terms of unit sales. The Mac Plus features the same clamshell design as the original Macs, but with an internal redesign that includes one megabyte of industry standard Single In-line Memory Modules (SIMMs) with the capacity for up to four megabytes, a new (at release time) and more powerful version of the Macintosh ROM software, a built-in SCSI port for large and fast hard disk drives and other SCSI devices, a new hierarchical file system, a new keyboard, and a double-sided internal floppy drive. Like the original Mac, the Mac Plus is based on an 8MHz Motorola 68000 processor; it has LocalTalk networking hardware, video hardware, a floppy controller, two serial ports, one mouse port, and one parallel external floppy port, all on its motherboard.

The Mac Plus offers all the benefits of the clamshell design (all-in-one convenience), but with the increased power of the SCSI bus, and with user-upgradeable memory. It has no expansion slots. Today there are hundreds of thousands of Mac Plus machines configured to the limit of 4MB of RAM, and driving SCSI hard drives formatted at up to 600MB or even larger. The Mac Plus, like the PC AT, continues to perform to the satisfaction of many of its original owners, who stick with the Plus despite the advent of more powerful hardware.

The Mac Plus supports today's network systems admirably, except that it has no provision for Ethernet. It does have the standard Apple LocalTalk hardware within its motherboard circuitry, and it supports very large SCSI storage devices. In fact, Apple introduced AppleShare jointly with the Mac Plus, and the Plus was used largely as an AppleShare file server in its earliest days.

While the Plus is more open than the original Macs, it is still very much a closed system. Again, it has no expansion slots. Its 68000 processor is soldered to the motherboard, there is no socket for a math coprocessor, and—like the original Mac—you need special tools to open the case.

While its hardware design prohibits modular extendability, the Mac Plus ROM software is extremely open and extensible. Thus, third-party expansion devices for the Mac Plus appeared on the market shortly after its introduction. Most of these expansion devices connect to the Mac Plus with a type of clip that overlays the 68000 processor. Such clips have metal leaves that come in contact with the 68000's pins—one leaf to each pin. Each leaf connects to a wire, and the wires join to a ribbon cable, which leads to the expansion device. Internal hard drives, faster versions of the 68000 (or even a 68020), RAM cache cards, and other types of devices are even today designed and marketed as expansions to the Mac Plus. As an expansion bus, however, the processor clip is unreliable. Changes in operating temperature, movement, and vibration can cause one or more of the clip's leaves to lose contact with the 68000's pins.

The Mac Plus has been plagued by an unusually high number of power supply failures. In fact, this is true not only the Mac Plus, but of the original Mac as well. The power supply failures are more prevalent in the Mac Plus simply because it has more memory and more circuitry than the original Mac. Incidentally, Apple manufactured the Mac Plus for a brief period in an off-white color, much lighter than any of the machines Apple builds today. If you run into a "white" Mac Plus, you're not seeing things.

The Macintosh SE

Apple introduced the Mac SE jointly with the Mac II. Although the Mac SE has a clamshell case, it is an open system and represents a total redesign of the Mac. Aside from its 8 MHz 68000 processor, the SE has almost no elements in common with the Mac Plus or with the original Mac. To begin with, the Mac SE is an open system, having one expansion slot and a special internal SCSI port, in addition to two internal drive bays. While you still need a special Torx screwdriver to open the SE's case, the SE's motherboard is designed to slide out of its bracket, providing you with easy access to the expansion slot and internal drive bays.

The SE has a new and unique version of the Macintosh ROM software that increases its graphical primitive video performance by around 25 percent, and a new, faster SCSI manager that causes SCSI throughput to be around 25 percent greater than with the Mac Plus. Significantly, the SE has a completely different and more vigorous power supply and analog system from the Mac Plus.

The SE has one other major enhancement over previous Macs: the Apple Desktop Bus (ADB). The ADB is a bus in the traditional sense; it has its own set of commands, and it provides expansion capability. The keyboard and mouse are the two most popular ADB devices, but there are many others, including trackballs, graphics tables, and so on. The SE has two ADB ports, located on its back panel. Apple keyboards have two ports. You can chain ADB devices in a linear fashion; for example, you can hook the keyboard up to the SE, the mouse to the keyboard, and so on. While the advantages of the ADB are self evident, its main disadvantage is that keyboards and mice designed for the Mac Plus and earlier Macs don't work with ADB Macs.

The SE's one expansion slot is based on a 16-bit proprietary bus that allows for almost any type of modification to the SE you can imagine. The most popular expansion devices for the SE are processor upgrades (to the full 32-bit 68020/68881 combination), video cards for large-screen monitors, and ethernet cards. However, there are scores of more obscure expansion options for the SE, and the expansion market for this machine continues to thrive. Be aware, however, that expansion devices for the SE won't work with any other Macintosh—not even the newer SE 30.

The SE 30

The SE 30 looks just like the SE. But don't be fooled. This is one of the quickest, hottest machines Apple has ever made. At the heart of the SE 30 is a Motorola 68030/68882 chip set running at 16MHz. Like the SE, the SE 30 has one internal expansion slot. But this is a full 32-bit proprietary bus. Because the SE 30 is a relatively simple machine (only one slot, integrated SCSI and video, true 32-bit integrated internals including memory and bus pathways), it is a surprisingly good performer.

One thing most people don't know about the SE 30 is that it has undocumented support for color video and other features of the Mac II line, because it uses the same ROM software as the Mac II family. Also, because the SE 30 is based on the 68030 processor, the SE 30 will support in full Apple's upcoming System 7 Macintosh operating software. This means the SE 30 will support true multitasking and true virtual memory. Unlike all of the other clamshell Macs, the SE 30 has a clear and promising upgrade path.

The Mac II

The Mac II is the original "Open" Mac—the first Mac that isn't a clamshell machine. It features six expansion slots, a 68020 processor running at 16MHz, a 68881 coprocessor, color video (displays up to 16.7 million colors), three drive bays, a new version of the Mac's ROM software, room on its motherboard for 8MB of RAM, and a full 32-bit architecture.

The Mac II's components reside in a rectangular box (slightly smaller than the PC-AT's box). There are two floppy drive openings on the front of the Mac II's case. The power switch is on the rear panel, right side. To turn on the Mac II, however, you don't need to reach around to hit the power switch. Instead, you need only to press a key located at the upper right corner of the Mac II's keyboard. That key sends a signal to the ADB, which then hits the Mac II's power supply and turns on the machine. Conversely, when you use the "Shut Down" command from the Finder, the Mac II powers itself down.

To open the Mac II, you must remove a single screw (you can use a regular Phillips screwdriver) from the top-center-rear panel. After removing the screw, look for two tabs on the top-rear panel—one tab on the left, another on the right. Finally, press in on both tabs and pull the top cover up in one motion. The cover should come off, starting in the rear. The cover is held into place along the front panel by a series of tension clips. These clips tend to be sticky, so you may have to tug pretty hard on the cover to separate it from the case.

Looking down into the opened Mac II case, you'll see six Nubus slots along the rear, starting in the left corner. (Nubus is a self-configuring, 32-bit bus protocol developed partially by Texas Instruments.) On the right side, you'll notice a raised platform that holds the floppy and internal hard drives. This platform rests on four pillars—one under each of its corners—and is fastened by four screws. Underneath the platform you'll see the Mac II's memory SIMMs. There are eight slots, each with capacity for one SIMM.

The Mac II has a socket for a Motorola 68851 Paged Memory Management Unit (PMMU). The 68851 provides the Mac II with demand-paged virtual memory capability. However, to take advantage of virtual memory, you'll need A/UX (Apple's implementation of Unix) or the upcoming System 7.

Expansion Cards for the Mac II

Installing expansion cards into the Mac II is simple. Once you've got the cover off, plug the card into any empty slot. You don't need to worry about interrupts, base addresses, or DMA. Every time you install a new card, Nubus negotiates an address and interrupt for that card with cards presently in the machine. In this way, the new card will always receive an address from Nubus that ensures smooth operation.

Because the Mac II is the first open Macintosh, it isn't a self-contained package, as the clamshell Macs are. For example, if you don't order a monitor and video card for your Macintosh, you'll end up without either. (When buying a Mac SE, for example, you don't need to order a monitor separately because the monitor is part of the self-contained SE design.) You also must specify drive configuration, network cards, and so on. Despite its slots, the Mac II (along with all its children) has LocalTalk networking hardware built into its motherboard, just as the original Macs do.

Expansion cards for the Mac II are plentiful, and include the standard network interface cards (ethernet, token-ring, ARCnet), in addition to more esoteric devices such as video frame buffers, data acquisition devices, and MIDI controllers. The original Mac II has been superseded by more powerful designs, but remains a vital machine because of its expandability. This is the first Macintosh with a wide-open and, currently, unlimited upgrade pathway. Moreover, any Macintosh Nubus card will work on any Macintosh with Nubus, regardless of ROM version, processor, and so on.

Nubus supports so-called bus mastering, meaning that an intelligent Nubus device can take control of the Macintosh and all its resources. Bus mastering makes it possible to use coprocessors and other intelligent devices by plugging them into one of the Mac II's slots.

All of the Macs discussed in the remainder of this chapter have 32-bit Nubus slots.

The Mac IIx

The Mac IIx is essentially a Mac II with a 16MHz 68030 processor (instead of a 68020) and a 68882 coprocessor (instead of a 68881). The IIx has the same case as the Mac II, essentially the same circuitry, the same number of slots, and the same memory architecture. One big difference between the Mac II and the Mac IIx is that the latter doesn't have a socket for the 68851. That's because the 68030 processor has the equivalent of a 68851 built into its instruction set. If you choose to use A/UX (or System 7 when Apple releases it), you'll be able to do so without adding a chip to your Mac IIx.

The Mac IIcx

The IIcx is essentially a slimmed-down IIx. The IIcx has the same processor and coprocessor as the IIx, runs at the same speed, and has the same RAM configuration, but has only three expansion slots. While functionally similar to the IIx, the IIcx has a much smaller motherboard, uses fewer chips, consumes less power, and has a more accessible arrangement of key components, such as drive bays and RAM. The IIcx also has a slot for an accelerator/cache card. By stacking the IIcx on its side, you can markedly reduce the footprint of the Mac IIcx.

Since you'll always have a video card in your IIcx, the IIcx has two open slots. If you install a network interface card, you'll have one slot left over.

The Mac IIci

The Mac IIci is a souped-up Mac IIcx. Both machines have the same case, and both have three slots. However, the IIci runs at 25MHz and comes with a graphics coprocessor and a separate video frame buffer as standard equipment. Despite its additional performance gear, the IIci has even fewer chips than the IIcx and has much empty space on its small motherboard, demonstrating the evolution of VLSI technology.

The Mac IIfx

The Mac IIfx is a server-class Macintosh with a 68030 running at 40MHz, six slots, integrated write-through cache, interleaved zero-wait-state memory, a faster SCSI bus, and more. The Mac IIfx's case is the same as that of the Mac II and Mac IIx. However, the IIfx's motherboard has a lot of empty space on it, indicating that Apple could shrink this machine just as it shrank the IIx (creating the IIcx).

Hardware Elements Common to All Macs

The 3.5" floppy

The original Mac was one of the first machines to feature the 3.5" floppy. Advantages of the 3.5" floppy include its smaller size and its sturdy plastic case, which protects the media from dust and other harmful matter. The 3.5" floppy also has a sliding tab which you can use repeatedly to lock and unlock the floppy. The first major DOS machines to use the 3.5" floppy were the IBM PS/2 models. You can use floppies from the same box for either a Macintosh or a DOS machine that has the appropriate 3.5" disk drive.

The Macintosh ejects diskettes from the floppy drive itself — there is no door or button for you to press or open. However, sometimes the Mac may crash without ejecting the floppy. Every Mac floppy port has a tiny hole on the right side of the slot into which you insert the floppy. The hole is there so you can eject diskettes manually. A good method is to use a straightened paper clip, inserting the end of the paper clip into the tiny hole and pressing firmly inward. The diskette should eject.

The SuperDrive

All Macs, beginning with the IIx and the SE30, have the so-called "Super-Drive." The Superdrive can read both Macintosh-formatted floppies and DOS-formatted floppies. If you insert a Macintosh-formatted floppy into the SuperDrive, it will recognize that floppy and place the floppy's icon on the Desktop.

To read a DOS-formatted floppy using the SuperDrive, you must first execute the Apple File Exchange program. With the File Exchange loaded, you can insert DOS-formatted 3.5" floppies into the SuperDrive, and the File Exchange program will recognize the floppy and give you options for translating the data from DOS to Mac format.

The Programmer's Switch

Every Macintosh ever sold came with a programmer's switch. While the design of the programmer's switch changes from model to model, the switch for every model is certain to 1) be made of plastic, 2) have two buttons, and 3) require the user to install it by mounting in the Mac's case.

The programmer's switch is actually two switches: One switch resets the Macintosh, while the other switch generates an interrupt that sends the Mac into debug mode. How your Mac behaves in debug mode depends on the particular debugging software you have running. Consult the Macintosh hardware manual for details on how to install and use the programmer's switch for a particular Macintosh.

18 Setting up a Macintosh Workstation: The Essential Skills

Although setting up a Macintosh workstation is a relatively clean and simple process, it is not necessarily intuitive to the network manager accustomed to configuring DOS workstations. Moreover, there are several critical steps in the process that, when omitted or botched, can cause eventual problems. Here, then, is an overview of the essential steps in setting up a Macintosh workstation.

The basic steps in setting up a Macintosh workstation are as follows:

1) Unpack the Macintosh; identify the operating system software, the system documentation, and the hardware documentation; unpack the network interface card or LocalTalk connector, its software, and its documentation.

2) Install the network interface card or LocalTalk connector; install the video card (Mac II family only); connect the keyboard, the monitor (Mac II family only), the power supply, and other peripherals.

3) Format the hard disk (if necessary).

4) Install the operating system, including printer drivers and AppleShare client software.

5) Test the setup by logging on to a NetWare for Macintosh server and printing a directory of a Macintosh folder.

This chapter will cover each of the five steps identified above. First, however, you need to know about a program called the Installer. The Installer is a special program Apple supplies as part of the Macintosh system software. In addition, Apple licenses the Installer to third-party developers. You will use the Installer continually to install the Macintosh operating system, drivers, system resources, and other Macintosh software. If you are familiar already with the Installer, you can skip this section.

The Installer

If you have installed much software on DOS systems, you have no doubt run accross scores of "INSTALL.BAT" files. These batch files typically execute a series of DOS commands that install a specific piece of software on the machine, create appropriate directories, modify the CONFIG.SYS and AUTOEXEC.BAT files when appropriate, and other setup procedures.

Rather than have each third-party developer create its own Macintosh version of INSTALL.BAT, Apple created a program that executes batch-style scripts, endowed it with a slick set of commands for installing all types of software, and released the program to developers. The program in question is, of course, the Installer—always the easiest, cleanest, and safest way to install operating system software, drivers, and system resources.

When you want to install a new version of the Macintosh operating system, a driver, or some other resource, always look for a copy of Installer on the installation disk for the software. In addition to the Installer, there should also be at least one "script" (a series of Installer commands for installing one or more pieces of system-related software: See Figure 7).

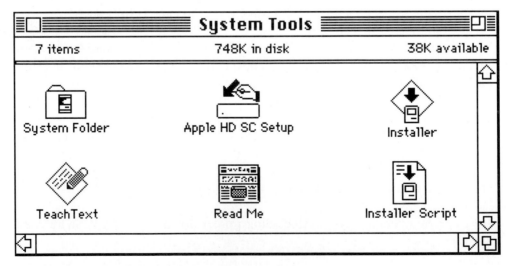

Figure 7: The Installer program is included with other system files.

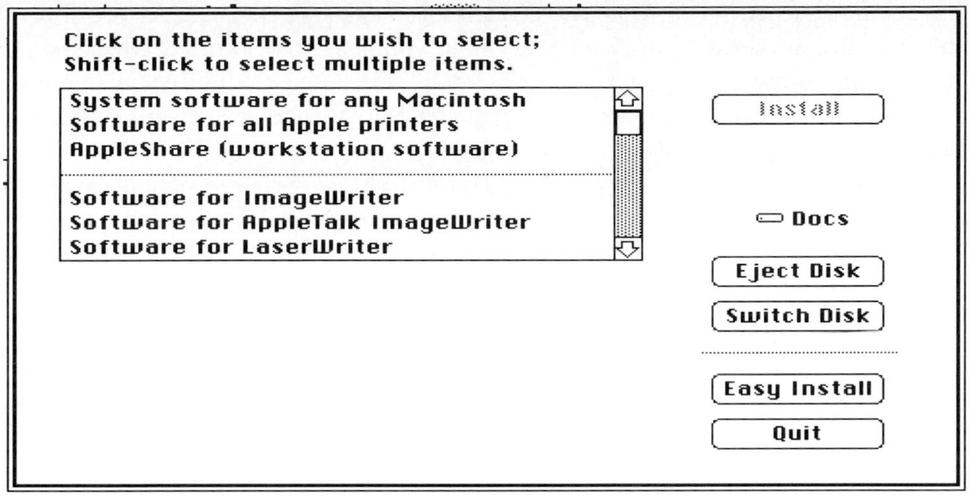

```
┌─────────────────────────────────────────────────────────────┐
│                                                               │
│   Click on the items you wish to select;                      │
│   Shift-click to select multiple items.                       │
│  ┌────────────────────────────────────────────┬──┐           │
│  │ System software for any Macintosh          │⬆ │  ┌──────────┐
│  │ Software for all Apple printers            ├──┤  │ Install  │
│  │ AppleShare (workstation software)          │▓ │  └──────────┘
│  │┄┄┄┄┄┄┄┄┄┄┄┄┄┄┄┄┄┄┄┄┄┄┄┄┄┄┄┄┄┄┄┄┄┄┄┄┄┄┄┄┄┄┄┄│▓ │           │
│  │ Software for ImageWriter                   │▓ │     ⬭ Docs  │
│  │ Software for AppleTalk ImageWriter         ├──┤           │
│  │ Software for LaserWriter                   │⬇ │  ┌──────────┐
│  └────────────────────────────────────────────┴──┘  │Eject Disk│
│                                                      └──────────┘
│                                                      ┌──────────┐
│                                                      │Switch Disk│
│                                                      └──────────┘
│                                                      ┌──────────┐
│                                                      │Easy Install│
│                                                      └──────────┘
│                                                      ┌──────────┐
│                                                      │   Quit   │
│                                                      └──────────┘
└─────────────────────────────────────────────────────────────┘
```

Figure 8: Options available for installation scripts.

The different options listed in Figure 8 represent different installation scripts. If the Macintosh has more than one hard drive, make certain the "target" drive is the correct one. The target drive is indicated by an icon on the right side of the Installer window. You can cycle through available drives by repeatedly clicking the "Drive" button. When you cycle to the target drive, stop clicking the "Drive" button.

Each script installs a specific piece of system-related software, or a specific group of system-related software. To install a specific option, first select that option by clicking on it with the mouse. Next, issue the "Install" command by clicking the "Install" button. That's really all there is to it—select the appropriate script and execute it.

The Installer is intelligent; it performs all the necessary system housekeeping before it modifies the Macintosh system software. For example, the Installer always checks for available space on the target disk before executing an installation script. The Installer can also warn you before replacing or removing crucial system resources. While the Installer is executing scripts, it always prompts you to insert disks or perform other actions necessary to the sucessful completion of the current script. You can run the Installer with confidence; it is a predictable utility that always gives you feedback regarding its state of execution, never taking ultimate control away from you.

Unpacking and Setting Up the Macintosh

For this step you should rely primarily on the Mac's packing materials. You may have unpacked computers that had unpacking instructions at the bottom of the box, forcing you to unpack everything in order to read the unpacking instructions. The Macintosh has an idiot-proof unpacking scheme: the first thing you see when you open the box is a folder that says "Open Me First." This folder contains the unpacking instructions for whichever Macintosh model is in the box. As you unpack the machine, be certain you have everything you need to network the Macintosh. Identify and browse through the hardware documentation, paying special attention to the segments explaining how to open the Mac's case and install expansion devices.

The "Open me first" portfolio contains five disks, four of which are necessary for the operating system installation, and one which contains an automated guided tour of the Macintosh. The disks are titled "System Tools," "Utilities Disk 1," "Utilities Disk 2," "Printing Tools," and "Mac Tour."

To run the Installer, you must boot the Macintosh using the "System Tools" disk. The surest way to do this is to turn the Macintosh off, insert the System Tools disk into the floppy drive, and turn the Macintosh back on. When the Macintosh desktop appears, the "System Tools" diskette icon should appear in the upper right corner of the Macintosh display. If another icon appears above the System Tools diskette icon, you didn't boot from the System Tools diskette. Try again.

To see a directory of the System Tools diskette, click on the diskette's icon (thus selecting the diskette) and select "Open" from the File menu. (Rather than selecting "Open," you can select the diskette and press Command-O, or simply double-click on the diskette's icon.) The Finder will open a window for the System Tools diskette, and the Mac's desktop should look similar to Figure 9.

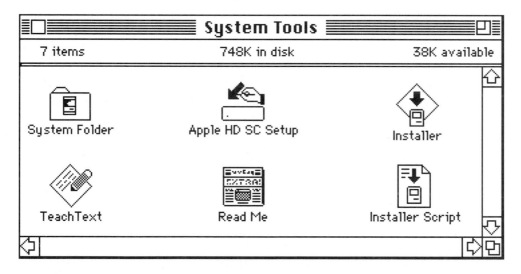

Figure 9: The System Tools window.

Each of the objects signified by the six icons in the System Tools window is important. The System Folder contains the operating system files from which the Mac booted. The tiny Macintosh portrayed within the System Folder icon signifies that the folder has been "blessed," or initialized to be the startup folder. "Apple HD SC Setup" is a utility that formats, partitions, initializes, and tests SCSI drives for the Macintosh. "Installer" is the program that actually installs the operating system and utilities. "Installer Script" is an Installer document that contains instructions for different installation tasks. "Read Me" is the ubiquitous text file that contains last-minute instructions for the other objects on the diskette. (The "Read Me" file will, of course, be different for each release of the System Tools diskette.) "TeachText" is a text editor and browser, included specifically for displaying "Read Me" files.

Initializing the Hard Disk

To open the case of a Mac II-class machine, you need only remove one screw, located at the center of the upper rear panel. (You can use a standard Phillips screwdriver.) Grasp the two tabs—one on the upper right side, another on the upper left side—and pull the case up and towards you. On some Macs, you will need to pull firmly.

Mac II-class machines feature Nubus, and therefore do not require you to set interrupt and base address jumpers on network interface cards. However, some Mac II ethernet cards require you to set a jumper to tell the card what type of cabling system it is hooked up to. Most Macintosh ethernet cards have two connectors—one DIX (thick ethernet) and one BNC (thin ethernet). The Novell (Excelan) EtherPort II card has a small switch located just above the DIX connector. (See Figure 10.)

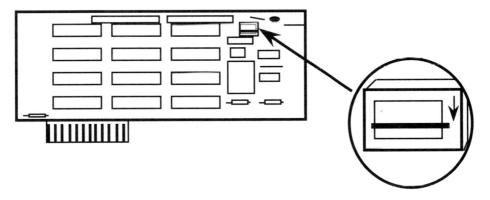

Figure 10: The EtherPort II card cable selection switch.

Some cards have connectors for RJ-11 twisted pair, others for fiber. Refer to the card's documentation for the correct jumper settings. Most cards are pre-set for BNC connectors. Some cards supplied by Apple don't have jumpers—they are intelligent enough to infer which connector you've attached to the network, and they configure themselves accordingly.

The Mac SE and SE30 present special problems. First, they're built with a "clamshell" case, requiring you to have a special Torx screwdriver to open them. Second, the form factor for SE expansion devices is too small for standard ethernet cards. Some ethernet cards for the SE, therefore, are actually two cards—one card attaches to the expansion slot, and the other card attaches to the inside of the SE's rear panel. You must rely heavily on the documentation that comes with any card for the SE family. Just be aware that expanding the SE is a totally different (and more involved) operation than expanding a Mac II-class machine.

All Macintoshes, beginning with the Mac Plus, use SCSI hard drives. Normally, these drives come pre-formatted from their manufacturer. However, you may face the prospect of formatting a Macintosh SCSI drive, either because of a drive crash or for some other reason. Relative to DOS machines, some aspects of Macintosh hard drives are simpler, while others are more complex.

Because the Mac's SCSI controller is part of its motherboard, you needn't worry about installing and configuring the controller. In addition, the Mac's built-in controller provides for a high degree of compatibility among different brand drives and different model Macintoshes. For example, you should be able to unplug any third-party external hard drive from a Mac Plus, plug that drive into a Mac IIci, and boot from it with no reformatting or reconfiguring. However, because today's SCSI drives have their own embedded controllers, many drive manufacturers place their own extensions to the SCSI command set on their drive's controllers. Manufacturers do this for a number of reasons, most of which have to do with increased performance or operating convenience. You can usually identify a drive that has a proprietary SCSI command set because its initializing software will not initialize a drive that has a different command set. For example, if you attempt to initialize a CMS drive with Jasmine DriveWare, DriveWare will return an error.

The first thing to remember, then, is to use a drive's own software to initialize the drive whenever possible. If you cannot locate the software for a specific third-party hard drive, you can always use Apple's hard-drive initializing software. However, if you do, you'll lose access to extra features added by the third-party manufacturer.

The Apple HD SC Setup Program

Part of Apple's standard system software for the Macintosh is the HD SC Setup program. Setup is located on the "System Tools" disk. (The "SC" stands for SCSI.) This software will initialize and partition almost any SCSI hard drive capable of working with the Macintosh. If the Mac's hard drive came installed from the factory, or if you've lost the drive's third-party installation software, you'll need to use the HD SC setup program.

The first thing to know about Setup is that it only works on unmounted drives. An unmounted drive is one that is present on the SCSI bus but is not currently addressable by the Macintosh operating system, except through Setup or equivalent third-party software. (Of course, if the Macintosh hard drive has suffered a media failure, you probably won't be able to mount the drive anyway.) To be certain the hard drive in question is unmounted, reboot the Macintosh by turning it off, inserting the System Tools disk into the internal floppy drive, and turning the Macintosh back on. When the Mac boots, it will display the System Tools disk icon in the upper right hand corner of its display. If the icon for the hard drive in question appears below the System Tools diskette, drag the hard drive's icon into the trash can (thus unmounting the hard drive).

Open the System Tools diskette and locate Setup's icon; it looks like a hand waving a magic wand over a SCSI subsystem. (See Figure 11.) Open the Setup

Apple HD SC Setup

Figure 11: The "Magic Wand" icon for setting up a Mac hard disk.

program by selecting its icon and choosing "Open" from the file menu. When Setup opens, it will display a dialog box similar to Figure 12.

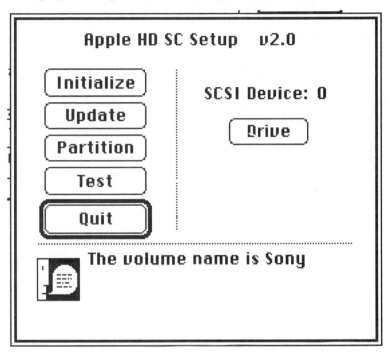

Figure 12: The hard disk installation dialog box.

      The first thing to look at here is the volume name listed in the lower portion of the dialog box. In Figure 12, the volume name is "Sony." The volume name listed in the lower portion of the dialog box is the current volume—the one that Setup acts upon when you execute a Setup function. In the middle of Figure 12 on the right side there is the text "SCSI Device: 0," and a "Drive" button. Remember that the SCSI bus can have up to seven devices on it, and each device has a number (valid numbers range from 0 to 6). On the Macintosh, device 0 is reserved for the internal SCSI port. If there are other SCSI devices present on the SCSI bus, you can cycle through those devices by clicking on the "Drive" button. Once you have confirmed that the active drive is the one you wish to initialize, you can proceed.

      Along the left side of the Setup dialog, you will see five buttons: "Initialize," "Update," "Partition," "Test," and "Quit." The "Quit" button should have a heavy black border. (Any button that has a heavy border can be activated either by a mouse click or by pressing <Enter> or <Return>. Buttons without a heavy border usually require a mouse click.) Clicking on the "Initialize" button will execute the hard disk initialization program. Initializing a hard disk destroys all data on the drive by rewriting each track, and then installing a SCSI driver on the volume. Most SCSI drives have embedded controllers, which store in the controller's firmware information about the particular drive's cylinders and tracks, including bad block information. In addition, initializing a hard drive detects bad blocks of media and maps those blocks out, and—on some drives—passes information about bad blocks to the drive's embedded SCSI controller. Usually when a hard drive suffers a soft failure (a media failure that does not involve the destruction of a physical component of the drive) you will want to initialize the drive, after which the drive will work as though it were new.

Clicking on the "Update" button updates the volume's software driver, usually located on track 0 of the drive. This is the software that the Macintosh operating system uses to mount the volume and perform the initial transfers of information. Sometimes when a Macintosh drive partially fails (appears to work under some conditions but not others) it only needs a new driver. In such cases updating a Macintosh SCSI volume's driver is often the first thing to try when troubleshooting a failed volume. Updating a driver has no effect on the drive's data, except for possibly replacing a corrupt driver that may have impeded communications between the Macintosh and its SCSI devices. Updating a volume's driver makes sense only when that volume is already initialized.

Once you have initialized a volume, you have the option of partitioning the volume. You can do so by clicking on the "Partition" button. Be aware, however, that partitioning a Mac using Setup does not give you multiple Macintosh partitions. Rather, Setup's partition function allows you to have an A/UX (Apple's implementation of Unix) partition co-resident with a Macintosh partition. Partitioning Macintosh hard drives has never made as much sense as it has for DOS drives, because (since the Mac Plus) the Macintosh operating system has never imposed upper limits on the size of a hard drive partition that are anything more than theoretical, given today's storage hardware.

Installing the Macintosh Operating System

To begin the installation process, start Installer by selecting it (clicking on its icon) and opening it. (You open programs on the Macintosh using exactly the same methods as for opening windows—double click, select the Installer and choose "Open" from the File Menu, or select the Installer and press command-O.)

After opening the Installer, your Macintosh will display a dialog box that explains what to do next. (See Figure 13.)

You can proceed by either clicking on the "OK" button or pressing <Enter> or <Return>. (Any button that has a heavy border can be activated either by a mouse click or by pressing <Enter> or <Return>. Buttons without a heavy border usually require a mouse click.) Next, the Macintosh will display an "Easy Install" dialog box, giving you the immediate option of intalling the default operating system and utilities on the disk listed along the left border of the "Easy Install" dialog box, about halfway down. To do so, simply press <Return> or <Enter>, or click on the "Install" Button.

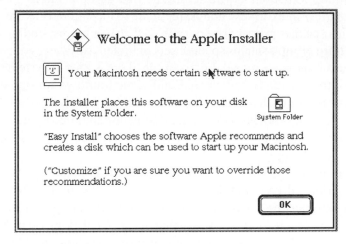

Figure 13: The Macintosh Operating System dialog box.

The Chooser and Appleshare Client Software

However, you may not want to install using the default options, because doing so will probably place inside the Mac's system folder unecessary files. Installing such files will cause no harm, but will take up disk space. By clicking the "Customize" button, you can be more exact in specifying which files Installer will place inside the Mac's system folder.

When you choose to customize the Mac's system installation, Installer will display a dialog box with two windows. The upper window is scrollable, and contains every installation option available to you. The lower window is dynamic; it displays detailed information about the installation option currently selected in the upper window. (See Figure 14.) You can select an installation option from the upper window by clicking on it. As you select different options, the lower window displays different information. The lower window always displays the size of the currently selected installation option.

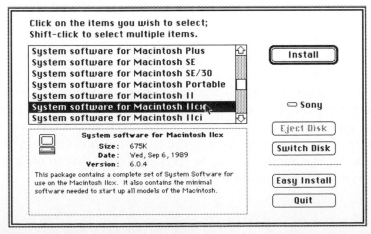

Figure 14: Choosing the operating system.

The different installation options are organized into four major groups. Moving from top to bottom as you scroll, the first group contains generic system software, generic printer drivers, and AppleShare workstation software. The second group contains specific printer drivers, with each driver corresponding to an Apple printer. The third group contains specific sets of system software, with each set corresponding to a Macintosh model. For example, there is a set of system software for the Mac Plus, the SE, the II, and so on. Finally, the fourth group contains minimal operating systems for each model of the Macintosh. A minimal operating system is one that contains only enough code to sucessfully initialize and boot the Macintosh. You would use a minimal operating system, for example, if you wished to boot the Macintosh from a floppy diskette.

As an exercise, assume you are installing an operating system, utilities, LaserWriter printer driver, and AppleShare client software on a Mac IIcx. First, scroll down through the upper window until you see an option titled "System Software for the Macintosh IIcx." Select that option by clicking on it. You'll notice that the lower window now shows detailed information about the Mac IIcx system software. Also, the "Install" button now has a heavy border. Press <Enter>, and wait while Installer does its thing.

The Installer will first check the target disk to be certain there's enough room to install the operating system. If there's enough room, the Installer will work for a while, then prompt you to insert a different disk. Follow the prompts until the Installer is finished, at which time it will display a message to the effect that the installation has been sucessful. Repeat the process for the LaserWriter driver and the AppleShare client software. Remember to have the "System Tools" disk, both "Utilities" disks, and the "Printer Tools" disk nearby before you run the Installer.

It's a good practice to install the operating system before installing AppleShare client software or a printer driver. However, there is a shortcut that (provided you have room on the target disk) will install more than one option at a time. You can take the short cut by selecting the first option you wish to install, pressing and holding down the shift key, and, still holding the shift key down, selecting any other options you wish to install. When you have more than one option selected, the lower window changes modes. Where it previously displayed detailed information about a single selected option, it now displays a description of options currently selected for installation. (See Figure 15.) Clicking "Install" or pressing <Enter> at this point will install the items you have selected.

When making multiple selections by holding the shift key down, you may accidently select an item you do not wish to install. If this happens, don't take your finger off the shift key; instead, click on the item you selected by accident. If you're still holding down the shift key, the item you accidently selected will become deselected when you click on it, and all other selected items will remain selected.

After you run the Installer using all the installation options you need, you must reboot the Macintosh without the "System Tools" disk in order for the new operating system and utilities to be active.

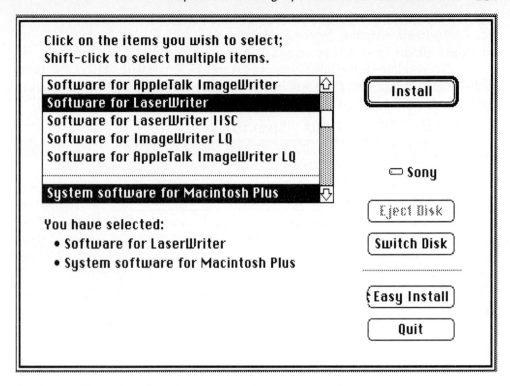

Figure 15: The currently selected operating system options.

Upgrading System Software

You will occasionally want to upgrade a Macintosh's system software—for example, when Apple releases a new version of the System, AppleShare, or Multi-Finder. While upgrading the operating system of a Macintosh is different than endowing a Mac with an operating system for the first time, you must follow exactly the same procedures in both cases.

The reason for both installing and upgrading in same way may elude you if you are not familiar with the Mac. Briefly, every font and desk accessory (with some esoteric exceptions) installed on the machine becomes linked with the machine's operating system when the font or desk accessory is first installed. If you delete an operating system or copy a newer version of the operating system over an existing version, you are replacing not only an outdated operating system, but also any fonts and desk accessories the user of that Macintosh may have installed. The Installer, on the other hand, extracts all desk accessories and fonts from the old operating system, builds a new operating system, and installs the extracted fonts and desk accessories in the new operating system.

Installing the Network Driver

By default, every Macintosh with an operating system has a LocalTalk network driver. However, if you are planning to hook the Macintosh up to an ethernet, a token-ring, or an ARCnet network, you must explicitly install a network

driver. Usually, the correct driver software comes packaged with the network interface card you are installing. For example, if you are installing an Etherport II card,
the EtherTalk driver should be on a disk within the Etherport packaging.

　　　To install the EtherTalk driver, restart the Macintosh with the disk that came
in the Etherport box. After you boot the Macintosh and open the disk, your screen
should look similar to Figure 16.

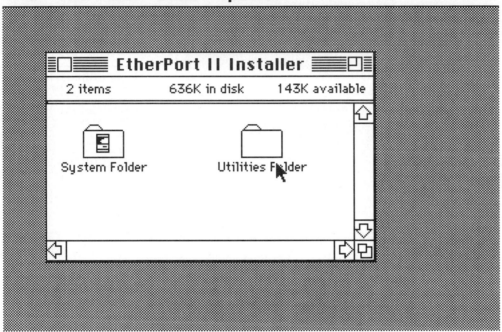

Figure 16: The Utilities Folder for Etherport II contains the Installer for the driver.

　　　Inside the "Utilities Folder," you'll find the Installer and at least one Installer script. You use the Installer to place EtherTalk on the Macintosh just as you used
Installer to place the operating system on the Macintosh. A primary advantage of the
Installer is simply that it allows you to install almost anything related to the Macintosh operating system using a familiar process. This is true for EtherTalk, in addition
to TokenTalk (the Macintosh token-ring driver), the Mac's ARCnet driver, and anything else.

　　　As soon as you restart the Mac with EtherTalk installed, you face a dilemma:
the Mac has two network drivers linked to its operating system (LocalTalk and
EtherTalk). How do you choose one over the other? The answer is something called
the Network CDEV.

　　　CDEVs, you may already know, are "Control DEVices"—miniature programs that initialize when you start the Macintosh, giving you the ability to control
one or more operating system parameters. The Network CDEV allows you to select
a network topology from among the networks currently installed in the operating
system. Figure 17 shows how to select EtherTalk rather than LocalTalk or EtherTalk
II. (EtherTalk II is the ethernet driver for AppleTalk phase II.)

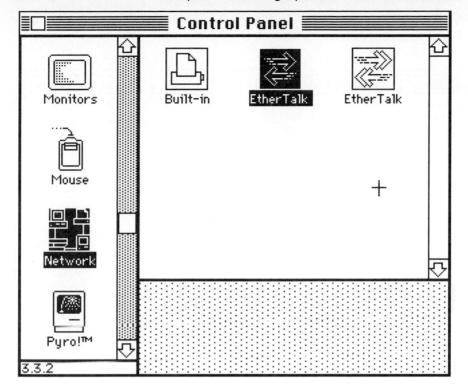

Figure 17: Choose the Ethernet icon to attach to the network.

The Network CDEV allows you install any number of network drivers, and to make one driver active at all times. You can change the active driver at any time by opening the Control Panel and selecting the new active driver. If you're logged in to a server over Ethernet, though, and you change the active driver to LocalTalk, you'll have to re-log in to the server using the newly active driver.

The Chooser and AppleShare Client Software

It's important not confuse the roles of the network driver and the client software. For example, on DOS NetWare workstations you have IPX.COM, which is the network driver, and NETx.COM, which is the client software. Likewise on the Macintosh you have LocalTalk, EtherTalk, TokenTalk, and so on; these are the network drivers. AppleShare client software is distinct from the network drivers on the Macintosh. If you were using a network other than NetWare, you would probably install client software other than AppleShare, but you would certainly use the same network drivers.

Because this is a NetWare workstation book, you need to know how to log in to a NetWare server from the Macintosh. In addition, you need to know how to select network resources such as printers and modems. One Desk Accessory, the Chooser, accomplishes both tasks. To open the Chooser, you must pull down the Apple menu and select "Chooser." The Chooser's position in the Apple menu varies, depending on the number of desk accessories currently installed in the Mac's operating system. The Apple Menu displays desk accessories in alphabetical order. When the Chooser appears on the Macintosh screen, it will look similar to Figure 18.

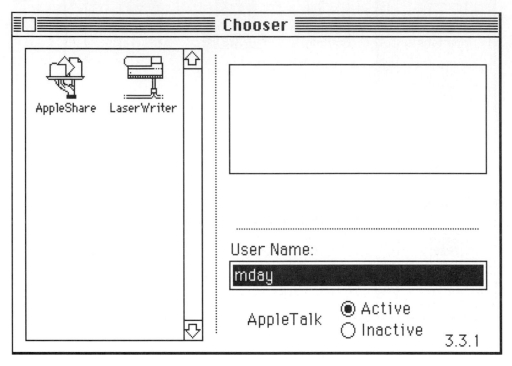

Figure 18: The Macintosh Chooser dialog box.

To log in to a NetWare server, you must first select the AppleShare icon listed on the left side of the Chooser's window. To select the AppleShare icon, click on it. After you select the AppleShare icon, the Chooser will list every AppleShare-compatible server it knows about. (See Figure 19.) (NetWare for Macintosh servers are AppleShare-compatible.)

Before selecting a server, be certain that AppleTalk is activated. You can check visually by looking at the two radio buttons in the lower right corner of the Chooser window. If the "Active" radio button is darkened, AppleTalk is active. Otherwise, AppleTalk is not active. You can activate AppleTalk by clicking on the "Active" radio button.

Next, select the server you wish to log in to. Selecting the name of a server by clicking on it causes the "OK" button to have a heavy border. As you know by now, you can activate a button that has a heavy border by pressing <Return>, <Enter>, or clicking on the button. You can select a server and activate the "OK" button in one action by double-clicking on the name of the server you wish to select. To select more than one server, hold down the shift key while making selections.

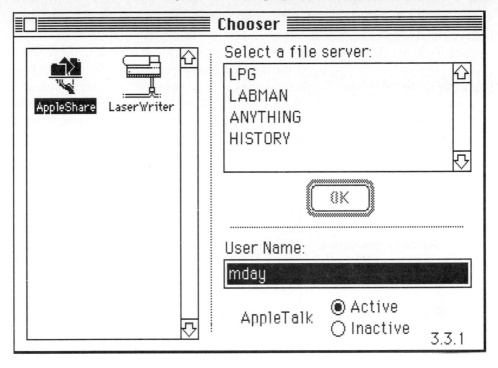

Figure 19: The Chooser will list every AppleShare server it knows about.

After selecting a server and activating the "OK" button, your screen should look similar to Figure 20. The name of the selected server is listed across the top of

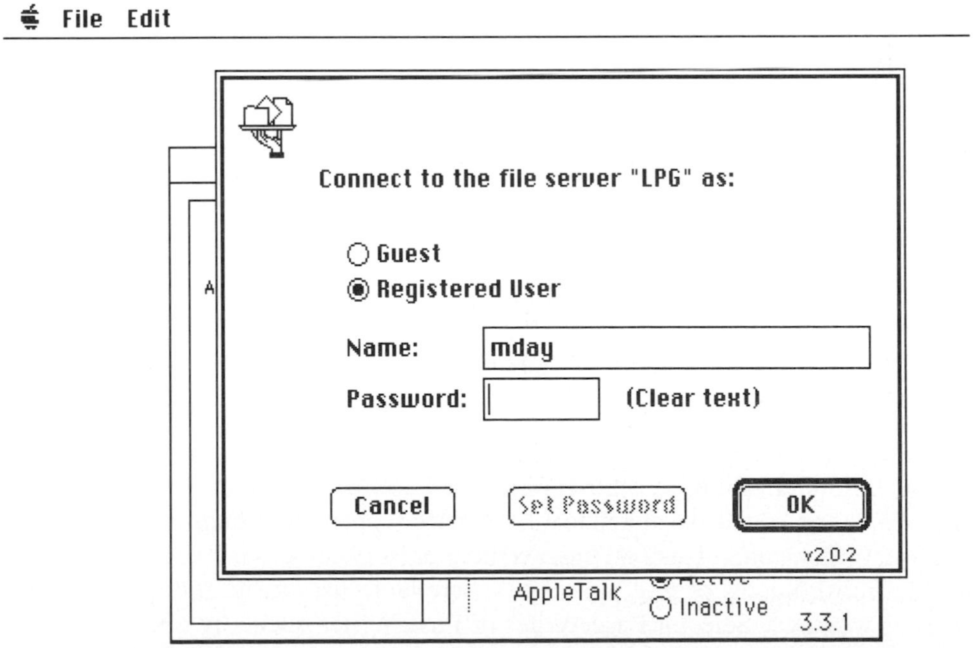

Figure 20: The selected AppleShare server will appear in the dialog box.

the login dialog box. If you wish to log in as a guest, click inside the "Guest" radio button. Otherwise, be certain the "Registered User" radio button is darkened. Next, be certain your name appears in the "Name" field exactly as it is listed in the server's bindery. If you have a password for the selected server, be certain to type your password in the "Password" field. As you type your password, the Macintosh will echo bullet characters. Unfortunately, the AppleShare login dialog box will accept only passwords of eight characters or less. Be certain, then, your users who will log in from a Macintosh have passwords of eight characters or less.

After you enter your password, activate the "OK" button by clicking on it, or pressing <Enter> or <Return>. Your Macintosh will then log you in to the selected server and display a list of on-line volumes for that server. Select a volume by clicking on it. As soon as a volume becomes selected, the "OK" button receives a heavy border; when you activate it, you will be logged in to the appropriate server, and the selected volume will appear on the Macintosh desktop. (See Figure 21.) You can select more than one volume at a time by holding down the shift key as you click on the server names.

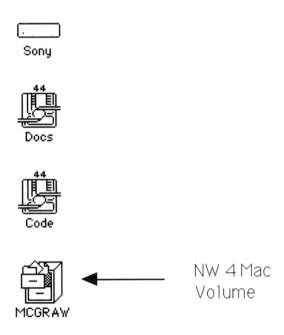

Figure 21: The selected volume will appear on the screen.

Before attaching to a LaserWriter or LaserWriter queue, be certain that AppleTalk is activated. To attach to a LaserWriter, open the Chooser and click on the LaserWriter icon. A list of all LaserWriters or NetWare LaserWriter queues that the Macintosh knows of will appear in a scrollable list on the right side of the Chooser window. Select a LaserWriter or LaserWriter queue by clicking on its name. Your screen should look similar to Figure 22.

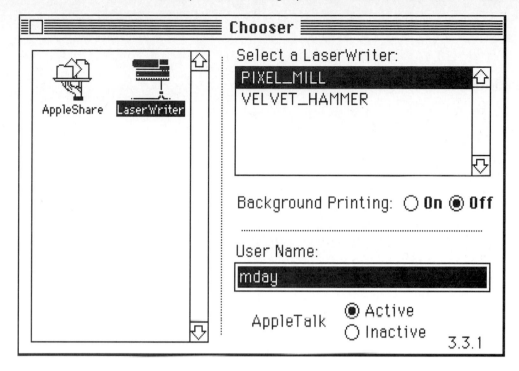

Figure 22: The printer selection dialog box.

Background printing is a MultiFinder feature that allows the Macintosh to print in the background while other MultiFinder sessions execute in the foreground. However, if you've selected a NetWare LaserWriter queue and most of your printing consists of conventional jobs, you may find background printing unnecessary. The NetWare spooler turns most Macintosh print jobs around quickly, reducing the relative benefit of the background printing feature.

Once you've selected a LaserWriter or LaserWriter queue, you're attached to that printer. Close the Chooser window. The next time you print from the Macintosh (regardless of the application), the print job will automatically go to the selected printer or queue. Using the Chooser to attach to a printer is analogous to using the NetWare CAPTURE utility from a DOS workstation.

To test the setup, open the NetWare volume you've logged in to and print a catalog of the volume to the LaserWriter. From the desktop, select the NetWare volume and choose "Open" from the File menu. The Finder will display a window showing the contents of the NetWare volume you just opened up. After the window is displayed, select "Print Directory" from the File menu. If the directory prints sucessfully, you have correctly installed and configured the printing software.

19 Macintosh Troubleshooting Tips

Many of the workstation troubleshooting techniques relevant to NetWare are the same for Macintoshes as they are for DOS. For example, any problems associated with the physical layer of the network (cables, cards, and so on) are usually common to both Macintoshes and PCs. However, there are several troubleshooting problems unique to the Macintosh that you need to be aware of. These include the Macintosh file system, corrupt Macintosh System or Finder files, memory fragmentation under MultiFinder, and conflicting INIT files. Finally, this chapter discusses the role of the Macintosh desktop files in NetWare for Macintosh.

Corrupt File Systems

The Macintosh file system is at once both powerful and fragile. It is powerful, because it is hierarchical, addresses huge hard drives, and maintains both data and resources for every file. It is also fragile because it relies on the accuracy of its resource directory and requires certain clean-up operations prior to a sucessful shutdown.

When a Macintosh file system becomes corrupt, you won't be able to mount the volume which contains the corrupt file system. If the corrupt file system contains the operating system from which you boot your Mac, you won't be able to get as far as the "Welcome to Macintosh" dialog box when booting—the machine will freeze first.

If the corrupt file system is on a non-boot volume, the Mac will attempt to mount the volume, but will fail with a dialog box message similar to "Volume Needs Repair—Repair It?" Clicking "yes," which causes the Macintosh to try a couple of basic repair routines, is always the first thing you should try. Before you click on anything, though, read the next paragraph.

Here's a second possibility: The Macintosh sometimes attempts to mount a volume and fails with a dialog box message similar to "This is not a Macintosh disk" and the buttons "Cancel" and "Initialize." Never select the "Initialize" button unless you want to wipe out all your data and start from scratch. Select "Cancel" instead.

The third possibility is that the Macintosh won't even be aware that the volume—corrupt or not—is available for mounting. In this case, the Mac will display a flashing question mark, or, if the drive in question is a non-booting drive, the Mac will boot and ignore the failed drive.

Here are some things to try when a file system becomes corrupted. Try them in the order in which they're listed.

1)   If the failed file system contains the System you use to boot the Mac, reboot the Mac with a floppy containing a valid System and Finder. As the machine is booting, hold down the option and command (cloverleaf) keys. This causes the operating system to rebuild critical files required to successfully mount a Macintosh file system.

2)   Run Disk First Aid on the failed file system. Disk First Aid is a program Apple ships as part of its system software.

3)   Re-install the driver for the particular drive on which the failed file system resides. For example, if you're using a Rodime drive, re-install the Rodime driver using the software that shipped with your drive. If you're using a GCC Technologies drive, re-install the GCC driver using the software that shipped with your drive.

4)   If none of these methods solve the problem, you can start to worry a little. The best thing to do here is to run the Symantec Utilities for Macintosh (SUM) to try to repair the drive. Read the SUM documentation thoroughly before trying to use the software. The SUM package contains two types of utilities; some utilities attempt to repair a damaged file system, while others attempt to recover data from an irreparable file system. If SUM can't repair the file system, you can still try one more thing before you run the data recovery utilities.

5)   Delete the desktop file manually, using MacTools (part of the PC Tools Deluxe for Macintosh package from Central Point Software). Then reboot the Mac, holding down the command and option keys.

6)   The volume is almost beyond hope—run the SUM data recovery utilities.

Good luck.

Most corrupt Macintosh file systems are easy to fix, using the first three steps above. Losing data to a failed Macintosh file system is much more rare than losing data to a physical hard drive failure.

To prevent corrupt file systems, always use the "Shutdown" or "Restart" items on the Finder's Special menu when turning off or rebooting the Macintosh. These two menu items clean up the file system and prepare it for being dismounted. In addition, you should periodically (once a month or so) boot the Mac while holding down the option and command keys. This process, called "rebuilding the desktop," purges the file system of obsolete or unneeded resource files.

Corrupt System Files

One hallmark of the Macintosh is that, occasionally, the System or Finder will become corrupt in one way or another, rendering the Macintosh unusable until you reinstall the System or Finder. This happens infrequently, but often enough to be an issue. When it does happen, the Macintosh doesn't cause any data loss, and the fix is fairly painless.

The telling signs that your System or Finder is corrupt are fairly straightforward. If your System is corrupt, the Macintosh will usually display part or all of the "Welcome to Macintosh" dialog box—and then hang. If your Finder is corrupt, the Macintosh will usually display a dialog box to the effect that it can't load the Finder, or the Finder is not valid.

Many DOS users assume that this problem occurs because of the inherent inferiority of the Macintosh operating system. It's simply not true that the Macintosh operating system is inherently unstable. The system occasionally becomes corrupt depending on how the user uses the system, and such incidents are the ultimate result of the openness and freedom the Macintosh operating system gives you to modify it. For example, every time you install a desk accessory or font, CDEV, or INIT, you're modifying the operating system. In the case of Desk Accessories and Fonts, you're performing a patch on the operating system; in the case of INITs and CDEVs, you're linking resources to the operating system at run time.

Patching and linking are not unique to the Mac—DOS also does that—but not to the degree that the Mac does. Depending on the applications he or she uses, the average Macintosh user installs, deletes, and reinstalls hundreds of fonts and desk accessories over the life of an operating system binary image, in addition to having a number of CDEVs and INITs. All of this places major strain on the operating system as its executable image shrinks and grows, and as it becomes fragmented over the storage device.

In fact, most intermittent corruptions of the System or Finder are the result of disk fragmentation. Under such conditions, part of the System's executable image becomes spread over hundreds of different locations on the hard drive. Fragmentation itself is a condition in which files on a drive become spread over disparate physical locations of the drive. The operating system must do more work to read or write fragmented files because they are harder to maintain logically. If there are any random media failures, or if just one block of the System's executable image becomes corrupt, the Macintosh won't boot. (The same goes for the Finder.)

Macintosh users contribute to this problem in two ways. The first way is changing the operating system frequently by adding or deleting fonts or Desk Accessories, INITs, or CDEVs. The second way is to allow the hard disk itself to become fragmented. Disk fragmentation is more likely to occur when the available free space on a drive falls below 20 percent of the total formatted space on the drive.

When the Macintosh operating system or Finder becomes corrupt, you won't, of course, be able to boot from the Macintosh's hard drive. To boot the Macintosh, simply insert a floppy containing a valid System and Finder and reboot the machine. The Macintosh will boot from the floppy and will mount the hard drive successfully.

The simple solution to this problem of disk fragmentation involves two steps:

• *Run a de-fragmentation utility on the hard drive.* These utilities rearrange files so that the files are located in contiguous physical blocks Two useful products for defragmenting Macintosh drives are the Symantec Utilities for the Macintosh and PC Tools Deluxe for the Macintosh.

• *Run the Installer and reinstall the System and Finder*, in addition to any system resources you need.

MultiFinder Memory Fragmentation

Because the current Macintosh operating system doesn't support virtual memory (System 7 will), memory is always a consideration under MultiFinder. When MultiFinder executes an application, it allocates a continuous block of RAM within which to run the application. The size of this block of RAM is determined by a parameter contained in the resource fork of the application file. Once an application executes under MultiFinder, the amount of memory devoted to that application is frozen until you quit the application.

It's possible, therefore, for the Mac's memory to become fragmented, just as it's possible for files to become fragmented over a hard drive. Memory fragmentation is most likely to occur when you repeatedly load and unload applications under MultiFinder. Ultimately, an application will fail to execute with the message "not enough memory," despite the fact that there is memory available. The problem is that available memory is fragmented to such a degree that MultiFinder fails to recognize it. The only solution is to save your data, quit your applications, and reboot the Mac.

The primary method for avoiding memory fragmentation is to know ahead of time which applications you are most likely to use, open those applications, and keep them open. (The cause of memory fragmentation is the continual opening and closing of applications.)

A less common memory problem with MultiFinder occurs when NetWare for Macintosh users attempt to open NetWare volumes that contain hundreds of files or folders while MultiFinder is also active. Because the Finder has access to a finite segment of memory under MultiFinder, it may not have enough memory allocated to it to open and display NetWare directories that have large numbers of files or folders.

The solution is to select the Finder icon by opening the system folder and clicking on the Finder. Choose "Get Info" from the File menu. The Finder will display a small window with miscellaneous information about the Finder, including the size of the memory partition MultiFinder allocates. Two sizes are listed in the "Get Info" window: the minimum recommended size and the actual allocated size. By increasing the actual allocated size, you can give the Finder more memory (see Figure 23). You must reboot the Macintosh in order for the Finder to enjoy its new memory allocation.

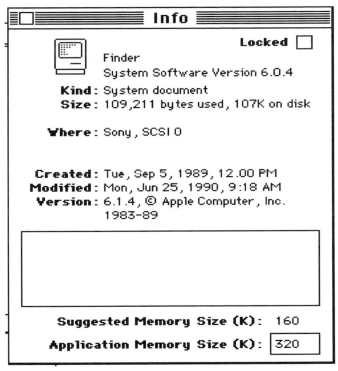

Figure 23: Allocating additional memory may solve getting NetWare directories to appear.

Conflicting INIT Files

INITs are special programs that link to the Macintosh operating system at boot time. To install an INIT, simply drop it into the System folder. The operating system links INITs in alphabetical order (ASCII-style) according to the name of the INIT.

INITs often conflict with each other during the linking process, preventing the Macintosh from booting. When this occurs, the Macintosh will display the "Welcome to Macintosh" dialog box, remove the dialog box and proceed with the booting process, but suddenly freeze. Here are a couple of things you can try when this happens.

1)   Most INITs display tiny icons along the bottom of the Mac screen, left to right, as they are linked. It's likely that the farthest right INIT icon represents the offending INIT. Identify that INIT. Reboot the Macintosh with a floppy and remove the offending INIT from the Mac's system folder by dragging it onto the root level of the file system. Reboot the Macintosh as you normally would (without the floppy you just booted it with).

If the Mac boots successfully, you've identified the problem and removed it. One thing to try now is to rename the INIT so it links in a different order. Sometimes the order in which INITs link causes problems.

2)   If the above method doesn't identify the offending INIT, remove every INIT from the system folder. Place a single INIT back into the system folder and boot the Mac. If the Mac boots successfully, place an additional INIT in the system folder and boot the Mac. Continue to do this until the Mac fails to boot. At this point, you've identified the last INIT you placed into the system folder as the offending INIT.

Macintosh Desktop Files

NetWare for Macintosh emulates a standard Macintosh file system using, among other tricks, four special files. These files are contained in the "DESKTOP" directory, which is located at the root of a NetWare for Macintosh volume. There are four files, each having the extension ".DTM": APPKEY.DTM, COMKEY.DTM, ICONDATA.DTM, and ICONKEY.DTM.

If a Macintosh workstation attempts to mount a NetWare for Macintosh volume, but doesn't have sufficient rights to the DESKTOP directory, the Macintosh Finder will return an error message similar to "The volume is damaged." Nothing will happen; the Mac won't mount the NetWare volume, and the NetWare volume won't be damaged in any way, so you can relax.

The solution is to ensure that all NetWare for Macintosh users have sufficient rights to the DESKTOP directory to mount the volume. Be careful, however, that in so doing you don't give the user unnecessary rights to the root directory of the NetWare volume.

Appendix A

Workstation Configuration Worksheets

Workstation Configuration for _____.

Make and type of workstation _____

Make and type of monitor(s) _____
_____

Make and type of network interface board(s) _____
_____
_____

Network interface board settings _____
_____

Network address _____ Node address _____

Memory configuration _____ KB/MB Extended? _____ KB/MB
Expanded? _____ KB/MB

ROM BIOS version _____ _____

Make and type of memory boards _____

Make and type of other internal hardware & settings (*mouse, modem, etc.*)
_____
_____

Floppy drives (*put drive letters in space*) _____ 360KB _____ 1.2MB
_____ 720KB _____ 1.44MB _____ Diskless

Hard Disk Drive Settings _____ Type _____ Head _____ Cylinder
_____ Tracks/Sectors _____ Size

Last local drive letter _____

Type and version of DOS (*NVER*) _____

Attach to this form	*To get it type*
Config.sys printout	A:Config.sys >PRN:
Autoexec.bat printout	A:Autoexec.bat >PRN:
WhoamI /A printout	WhoamI /A >PRN:

Server Configuration

Make and type of server _____

Make and type of monitor _____

Make and type of disk subsystem(s) _____

Number and configuration of serial and parallel ports _____

Make and type of network interface board(s)
　　　　　　　　　　　　1. _____
　　　　　　　　　　　　2. _____
　　　　　　　　　　　　3. _____
　　　　　　　　　　　　4. _____

Network interface board settings
　　　　　　　　　　　　1. _____
　　　　　　　　　　　　2. _____
　　　　　　　　　　　　3. _____
　　　　　　　　　　　　4. _____

Network and node addresses
　　　　　　　　　　　　1. _____
　　　　　　　　　　　　2. _____
　　　　　　　　　　　　3. _____
　　　　　　　　　　　　4. _____

Memory configuration _____ MB　　　　ROM BIOS version _____

Make, type, and settings of memory boards _____
_____

Type and settings of add-on boards _____
_____

Make and model of drive controllers _____

Disk coprocessor board(s) (*include revision #*) _____

Disk interface board (*include revision #*) _____

Disk Drives
Make and model of disk drive _____
Disk drive settings _____ Type _____ Head _____ Cylinder _____ Track/Sector _____ Size
Make and model of disk drive _____
Disk drive settings _____ Type _____ Head _____ Cylinder _____ Track/Sector _____ Size
Make and model of disk drive _____
Disk drive settings _____ Type _____ Head _____ Cylinder _____ Track/Sector _____ Size
Make and model of disk drive _____
Disk drive settings _____ Type _____ Head _____ Cylinder _____ Track/Sector _____ Size

Appendix B

Hard Drive Type Table for IBM AT BIOS

Hard Drive Type Table for IBM AT BIOS

Type	# Cylinders	Heads	Precomp	Landing	Sectors	MFM/FZoneMB
2	615	4	300	615	17	20.4
3	615	6	300	615	17	30.6
4	940	8	512	940	17	62.4
5	940	6	512	940	17	46.8
6	615	4		615	17	20.4
7	462	8	256	511	17	30.7
8	733	5		733	17	30.4
9	900	15		901	17	112.1
10	820	3		820	17	20.4
11	855	5		855	17	35.5
12	855	7		855	17	49.7
13	306	8	128	319	17	20.3
14	733	7		733	17	42.6
15	reserved					
16	612	4	0	663	17	20.3
17	977	5	300	977	17	40.5
18	977	7		977	17	56.8
19	1024	7	512	1023	17	59.5
20	733	5	300	732	17	30.4
21	733	7	300	732	17	42.6

Type	# Cylinders	Heads	Precomp	Landing	Sectors	MFM/FZoneMB
22	733	5	300	733	17	30.4
23	306	4	0	336	17	10.2
24	612	4	305	663	17	20.4
25	306	4		340	17	10.2
26	612	4		670	17	20.4
27	698	7	300	732	17	40.6
28	976	5	488	977	17	40.5
29	306	4	0	340	17	10.2
30	611	4	306	663	17	20.4
31	732	7	300	732	17	42.6
32	1023	5		1023	17	42.5

Appendix C

NetWare Requester Error Codes

Appendix C

NetWare Requester Errors

Hex Value	Unsigned Decimal Value	Signed Decimal Value	Description
0x8800	34816	-30720	Already attached
0x8801	34817	-30719	Invalid connection
0x8802	34818	-30718	Drive in use
0x8803	34819	-30717	Can't add CDs
0x8804	34820	-30716	Bad drive base
0x8805	34821	-30715	Net read error
0x8806	34822	-30714	Unknown net error
0x8807	34823	-30713	Server invalid slot
0x8808	34824	-30712	No server slots
0x8809	34825	-30711	Net send error
0x880a	34826	-30710	Server no route
0x880b	34827	-30709	Bad local target
0x880c	34828	-30708	Too many req frags
0x880d	34829	-30707	Connect list overflow
0x880e	34830	-30706	Buffer overflow
0x880f	34831	-30705	No connection to server
0x8810	34832	-30704	No router found
0x8811	34833	-30703	Invalid shell call
0x8830	34864	-30672	Not same connection
0x8831	34865	-30671	Primary connection not set
0x8832	34866	-30670	No capture in progress
0x8833	34867	-30669	Invalid buffer length
0x8834	34868	-30668	No user name
0x8835	34869	-30667	No NetWare print spooler
0x8836	34870	-30666	Invalid parameter
0x8837	34871	-30665	Config file open failed
0x8838	34872	-30664	No config file
0x8839	34873	-30663	Config file read failed
0x883a	34874	-30662	Config line too long
0x883b	34875	-30661	Config lines ignored
0x883c	34876	-30660	Not my resource
0x883d	34877	-30659	Daemon installed
0x883e	34878	-30658	Spooler installed
0x883f	34879	-30657	Connection table full
0x8840	34880	-30656	Config section not found

These error codes can also be found in the NetWare OS/2 API Reference manual.
That reference work also lists error codes specific to NetBIOS, IPX, and SPX.

Index

Section 1 - DOS and NetWare

Section 2-
OS/2 and NetWare

Section 3 -
Macintosh and NetWare